Colour, Culture and Consciousness

Immigrant Intellectuals in Britain

Colour, Culture and Consciousness

Immigrant Intellectuals in Britain

Edited by

BHIKHU PAREKH

Senior Lecturer, Department of Political Studies
University of Hull

LONDON · GEORGE ALLEN & UNWIN LTD

Ruskin House   Museum Street

First published in 1974

ISBN 0 04 301067 9

Printed in Great Britain
by T. & A. Constable Ltd
Hopetoun Street
Edinburgh EH7 4NF

Acknowledgements

Not being a sociologist or a political activist working in the field of race relations I had to draw on the goodwill of a number of scholars for suggesting names of people who could be invited to contribute to this collection. Among them were Professors Ernest Gellner, C. H. Dodd and Michael Banton, and Mr Andrew Salkey, to all of whom I am most grateful. My greatest debt, however, is to my good friends Mr Trevor Smith who invited me to edit the volume on behalf of the Acton Society Trust and helped in several ways towards bringing the project to fruition, and to Professor Preston King and Mr Edward Goodman who were both closely connected with the planning of the volume and have been most helpful throughout its slow progress. I am also most grateful to all contributors for agreeing to write and for sending their contributions in on time. I am especially grateful to the contributors to the second section for writing their essays at short notice; they were all very encouraging and no editor could have wished for more friendly and co-operative contributors. I am most thankful to Miss Charmian Hall of Hull University and Miss Jackie Eames of the Acton Society for coping with the typing with remarkable patience and efficiency, and to Raj for preparing the index.

Contents

10 CONTENTS

Introduction

This volume is about the experiences of non-white intellectuals[1] resident in Britain. Each contributor was invited to reflect on his life in England and on the problems he has encountered. Each of them, born and raised outside Britain, was asked to articulate and analyse the tensions generated by the conflict between his own native culture and that dominant in Britain, and the ways in which and the degree to which he has coped with them. He was invited too to comment on British life and society, to elucidate what struck him as their distinctive characteristics, and to analyse the extent to which he felt sympathetic to them. As the reader will see, each contributor discusses these and other cognate questions in his own way, and expresses concerns which are unique to him. Collectively they represent a wide variety of views. Some clearly love England and feel at home here, while others find life here an agony; of the latter, some are interested in resolving inevitable existential conflicts at a personal level, whereas others see the problem as essentially racial and political in nature. This should be enough to show that immigrants do not constitute a solid and cohesive group thinking and feeling alike on the issues affecting their life.

It was felt that the value of the volume would be greatly increased if philosophers, sociologists and students of English character were invited to respond to the problems immigrant intellectuals raise in their essays. Some were invited to comment on the immigrants' accounts of their experiences, and others to discuss the general questions raised by these. As the reader will gather from the second section, their responses are as varied as those of the immigrants themselves, and predictably they sympathise with the latter's accounts in different degrees.

The volume was recognised to have two deficiencies. First, the papers composing it are largely analytical and/or descriptive in nature and do not explore the ways in which Britain could best deal with immigrants settled in her midst. Second, the papers are largely accounts of the experiences of immigrant intellectuals, and do not discuss the experiences and problems of their working-class co-nationals. The postcript, in which the editor analyses the British scene against the background of the preceding chapters, is designed to rectify these deficiencies.

Whether the volume succeeds in achieving its objective of offering an insight into the immigrant's complex relationship with British society, only the reader can judge. The editor is all too aware of the volume's limitations. He regrets that there is no woman contributor, though that is not for want of trying. He regrets too that despite his efforts, the volume is not fully representative of the immigrant community; there are, for example, no Chinese or Arab contributors, and only one African. In many ways therefore the volume is incomplete and does little justice to the vast pool of experiences struggling to find an articulate utterance. The editor hopes that other more competent hands will one day produce a fuller and richer account of these experiences, though he must warn that we immigrants sometimes take several months, and at least three reminders, to answer a letter.

1. An apology is due for the use of this term in the sub-title of this volume and elsewhere. All the contributors to the volume earn their living by selling their intellectual labour in diverse forms, and there was no other term that could describe them all.

PART ONE

Viewpoint

1 Another Kind of Minority

DILIP HIRO

I remember the first time I met a white man: it was in Kalol, a small town north of Bombay. He was a Dane, an employee of a European firm in Bombay, who had travelled to Kalol on business. I was introduced to him as a government overseer, my position in life then, but I did not say much to him. I could not. I was too awestruck. That happened more than a decade ago: but, if the same situation were re-created today, with another government overseer in my place, it would happen again. I am not speculating. I am basing my statement on evidence as I found it during my visit to India last year — my first since I left it. I noticed the nervous pleasure mingled with excitement that overcame Indians, mostly urban middle class, when they came into contact with white men or women.

Why is this so? Because of the historical experience of the blacks[1] having been ruled, until recently, by the whites; and because of the current fact that the white world is rich and technologically advanced whereas the coloured world is poor and economically backward. Given this, it is easy to understand why being white in a coloured society is an asset which a white person can start capitalising on the moment he enters a non-white country; and the reverse is true when a black arrives in a white country. In other words, present attitudes regarding race and colour are rooted mainly in the history of colonisation of the non-European world by Europe.

The colonisation process was closely tied up with the development of the economies of European nations from feudalism and commercial capitalism to fully-fledged industrial capitalism at the cost of keeping the economies of the non-European colonies at a pre-feudal or feudal stage or, at best, allowing these to progress towards commercial capitalism. This progression, or stagnation, was reflected correspondingly in the change in social values, or absence of it. Both these points are pertinent to the subject under study—the relationship between whites and blacks in contemporary Western societies.[2]

The whites (in West Europe) today constitute advanced capitalist societies whereas the blacks, i.e. the ex-colonials, who have settled among them, have come from societies which exist in pre-capitalist environments. In short, what divides these two groups is not only race but also the widely different historical experiences and contemporary socio-cultural backgrounds.[3] The following points need therefore be borne in mind: we can understand the present only in the light of the past; industrial capitalism is an advancement over feudalism and commercial capitalism; and social values are closely related to the stage of economic development of a society. I state this at the outset because these points underlie practically all that I am about to say (descriptively or analytically) about my experiences, as a black man, in Britain and America.[4]

I was born in Sind, a province of the present-day Pakistan, in a middle middle-class family. My father was a civil servant, and a property-owner—agricultural land and buildings. As a group, we, the Hindus in Sind, valued education which, among other things, meant learning English. There was indeed a premium on learning English and being fluent in it.[5] My father, for instance, encouraged me to read *The Sind Observer* every day in order to improve my English. We also prided ourselves on habitually wearing trousers or 'knickers', that is, *not* wearing the traditional *dhoti* or pyjamas. We often sat in chairs and ate rice with spoons: very wisely, we did not attempt to eat *chappatis* with such implements as forks. That was about the extent of our anglicisation while we were in Sind.

Then came independence and the creation of Pakistan in 1947, and our migration to India, to an outer suburb of Bombay. I went to live in a college hostel in Bombay. Residence in a metropolitan city hastened the process of superficial anglicisation. My use of English, both as a source of information and as a medium of expression, increased, and, more importantly, for the first time, I was exposed to films in English, mostly made in Hollywood. These became my window to the West.

Thus seen, Western society appeared orderly and efficient. Even the violence that was depicted seemed, to me anyway, clean and intelligent. Rationalism seemed to permeate the Western world which was not the case with the society in which I then lived. The Western people seemed generally affluent and well-mannered. They looked beautiful, especially the women—vivacious, exuding vitality, health and sex, their bodies an inexhaustible source of sensuous pleasure. What was particularly meaningful to me, a young man starved of female company, was that women in the West, whether married or not, were individuals in their own right, free to make their decisions; free to mix with men, to date, even to copulate —an unimaginable situation in the feudal society in which I lived and where women remained, and still remain, essentially 'property'.

Of course we had left the feudal Sind and were now living on the outskirts of the commercial-industrial city of Bombay but we had not been there long enough for our family structure, or social attitudes, to change. These remained feudal. Our families remained close and tight-knit where ideas of individualism and individual development, independent of parents and brothers and sisters, were simply unknown.[6]

Our flight from Sind, and property, had turned us into paupers. I had therefore to share the burden of supporting the family of six school-going brothers and sisters while simultaneously pursuing full-time studies at the university—an overworked existence, full of worry and anxiety. This burden remained with me as long as I was in India. It was all a part of being a 'dutiful son', ever ready to meet his never-ending obligations towards parents, brothers and sisters, and near-relatives.

This subservience of oneself to others was an integral part of one's existence. One even allowed oneself to be married off, by one's parents, more as a means of enabling them to forge an alliance between families rather than a consummation of one's love for someone of the opposite sex. Or, seen from the parents' point of view, it was their 'duty' to marry off their children, a duty which, in the case of a son, they got ready to perform only after he had secured a job. Now I had a job, first as a government overseer, in Kalol, and then with a foreign firm, in Bombay. I thus became eligible for marriage to be 'arranged' by my parents.

I detested the very idea of 'arranged marriage' even though, in my case, the final say was to have rested with me. That was a poor consolation. I wanted to date girls just the way I had seen it done in Hollywood movies and knew to be the custom in the West. At the same time I was despairingly aware that this was beyond my reach. Had I been a member of Bombay's westernised rich class it would have been different: but I was not. I could barely manage a middle-class existence. There was thus, sadly, no chance of translating my romantic ideas into reality. So, I concluded, I should be where dating is—in a Western country, in Britain.[7]

By then I had acquired more than a cursory interest in under-standing Western life, an interest that, in part, was engendered by reading Somerset Maugham's novels and short stories. Also I wanted, desperately wanted, to free myself from the repressive, restrictive embrace of my family. Moreover, I argued (mainly with myself), a few years in Britain, followed by a few years in America, would help me in my profession, which then happened to be engineering. So I left for Britain.

In retrospect, I can say that the following factors led me to travel to Britain: economic deprivation at home; a desire to improve my professional status; intellectual curiosity about the West; and a spirit of adventure, sexual and otherwise. One or more of these may be seen as the reason(s) for migration, to Britain, by the people of the Indian sub-continent.

On arrival in England, I decided, as a matter of policy, not to work in London; it was only in a provincial town that I felt I could come to grips with the real England.[8] I had an introduction to a firm in Stockton-on-Tees, which my employer in Bombay represented in India, and used it. The Stockton company offered me a job which by no means matched my qualifications and experience, but I accepted it, mainly to keep myself away from London. Luckily, this firm had a hostel of its own: so I did not have to knock on doors for accommodation.

I did have my share of racial discrimination, however. I went to a private dancing class in town to enrol, but was refused. That really shook me. I remember walking away from the place, in anger and hurt, going here and there, without purpose or aim, walking, walking, until I was too tired to walk, and then taking a bus to the company hostel. After that, the occasional 'black bastard' whisper or shout, thrown at me often by teenage boys, seemed almost innocuous.

The first few weeks in Stockton were hell. A most dramatic change had occurred in my life. Except for the language spoken, English, everything was different from what I had been accustomed to: the weather, buildings, food, work, people, the very atmosphere. The buildings looked, and were, grey and sombre, tightly shut, with only a few people about in the streets, a total contrast from the situation in Bombay. At the office, instead of designing, which I used to do back home, I was now engaged in drawing, a tedious, boring job. The food I ate was monotonous and insipid. So were the people around me—at work and in the hostel—all British, all white. Their extreme formality and reserve intimidated and depressed me. It was always cold, with the sun shielded by clouds, grey and threatening. In the midst of white people I felt alien, inferior and exposed. More, I felt paralysed, not physically, but mentally; and yet, for all the trauma that this experience caused me, I would, given the same chance again, opt for it without a moment's hesitation.

There was of course an easy way out—into the outstretched arms of fellow-Indians in town, some of them employed by the same firm, who constantly flashed their friendly smiles at me. If nothing else, this would have cushioned the cultural shock that I was then suffering; but I refused to compromise. I stood firm by my original resolve to come to grips with Britain and the British people. For this, the company hostel was to prove an ideal place. Here I listened to the conversation in the lounge, often listless and sparse, which acquired some life when local housing and house purchase were considered from various angles, and became positively animated, even heated, when football was discussed. Both these subjects bored and puzzled me, and still do. Politics and political parties, which interest me, seldom figured in these conversations and, when they did, they were discussed, cursorily, at an emotional, yet super-ficial, level.

As a group, those at the hostel—all of them middle middle-class, white-collar workers—had little or no feeling for the non-European world, although some of them, finding themselves sitting next to me in a pub, would often make feeble, rather pathetic, attempts to talk about India. With very few exceptions, they all shared a notion that the British, called by some Higher, Nobler Deity, gave the 'natives' railways, hospitals, schools and roads, and what is more, taught them how to administer their countries, an altruistic mission that the British had willingly and honourably accomplished. I found the idea, and the smugness with which it was conveyed, preposterous and infuriating. I reacted to this rather noisily which caused no more than a ripple of mild irritation and amusement among my British acquaintances. At first I was puzzled by this. But later I realised that a Briton dreads to make a scene and that he seldom, if ever, loses his nerve or temper, a victim of self-imposed repression. I also learnt to translate British reactions, or lack of them, and to understand the nuances of British understatement and circumlocution. When someone said, 'I wouldn't go near the door', he was actually saying, 'You better stay away from that door'. Stockton proved delightfully generous in providing me with opportunities to under-stand the British character but woefully short on meeting my need for female company.

A male migrant can often connect, literally and metaphorically, with the host society by establishing contact with its female mem-bers. The woman in such cases becomes more than a sexual mate: she becomes the agent who eases the man's entry into a new social order. However, I was not seized with such analytical thoughts then. All I knew, and knew it well, was that I needed female companionship. Although I managed to get a few dates, and finally a girlfriend, it was not easy.

The size of the place had something to do with it: the smaller the place, the greater the chance of it being known that you, the girl, were going out with a 'coloured bloke'; and most girls simply did not wish to be so labelled. Most of them did not mind a dance or two in public dance hall, a brief contact, with a 'coloured bloke'; but nothing more. I knew this from personal experience. Often a girl would be delighted to dance with me[9] but would turn down flat any suggestion for a date. Sometimes when a girl came out with me she felt rather brave about it, and I could sense it, and when, even after a few dates with her, the girl did not invite me to her house, I realised that most likely her parents did not approve of her (unconventional) behaviour. All this was very sobering, and depressing too. It was certainly far removed from the romantic notions that I had entertained while in Bombay.

I visited dance halls frequently and began to view them as open markets, acutely sensitive to the law of supply and demand. Early in the evening, when there was an excessive supply of women, a man could dance with any woman he wished; but later, after the pubs closed and men, light-headed with drink, came pouring in, the situation changed. Towards the end there was a scramble among men to find a girl to escort home. It was, to put it mildly, a highly competitive situation where, whether you were a man or a woman, you were constantly scrutinised and judged.

As for me, for the first few months, my critical faculties were, to say the least, underdeveloped. *All* girls appeared beautiful to me. There was an apparent confusion in my mind—something that I shared with most people from the Indian sub-continent—of equating fair skin with beauty. To me, then, being white meant being beautiful. I was still too dazed by the clear, white skin of a woman to examine her facial features and figure. It was only after many exposures to a bevy of young women in dance halls that I began to distinguish the plain-looking from the merely presentable, and the attractive from the really beautiful: but I still failed to notice their class background (not that it mattered then, or does now). Accent was no guide. Many of them with a standard accent often had a working-class background.

The social situation improved when some months later I moved from Stockton to Hull, a city with a university and two teacher training colleges. It was here, in an academic environment, that for the first time in England, I found I could, without much effort, get along with young men and women. At last I seemed to have found a niche. It was also in Hull that I began attending the monthly meetings of the Tribune Club: this partially satisfied my political curiosity and interest.

I have always been interested in politics. I began reading a daily paper at ten, and delivered my first public speech (at an open-air rally) at twelve. I sympathised with the nationalist Congress Party and was against British imperialism. By the time I left India I was a social democrat and, as such, held the British Labour Party in high esteem.

One of the first things I did on arrival in Stockton was to write to the local Labour Party agent suggesting a meeting. He never replied. I remember going to a half-day seminar organised (on a Sunday) by the Workers' Educational Association in Middles-brough. While we were being served 'high tea' I told my neighbour at the table, a young trade unionist, that I admired the Labour Party because it had synthesised the noble principles of democracy and socialism. He was frankly puzzled by this abstraction. 'The Labour Party agent's office', he said, 'is around the corner'. My respect for the active supporters of the Labour Party suffered a severe blow.

Nonetheless, during the 1959 general election, I did some envelope-licking and voter-slip-writing for the Labour candidate for the Hull West constituency. What impressed and puzzled me was the precision with which the candidate and his canvassers could count their supporters: almost every voter's political loyalty was known! This robbed the electoral process of suspense and excitement, making it quite dull. The ease and speed with which party machines were geared into action indicated to me that elections in Britain were an old, established, and therefore an un-exciting, ritual.

The overwhelming reaction of the voters seemed to be boredom mingled with a touch of cynicism. The election meetings in Hull were thinly attended, except the one addressed by Hugh Gaitskell. It was an effort to draw even fifty people to listen to the local candidate. This was a contrast from the situation prevalent in India where even a mediocre politician could draw a crowd of 100,000. I was, of course, aware that television and popular newspapers in Britain had made political meetings unnecessary whereas, in a largely illiterate India, rallies are often the only means of political education. But, despite the professional smoothness of their presentation, the party political broadcasts on British television were far from popular.

How was one to explain this disinterest in politics? One could simply, and sweepingly, say that British people were apolitical *per se*, a statement that would be impossible to square with historical facts. A more tenable explanation was that, during the late 1950s, British people did not feel an urge to express themselves politically because, for the vast majority of them, the fundamental problems of food and shelter had been, more or less, solved. This amounted to saying that our socio-political behaviour is rooted in our economic existence, a viewpoint that I, gradually, came to regard as both profoundly important and widely applicable.

This viewpoint, combined with a historical approach, enabled me to properly understand such social phenomena in Britain as orderliness, punctuality, punctiliousness and speed which earlier I had, mistakenly, attributed to the British 'national character'. I began to connect these social and personal characteristics with the historical experience of an industrial society. I could see how factory work day after day, and generation after generation, engendered orderliness, precision and time-consciousness, the characteristics which are absent in non-industrial societies (and understandably so).[10] I could also see that the modern Western man, with a high degree of organisation and precision in thought and action, is the end-product of many generations, who lived and died in an increasingly industrial environment; and that there was nothing *inherently* superior about him.

I felt that non-Western people, if transferred to an industrial environment, would acquire the characteristics that one commonly, albeit vaguely, associates with being Western. Since then, I would say, my hypothesis has been tested and proved. Consider the case of the immigrants from the Indian sub-continent, most of them with a rural, agrarian background. Once they took up industrial employment they became time-conscious and lost their traditional leisurely way of living. Their ryhthm of life changed from the loosely defined seasonal cycle of (agrarian) work and leisure to the tightly regulated weekly cycle of (industrial) work and relaxation. In their dealings among themselves and with others they became less sentimental, more practical and businesslike.

I could say the same about myself. Residence in Britain brought about certain changes within me. My thinking became sharper and faster; my mind more analytical, less descriptive; and my expression, both verbal and written, more precise. This happened during the first two years in Britain by which time I had concluded, from more than one viewpoint, that I had gained as much from being here as I ever could. It was time to move on—to America, a speedier, capitalistically more advanced country. However, it took me another year before I could undertake that journey. I needed time to save enough to finance my studies in America, as a post-graduate student, the *only* way I could enter the country and stay there for a year or more.

In America, my view that contemporary intergroup attitudes can only be understood in an historical context was reinforced. Prejudice against negro Africans was, and is, rooted in slavery and the plantation economy which thrived on slave labour. By the same token, just because there had been no historical contact between America and the Indian sub-continent the average American's attitude toward the Indian or Pakistani in their midst was nebulous. They knew vaguely that East Indians (as they often call the people from the Indian sub-continent) do not have kinky hair and that their skin colour varies from pale golden to jet black: so, often, the degree of acceptance/rejection depended on the degree of darkness of the East Indian's skin. The Americans do not call, or consider, the East Indians as 'coloured', a term which to them meant, and still does, a negro African or Afro-American. This, as we know, is not the case in Britain. Here people from Asia, Africa and the Caribbean are all broadly called 'coloured'.

During my stay in Britain I had been made to consider myself 'coloured', and the realisation remained with me in America. So when, while filling an application form for a driver's licence in Baltimore, Maryland, I was confronted with the question 'Race?' I ticked off 'Colored', The white official at the counter was confounded. 'You are as coloured as I am', he said to me. I smiled, looked hard at the application form but changed nothing. That only spurred him into a long, tortuous explanation which meant, in essence, that many years ago they had four colours printed on these forms: white, yellow, red, and black. 'None of these would have fitted me,' I said, 'only a *mixture* of yellow and red can describe my colour precisely.' Exasperated, he initialled my form with an angry stroke.

One of the blatant contradictions in the American racial scene that I noticed was that, despite prejudice, blacks were to be found in some of the most intimate situations of white American life: as valets, often to Southern 'gentlemen', nannies, cooks and waiters. I could unravel this paradox only by taking an historical view. Racial relationships had been formed during the period of black slavery and within the plantation economy. This enabled the white masters to successfully combine economic exploitation with a paternalistic attitude towards their slaves whom they had managed to reduce, through terror and oppression, to shadows, 'invisible men'. As such, a black could be allowed to exist close to the master, forever serving him, without the master visualising him as a threat or an adversary. This pattern had continued, more so in the South than elsewhere. Here many of the segregated restaurants had black cooks and waiters! However, blinded by their traditional attitudes, the managers of these restaurants failed to see the irony. Such instances, although rare, were not unknown in the 'border' states like Maryland, where I lived.

I used to frequent a night club in Baltimore, Maryland. As long as I went there with a white girlfriend there was no problem. But when I took a black girlfriend with me, we were barred, subtly, not crudely, because, believe it or not, there existed, then, a local law against racial discrimination. The clerk at the counter told us that we needed reservations which, of course, we did not have. It was a lie. The clerk knew it; and I knew it; and my black girlfriend knew it. So we stared at one another and at the smooth black face on the poster at the counter, billed as the 'star of the night', for a while, then walked away, furiously aware that while a black girl had been kept out, the all-white audience inside were being entertained by a black comedian!

Who *exactly* did the clerk at the night club think I was, I wondered. It was a mystery that was soon to be solved when later I fell into conversation with a wiry old man in a bar in the South: this soon turned into an argument about the civil rights movement. At one point I mentioned my East Indian origin. The old man gave a sigh of relief. 'Jesus,' he said, 'I thought you was a Jew, a kike.' It struck me then that, to many Americans, I might as well be a Jew, an Italian- or Greek-American. As it happened, there was a Greek-American employed in the firm where I worked, who was a few shades darker than me. That gave me an idea.

I became a Greek from Cyprus, who had spent many years in London and had thus lost touch with the Greek language. For the rest, I devoured the pages on Cyprus in *Britannica*, memorised the vital statistics of Venus's birth-place and talked glibly about the Cyprus 'problem', which was very much in the news then and which I found far more interesting and challenging than answering the stereotype questions on India that were often thrown at me. I suddenly found myself being treated deferentially by white Americans as an heir to a superior (European) culture, and I noticed with surprise that I was genuinely touched by the inadequacy that many educated Americans of liberal disposition feel about their lack of 'background'! After an apologetic and marginal existence in Britain, I found my American experience exhilarating.

Changeling nationality apart, the situation regarding a job and girls—two reliable indicators of a society's reaction to a newcomer —was quite satisfactory. Had I wished to continue in the profession I then had—I held a M.Sc. in industrial management and was being groomed for a managerial position—I would have stayed on in America. The prospects were very good indeed, but I decided to give this up to write a novel that, I thought, I had in my head. I wanted to devote myself exclusively to writing. So I returned to England—to London—in 1964: it was then cheaper to live in England than in America.

I spent the first three years in London writing a novel and a stage-play. I had great difficulty in getting my novel published.[11] This, I am told, is the experience of almost all writers trying to sell their first novel. I do not know the reasons in the case of others, but I do know what happened to me, and why. My novel was not, technically speaking, sub-standard, nor was it exotic or written in 'Indian English'. It was, indeed, a serious, taut, well-written piece of work, set in modern Britain. But it was my point of view and tone of writing that proved unpalatable to the readers of the manuscript, almost always housewives in the Home Counties, on whose judgement the publisher's editor based his decision. One reader wrote in her report:

'Leaves (at least with myself) a distinct feeling that we might be better off without Indian immigrants. I don't think we are ready for an Indian anti-hero, certainly not in our setting. For myself I prefer not to think of Indians as men who get drunk too quickly and talk too loudly.'[12]

Another reader wrote:

'The characters are well drawn, and much of the detail is good. I like the humour too, but the reader is not encouraged to be properly sympathetic to the main character.'

During a meeting with the chief editor of a publishing house, who was apparently favourably disposed towards me, I asked how I could arouse the readers' sympathy towards the central character. 'If after reading the novel,' he replied, 'I felt glad that I was not the hero that would arouse my sympathy'. So there we were, back to the days of Rudyard Kipling. What the publisher found difficult to accept was the idea of presenting a black central character who was more than a match for most of the members of the (one-time) master race in intelligence, wit, articulation and simple verve.

I knew that such an attitude existed and was widely held; but, as yet, there was no acknowledgement of this fact among the politically powerful middle class. This was the case until the PEP (Political & Economic Planning Ltd) published a report, in April 1967, which established, beyond a shadow of doubt, that racial discrimination existed in England, and that it was widespread. This caused a perceptible change, particularly in the middle-class environment to which I was, and am, personally exposed.

It is worth noting that my freelance journalistic career started with a summary of the PEP report for the *Tribune*. After that I went on to write for other British papers, and compile programmes for BBC radio, often, but not always, on race relations in Britain and America. Simultaneously I stayed with my earlier vocation: writing books, a job that demands a high degree of stamina, patience and devotion, and which is becoming, financially, less and less rewarding. The only consolation is that, unlike newspaper articles or broadcasts, which are ephemeral, books are durable and remain available for at least a few years.

Living in London and being in touch with people in mass media have given me further insight into the working of British society. I realise, more than ever before, the supremacy that the middle class enjoys in practically every facet of British life, be it accent, fashion, education or Parliament. I wrote about it in my book *Black British, White British* thus:[13]

'Although a numerical minority, the middle class is relatively over-represented in the seats of power and persuasion—in Parliament, civil service, communications media and the universities. A study made in the late 1950s revealed that whereas nearly 75% of the population was working class, less than 10% of the students at Oxford and Cambridge (which then produced nearly one-quarter of all university graduates each year) had a working-class background. Also, nearly 40% of all MP's had Oxbridge degrees. Since then the situation has hardly changed. At present 39% of all MP's have Oxbridge degrees. Of the 630 MP's only 61 are 'mineworkers, engineers, railwaymen and other manual workers'; the remaining are 'barristers and solicitors (115), company directors (110), teachers and lecturers (65), journalists (60), landowners (42), managers and administrators (41), businessmen (36) and other professionals'.[14]

Even the trade union movement, a citadel of the working class, has not remained immune from middle-class influences. The upper ranks of the movement tend to manifest middle-class mannerisms, styles and attitudes. Almost invariably, the attachment to middle-class values among the leadership of British institutions (no matter what the economic and class profile of the institution's members) is related directly to the level of leadership: the higher the rank, the greater the obeisance to middle-class mores. This explains the divergence that exists, for instance, between MP's and local councillors, national and local trade union leaders, and the editors of the national quality and the provincial and local papers.

A central characteristic of the British middle class is its preference for gentility, moderation, pragmatism, subtlety and intellectualism over passion, radicalism, dogmatism, forthrightness and emotionalism. In short, the middle class aspires to remain 'civilised' to the point of blandness. It prefers to say, for instance, 'lavatory' to 'toilet', 'making love' to 'fucking'. Against this background, it is understandable why many MPs, civil servants, academics and journalists are averse to saying 'coloured immigrants', 'coloured' or 'blacks' instead of 'immigrants', 'Commonwealth immigrants' or simply 'newcomers'. Sometimes this evasiveness drives such moderate bodies as the Wolverhampton Association of Schoolmasters to blurt out in despair 'Instead of talking about this problem as if it were something indecent (the kind of thing that must not be mentioned on a Department of Education and Science Course where there are only 'nice, middle-class people' present)—present it to the profession and the nation as the major challenge of the 1970's'.

A personal experience brought home to me the dichotomy that exists between the middle class and others. I appeared once, during the early 1968, on BBC television's *Talkback* concerning its treatment of race and immigration in news and documentary programmes. I felt the cold hostility of the all-white audience in the studio focussed on me. One of the British participants sharing the platform with me told me bluntly, albeit privately, that the BBC ought not to invite 'foreigners' like me to its studio. I told him, equally bluntly, that he ought to say this to some higher-up in the BBC, not me, and that he should restrict himself to discussing the *issue* on hand and not personalities. At the end of the programme came the 'treatment' from the BBC producers, their assistants and 'hospitality' girls: drinks, wide smiles, and correct liberal sentiments: a different world altogether.

This incident illustrated to me, if any illustration was indeed required, that no matter what passport I possessed, I— or, for that matter, any person of Afro-Asian[15] origin—would be considered a 'foreigner'. I say this without any sense of anger, disappointment or despair, because, to be honest, I have never tried, or will ever try, to win the 'acceptance' of the natives here, collectively or individually. I do not really give a damn. All I care about is that I should be able to do what I most wish to do—to write—in comparative peace.

As far as the Afro-Asians, as a group, are concerned, I have never taken seriously the slogan of integration—by which is meant social integration—raised by the Establishment, especially the Establishment liberals. I do not see social integration of different races in Britain taking place for the next few generations and say as much, but at greater length, in the last chapter of my book *Black British, White British*.[16] What I see existing now, and continuing to exist for quite some time to come, is the pattern of social pluralism whereby, as Professor Michael Banton explains, 'members of different minorities enjoy equality in respect of civil rights and obligations, but keep themselves separate in marriage and mutual hospitality, while rivalling one another in other contexts—such as in political organisation'. This definition includes not only racial but also religious minorities, such as the Catholics in Northern Ireland.

Continued realisation of being a member of a minority, in my case, has engendered what I would like to call 'minority-mindedness'. That is, I tend, almost by reflex, to identify myself with minorities whether they be gypsies, Ulster Catholics, hippies, homosexuals or 'hash'-smokers. Actually, I stopped being a member of the majority community so long ago that I have lost the feeling.

It was only recently, when I returned to India to collect material for a socio-political book, that a feeling of belonging to the mainstream was revived. It was, in fact, more than that. My hair style, dress and accent led the Indians who came into contact with me to place me intuitively in an upper middle-class bracket, a member of the elite. This was a novel experience for me, quite unsettling. It was also ironic. Because, while in India, I soon came to regard myself not as a conscious, or sub-conscious, supporter of the ruling elite, but its uncompromising critic. Having perceived the subtle means by which the rich and upper middle classes in Britain have succeeded in establishing, and maintaining, their hold over the cultural and political consciousness of other classes, I found it comparatively easy to perceive the not-too-subtle means employed by the elite in India to achieve the same result.

A question arose in my mind: would I have perceived this if I had not left India and lived in the West? I could not answer this in categorical terms: 'Yes' or 'No'. Instead, I could say without hesitation that, but for my experience and intellectual growth in the West, I would not have perceived the class relationships in India as clearly, and quickly, as I actually did.

Indeed, this heightened perception has led me to regard the term 'West' as inexact and substitute it with the phrase 'an advanced industrial capitalist society' (which happens to exist only in the West[17]). By the same token, I find it more meaningful to say that I was born in a feudal society, grew up in a pre-capitalist environment and have passed my adult years in an advanced capitalist society rather than say that I was born in Sind, educated in Bombay, and have lived and worked in the West.

Thus seen, I realise that I emerge as a member of another kind of minority, one of those comparatively small number of people in the world who, for whatever reasons, have found themselves moving, within a generation, from a feudal environment to an advanced industrial society—a remarkable phenomenon by any standard, past or present.

NOTES

1. By 'black', I mean anybody, and everybody, who is not white. I mean the same when I use the term 'coloured'.

2. Particularly the West European societies.

3. The absence of racial difference does not eliminate the possibility of conflict between immigrants and host society. Note, for instance, the conflict that has arisen when people from the semi-feudal Southern Italy and Sicily have migrated to (the advanced capitalist) West Germany.

4. The blacks in America may be considered as colonial people who, over the past generation, have been actively engaged in liberating themselves.

5. It is worth noting that Zulfikar Ali Bhutto, the present President of Pakistan—with whom, incidentally, I share the birth-place—delivered his first broadcast, as the President, in English *only*!

6. It was much later, after many years of residence in the West, that I realised that the concept of individualism was closely bound up with the capitalistic system of production. It was therefore unrealistic of me to have expected my family members to behave differently from the way they actually did.

7. Britain was the only country 'open' to the Indians then.

8. Having worked in both the rural and urban India, I had known that the real India exists outside the cities. And so I presumed that the real England lay beyond London.

9. Almost always the girls took me to be a doctor.

10. Many Asians and West Indians, when back in their countries of origin, either temporarily or permanently, right away feel the absence of speed and orderliness of the Western world. This makes them often angry and frustrated, and sometimes sharply disparaging of 'the natives'.

11. My novel, *A Triangular View*, was finally published by Dobson in 1969, was widely noticed and generally well received. The following year my play, *To Anchor A Cloud* (Writers Workshop, Calcutta, 1972), about the Moghul emperor who built the Taj Mahal (a subject far removed from modern race relations) was produced in London.

12. This statement was apparently based on a brief scene in the novel where the 'anti-hero' pays for getting 'drunk too quickly' and for 'talking too loudly': he is beaten up inside the pub.

13. Eyre & Spottiswoode, London, 1971, pp. 315–6.

14. *The Times*, June 20, 1970.

15. The term includes people from the Caribbean because almost all of them originate from Africa or Asia.

16. *Op. cit.*, see pp. 350–62.

17. Japan is probably the only exception.

2 Through a Glass Darkly

J. AYODELE LANGLEY

'If you no know who sie you commot, mus know who sie you dey go'; 'ham sa bop si topa yal labok'. These are Krio and Wollof aphorisms nearly every Gambian has had drummed into his or her head by the elders from childhood to adolescence. Very loosely, they mean 'if you don't know your origins, you must at least know where you are going' and 'self knowledge is next to Godliness'. It is odd, but the real meaning of these common Gambian sayings only began to dawn on me with unusual force and clarity only two years after my entry into British society some nine years ago.

I was then a student on government scholarship and was considered one of the fortunate few to have this boon bestowed on them by the benign, all powerful, paternal masters of the day, the local representatives of Her Majesty's Britannic Empire. This was the opinion of the colonial society in which I was born, a society which had experienced and has partly been shaped by, 300 years of British overrule; a society the urbanised and educated members of which had become so British in certain modes of thinking and yet so stubbornly African (or rather, Gambian) in others that it would probably require a monograph to analyse its split personality. In short, I was born into the colonial society of Bathurst, the Gambia; the very name of the town is a clear indication of its strong British colonial connection and of the attitudes of its members. Up to the age of sixteen, I knew very little about the rest of the country outside Bathurst; all I knew were names of places there and I often heard some of my Wollof and Krio relatives say that 'they' were ignorant and backward and that our town was more 'civilised'. They said it with such finality and authority that I simply came to take this 'fact' as given. We all did—I mean my parents, relatives and schoolmates. Whatever the older ones said was true. After all, did not the white men bring education to them first? That group of people in the town who believed this most fervently and lost no opportunity in asserting it were the Creoles or Akus, most of whom could trace their origins to Freetown, Sierra Leone. The other section, the Wollofs, generally subscribed to this attitude, adding to it their ancient pride and dignity. Through my parents, I was a member of both groups: the former were mostly Christians, very Victorian in outlook and with a strong predilection for out-moded English manners; the latter were mostly Muslims, generally caste conscious, and needed no European to lecture them on the virtues of being loyal to one's traditions. In spite of the differences in religion and acculturation, both groups did have certain values in common—mutual aid, respect for one's elders, loyalty to the Empire, responsibility for relatives, however distant, hospitality and the dominance of the men. More importantly, through intermarriage, a series of bewildering family ties sometimes made one wonder whether Islam, Christianity and colonialism have in reality created any fundamental divisions in African society.

School for me began at five; curiously enough, my mother who was not literate in English, was instrumental in sending me to one of the elite schools, the Methodist Girls (yes, Girls!) High School—I learnt years later that my father, then a police sergeant, intended sending me to the school where the pupils went barefoot and wore khaki shirts and shorts. I suppose he wanted to make a man out of me. Whatever the reason, I found myself at kindergarten in the girls school; school lunch was prepared by an ambitious mother, brown (Clarks) sandals were bought, blue shirt and shorts, and white helmet, and I was off to school. I really cannot remember much about those days, except that (thanks to the kindness of the Methodist Mission and their supporters in England) we had a band, rode tricycles; played at drinking tea (we had miniature cups and saucers from England, and even a few grains of sugar) and slept soundly in campbeds on the verandah outside the classrooms, after which we were woken up by the teacher, said 'Ah Fallah' (our father) sang 'Now the day is over . . .' and then trooped off in small groups to our homes. Sometimes we lost our helmets, or we would go home with a helmet size too big or too small. I always went home with a dirty uniform.

From Kindergarten, through prep school to high school (I mean the Methodist *Boys*' High School), one always knew instinctively that one belonged to a fortunate privileged few whose parents could reasonably assume that their sons would achieve the height of their ambition—a 'high post' or a 'big man' in government service, i.e. an administrator (civil service), a doctor, lawyer, or at least some sort of big clerkly job. One hardly heard mention of technical jobs like engineering or agriculture, as these to our parents' thinking, were not white men's jobs. No, the white men they knew all wore white shirts and shorts, drove cars, lived in bungalows, had servants and worked in big offices equipped, among other things, with messengers and electric fans. One's education was therefore one big effort towards this goal. Yet, one had no idea just what the colonial government was educating us for. It is against this background of social attitudes and expectations that at the age of nineteen I was awarded a government scholarship to complete my education or rather, obtain a certificate in a British University. It had to be a British University in those days, and probably still is.

Looking back almost ten years, I still find it difficult to analyse fully my reactions to those areas of British life and thoughts to which I was exposed as a young student. Six months ago before I left Britain to return home finally, I could have written one long angry monograph of negative experiences and reactions; my reactions are so mixed that even after nine years in Britain, I am tempted to say 'never again'! I am tempted to say that I was merely there physically, and that even my physical movements and encounters were severely limited. I had very few British friends, nearly all of whom I knew principally as classmates or research colleagues with whom I came into daily contact and to whose homes I was invited a few times. The vast majority of people outside the University I did not know at all, except perhaps the grocer down the road with whom I would exchange a few jokes whenever I went to purchase biscuits, coffee, newspapers or cigarettes—oh yes, and the barmaid and sales girls who always greeted me with 'hallo luv' and even occasionally engaged me in brief conversation about the nasty weather and about the sunshine they thought I was missing in Africa. My encounters with the public were often silent encounters —in the streets, on the buses, in cinemas, restaurants and, quite often, even on the campus. You were visible and invisible at the same time. They stared at you, sometimes directly but usually quite often furtively, out of curiosity (or fear?) and you either stared back, ignored them or pretended to look elsewhere. Occasionally, a few brave ones among them, the ones we foreign students jokingly called 'human', would ask you questions about what you were studying, how you were settling down, where you came from, etc., and would even comment on some aspects of their society. For the most part, however, it was like sojourning in a strange land. Talking about strange land, I can now understand some of those West Indian reggae like 'Rivers of Babylon' and 'Hard Road to Travel', etc. They are the black man's cry of pain in the socio-cultural wasteland in which he has to exist but of which, try as he may, he cannot become a member. To be more exact, it is a technological wasteland in as much as the very colour of their skin condemns them to the status of observers on the periphery of a society whose ideological barrier of race and colour is proof, if indeed proof was needed, of that society's denial of the black man's humanity and potential contribution. Inevitably, the foreigner is forced back into the castle of his skin. '*They* are so different', 'he's got a chip on his shoulder', 'he doesn't mix', 'go back to the trees you came from!' and quite recently 'blacks go home', 'voluntary repatriation', etc. All this one had to swallow in silence—at least in public. A few of us students would protest occasionally, but the majority, protected as they were by the relatively liberal atmosphere of the University, merely got on with the business of passing exams and returning home—most of them to ape the manners of the very natives who had made life in Britain such a hell for them. In fact, a few ignorant African and Asian students, perhaps out of a peculiar perversity I still cannot understand, deliberately shut their eyes to the *fact* of racial discrimination, and religiously ingratiated themselves and strove with might and main to be perfect images of God's own Englishmen. The natives were not impressed; neither was I.

I cannot really say that I learnt or understood much about Britain and the British during my first three years. I only knew I was different; in fact consciousness of my being different was literally forced upon me. I came, I should think, with an open mind, colonial as I was. School, British and Empire history of which we had a good dose, British Council and the church had taught me to believe, naively of course, that the British were friendly, especially towards their colonial brethren. There was no reason to believe that I would encounter any difficulties there. I merely thought I would go there and benefit from the best they could offer. The first hint of things to come was when, immediately upon my arrival in London, the British Council saw fit to organise a one-week 'introduction' course. We were told in so many lectures things like how to use the toilet, how to eat with knives and forks, what to wear, how to behave, etc. That was the first shock. Then came the frequent attempts by our British Council friends to organise the foreign students' activities, the invitations requesting you to wear your 'national costume', and the general patronising attitude of some of the officials who explained things so elaborately as if they were talking to children in a nursery. After about a year I rebelled. I had had enough of the British Council and other cultural empire loyalist organisations. In spite of this initial disillusionment, however, I remained as correct in my behaviour as our hosts could desire. In short, I was determined not to be labelled 'different'. Outwardly, I adopted their reserve and correctness of manner, simply to avoid trouble and get on with my studies. The food was not too bad, the only trouble, for one accustomed to hot stews and sauces, was that much of it was boiled—all those potatoes, Brussels sprouts and strange vegetables. I just could not bear the salad; a Nigerian friend used to call it grass, and whenever it was salad time we would make polite excuses and dash off to the Indian restaurants.

The vacations were always something to look forward to; after exams I would spend a week or so relaxing in the hall of residence which had become my home before going down to London where my Gambian friends, especially the married ones, would invite me to all those delicious dishes I had missed so badly. That too was the time those of us on vacation would meet those who were working and exchange experiences, make fun of the British and their ways and damn them all for our problems, often ending our evenings with one of their great pastimes—in the pub. Quite often we would go into a Wimpy Bar or a fish and chip shop after a good session in the pub. I wonder what the whites thought of this?

I went through my first University in Wales as quickly as I came in. In general, those three years were pleasant, particularly as I got on well with my fellow students in the small student hall where I stayed. I made friends quite easily there; there was much social and intellectual activity there, although I rigorously eschewed student union politics. My favourites in hall were Alec the porter-cum-home spun philosopher, always regaling me with his fantastic stories about Martians, and the matron who insisted on mothering me and always made sure I was well fed. Anticipating my later experiences in Britain, I shall always remember my first encounter with Alec; I had just arrived to start my first year, and after showing me my room he introduced himself with: 'Look son, to me a man's a man until he proves himself otherwise'. I think Robert Burns would agree with that. Which takes me to Scotland, where I spent my next six years as a post-graduate student and as a University lecturer.

Without planning it, I found myself moving from a Welsh University to a Scottish one. Perhaps it was this attachment to the Celtic fringe that has stimulated my nationalism. I had always identified myself in a vague way with the aspirations of the Welsh nationalists, and to a lesser extent with Scottish nationalism. Perhaps it was the anti-English and anti-colonial aspect that interested me. But I always had a liking for the warmth, cultural autonomy and rhetoric of the Welsh. Friends and colleagues often commented on my Afro-Welsh accent. I still have a certain nostalgia for Wales and the Welsh. I found Scotland too cold and the University system

rather different. The intellectual community was particularly stimulating. Apart from academic connections, I must say, however, that
I found the city rather dull and uninteresting possibly because as a
research student I had very little time to get to know the city well.
In fact, apart from the University and the student areas, my knowledge of the city was very limited. My research trips to London and
West Africa must have contributed to this lack of feeling for this
cold conservative northern city. Most of the time one was in a state
of anomie; one could hardly make contact with the locals without
appearing to intrude or break an unwritten understanding not to
come too close to them. At least that was how I felt. Perhaps the
cold weather was responsible for this social inaccessibility. The
African students would organise a few dances and then disperse into
their various national unions and social groups. A few who probably found it difficult to adapt chose to remain under the aegis of
the British Council: they were always there, playing table tennis,
scrabble, watching indescribably boring films or going on organised
tours. I hardly ever went there, as I felt their activities were artificial and totally irrelevant to my problems and needs. What I
needed was communication with individuals who interested me and
not with anonymous organised groups. Social relations tended to be
too formal and artificial, and one always detected the clumsiness
and unease of the majority of people one came into contact with.
As time went on I even began to doubt the sincerity of most of those
who professed to be acquainted with me. Did these people know
and accept me as an individual and not as a bright black chap they
considered unusual and interesting? What about all those locals
who usually looked at you with that combination of curiosity and
hostility (I wonder whether they also pitied me?), as if they were
questioning my right to be in their country at all?

No, it was not entirely like that; one occasionally noticed an old
man or woman who would smile and nod approvingly as if he or
she was pleased to see a serious looking black student who might,
benefit from higher education in Britain. Most of the time, however,
even before the rise of Powellism in the late sixties, one was conscious of the indifference bordering on hostility. My own attitude
was simply to get on with my business so long as they did not bother
me, and to value the friendship and comradeship of those who
offered it sincerely. As a result I had only very few friends among
them and these, except one, were academic colleagues. Local girl
friends? Only once did I make the error of breaking a seven-year
rule of not dating local girls. The affair lasted exactly two months.
The 'lassie' in question, although a University student, was as pre-

judiced as I expected, even though she wanted to marry me! What really shocked me was the reaction of some of the white males to the affair; one of them who professed to be my friend took it so badly that he resorted to all sorts of mischief, including deliberate misrepresentation, to end the relationship. I watched in amazement. 'Whatever else you do when you go there, always remember, leave their women alone.' Yes, my mother told me that before I went to their country. My brief experience merely strengthened my doubts about interracial marriage; dating local girls could sometimes be a waste of one's time and often a humiliating business involving so many compromises as to make one lose one's identity and autonomy. I was determined to be myself even if I was dating Miss U.K.

Teaching at the University had its rewards and problems. Naturally, I was pleased, even surprised, with the appointment. I would have returned home had my Government required my services. It appeared that they did not. All the more reason why I spared no effort to accomplish the task expected of a University teacher and satisfy the expectations of those who had enough confidence in me to appoint me to that post. I am grateful for the opportunity I was given to contribute to the intellectual life of the University community and for all the opportunities offered me by a great and liberal University.

Surprisingly enough, I encountered only a few difficulties with the students. If I may be permitted to say so, I even forgot my colour, as, I think, did some of the students. A few, of course, took some time getting used to me. Then there were others who would constantly refer problems to me, the general idea being that I was more sympathetic. Exactly what that means I do not know. I will always remember the visiting white American student who, after attending a political thought tutorial on Plato, immediately requested the Director of Studies to transfer him to another tutorial class. Perhaps I was a bad teacher, or perhaps he could not get over the shock of a black man explaining the analogy of the cave to whites—I suspect it was the latter case.

It was exciting explaining African social, political and economic problems to the students, but there were problems too, as some of the students, brought up with so many myths, stereotypes and fantasies about Africa and the Africans, simply found it difficult to grasp the geographical and socio-linguistic diversity of the continent. These had to be thoroughly emphasised before one could talk about economic development, politics, etc. I even went so far as to confess my ignorance of certain parts of modern Africa so as to emphasise the impossibility of generalising about a whole continent, even by one who was born in a part of it.

How did I react to the students generally? I felt that compared to the students in some African Universities I know they took University education less seriously, although I liked the relatively informal relationship between teachers and students, as opposed to the practice in African Universities where the lecturers and Professors are almost gods. But I was a little uneasy about just how much freedom was being accorded to the students who demanded more say in the types of courses taught, the relevance of the subjects, University discipline, appointment of University lecturers, assessment of lectures and lecturers, etc. While I broadly sympathised with their views (and I taught some interesting students in this group of radicals) and agreed that courses must as far as practicable take account of the social and moral concerns of the students and that staff and students must engage in constant dialogue, I had the feeling that this could turn some academics into pop performers more interested in 'student interests' and other peripheral matters. I also felt that too much valuable time was being spent on the many committees dealing with the problem of student demands. Whatever one's views, I do not think that students are the best judges of a lecturer's ability or of the contents of courses. Any lecturer worth his salt should be able to teach his subject(s) at the highest level possible while taking, wherever possible, due account of contemporary problems and policies. In African Universities, I believe this search for relevance should be initiated by the lecturers themselves within the Universities, in the schools and in the local press.

My reactions to University life in Britain lead me to the problem of the role of black intellectuals in Britain. Do they in fact have a role? The answer to this question depends, I think, on the individual and his circumstances. Some foreign intellectuals choose to stay for a variety of reasons—some may be refugees, others, by virtue of high academic attainment, may have priced themselves out of the employment market in their home countries; others probably lack suitable opportunities in their home countries. In some cases their families may have settled in Britain permanently. As stated earlier, my original aim was to return home immediately I completed my post-graduate studies. As I could not do so, I came to regard the employment I had in Britain as an opportunity to contribute to research in African studies as well as an opportunity to gain wider experience to enable me to contribute, at a later stage, to my country's development. In retrospect, I may also add that I was more concerned during this period with a critical appraisal of the role of

intellectuals in Africa and the problems of development in Africa
than with my host country. The dilemma lay in the fact that I valued
the intellectual freedom I enjoyed in Britain as well as the respon-
sibilities entrusted to me but felt I had little to contribute to my host
country except as an academic. On the other hand, I was deeply
pessimistic about any real opportunities I would be given to contribute to my country's development. I began to feel that the most
I could do in Britain was to interpret modern Africa, through the
University, to the students and, wherever possible, to the public.
But I gradually abandoned this idea with the worsening of race
relations in Britain over the last three years. Six years before that,
I would have attributed it to the traditional reserve of the British;
but the new xenophobia, sanctioned by certain politicians and
given a semblance of respectability by certain newspapers, was
altogether different and somewhat frightening. One could not say
exactly whether the myth of the traditionally polite and tolerant
English had suddenly been replaced by a new post-colonial Little
Englandism. One academic, fortunately not a fellow member of
staff, even told me to go home during a discussion at a party. This
man had taught in an African University. Yet another said within
my hearing *a propos* an anti-Powellite remark by a colleague, 'Let
them (i.e. the Asians and Afro-West Indians) go home if they don't
like it.' He meant it. Many were the other social aggressions against
immigrants—in the press, in public and even on television. We
were called a problem, we were told to integrate (plans for our
'integration' or, failing that 'voluntary repatriation', were even
discussed in the mass media), there were learned monographs,
books, articles, symposia, television documentaries on the 'racial
problem'—but except for a few accepted spokesmen, we were
hardly consulted. It was impossible for me to be indifferent.

Re-entry into my society did not pose serious problems as far as
adaptation was concerned. I was never a black Englishman. My
great fear of the return centred on the difficult problem or art of
retaining one's autonomy in a small intimate society. Here, as elsewhere in Africa, one finds an ambiguous coexistence of tradition
and modernity. One found one's roles already defined by the
society; you could not disagree with traditional wisdom; you are
not supposed to have changed during your stay abroad; you were
supposed to return to the same social arrangements you left nine
years ago. Your relatives take it upon themselves to re-orientate
you, by a series of visitations and briefings to the permanent realities and obligations. You become a human showpiece if you have
'achieved' something; no, you are not seen as an individual but as

so and so's son who will be 'taking up appointment' in such and such Ministry, starting at such and such salary. 'You see' some would say, 'he received his parents' blessing. Now they can reap the fruit of their labours. . . . May we all live to see our children's labour. . .'. Some would congratulate and welcome you back, but really your father got all the congratulations. Freud was right, after all. The welcoming and re-orientation ordeal lasts a month or so. You may survive it either by agreeing with everybody or by remaining passive and quietly getting on with your business. It is not so easy. Half the time immediately after your arrival you experience a certain difficulty in thinking out your personal problems clearly, as every decision you take may involve several other people whose conflicting advice and interests only serve to limit your freedom further and create more confusion. Break out of this social prison and you are immediately branded a deviant, a 'white man', and even sometimes a mentally unstable person. The secret seems to be to conform while not actually conforming! You are not even allowed to forget some aspects of the Britain you left behind; the pre-occupations of some members of the new elite remind you of it: their material concerns—cars, new fashions, modern houses, elegant Western-style dinners, and the social competition. Some fashions, even among the men, startle me: am I in Chicago, Harlem, Carnaby Street or Paris—or is it all a dream?

> The smart professionals in three piece,[1]
> Sweating away their humanity in driblets
> And wiping the blood from their brow
> We have found a new land
> This side of eternity
> And our songs are dying on our lips.
> Standing at hell's gate you watch those who seek admission
> Still the familiar faces that watched and gave you up
> As the one who had let the side down.
> 'Come on, old boy, you cannot dress like that'
> And tears well down in my eyes for them
> These who want to be seen in the best company
> Have adjured the magic of being themselves
> And in the new land we have found
> The water is drying from the towel
> Our songs are dead and we sell them dead to the other side
> Reaching for the Stars we stop at the house of Moon
> And pause to relearn the wisdom of our fathers.

1. George Awoonor-Williams: *We Have Found a New Land.*

3 The Spectre of Self-consciousness

BHIKHU PAREKH

> I think if we are to feel at home in the
> world . . . we shall have to admit Asia
> to equality in our thoughts, not only
> politically but culturally. What changes
> this will bring about I do not know, but
> I am convinced they will be . . . of the
> greatest importance.
>
> Bertrand Russell

My concern in this paper is threefold: first, to elucidate what have struck me as some of the important features of English character and society; second, to outline some aspects of Indian character; and third, to explore the inner tensions and anxieties of an Indian when he finds himself living in England. By its very nature such an enterprise is fraught with dangers and difficulties, and therefore some clarifying remarks concerning its nature and limits will not be inappropriate.

It is always an impertinence for a man to claim to write about a community of men, whether his own or another. He cannot avoid talking about them as if they were objects under a microscope, and this denies them their subjectivity and dignity. Further, he cannot avoid making general observations about them, and that involves denying them their uniqueness. Such general observations again have an air of unreality about them. While they might describe some members of a society accurately, they never fit all.

Despite all these and other difficulties, however, a study of a community of men has some point. It helps us to know how it is held together and what makes it a distinct and unique community. Although individually unique its members share a family of characteristics, a common national character, to understand which is to gain some appreciation of how and why they think and live the way they do. In comparing and contrasting the character of two societies we are able, further, to observe their unique achievements as well as their partialities and limitations. We can see how every culture or way of life develops only a limited range of human powers and sensitivities, and how therefore it can benefit from coming into contact with another that has developed different types of human capacities and emotions. A study of the character of different societies, in other words, offers us an intellectual vantage point from which to explore the possibility of a higher, more universal, and in that sense more fully human, form of life. It is a widely held belief among moral philosophers in the English-speaking world that a form of life is a self-enclosed unit which cannot be criticised from outside nor compared with others and evaluated. I hope to show, not by directly attacking it, but indirectly by examples, that the cultural solipsism underlying this view is seriously mistaken and that forms of life can be compared and critically evaluated.

Having lived in India for over twenty years and for over half as many in England, these are the two societies or, rather peoples, that fascinate me most. Life in England has changed me profoundly, in some cases for the better, in others for the worse, and has given rise to profound personal experiences which have, for lack of clear comprehension and articulation, remained a dark part of my mind which I can neither live with nor exorcise out of existence. Sometimes they appear to be an inseparable part of me, indeed a far more authentic and meaningful part, than anything that had happened to me before coming to England. At other times they appear unreal, almost like a dream that has left no trace behind. This paper is a foolhardy exercise in mental archaeology, and is inspired by the twofold hope that it might have a therapeutic value for its author and might even contribute to the much-needed self-knowledge of men sharing my predicament.

Naturally, therefore, this is a personal statement, but I hope it is not merely that. It draws on what I have seen and heard happen to other people and therefore is representative of their experiences as well. Indians and Englishmen to whom it refers are those whom I have encountered in the normal course of life, and they are mostly middle-class men. My analysis of English character is therefore largely an analysis of English middle-class character. But in a society as much dominated by its middle-class as England, an analysis based on the study of middle-class character is likely to be substantially true of the society as a whole. While I would readily admit that what I take to be the constitutive characteristics of English character are not to be found in equal degree in all classes, professional groups, or regions, they seem to me to be present in varying degrees in all Englishmen. This also seems to me to be the case with what I say about Indians and their experiences in England. Not all Indians feel exactly the way I have described, but there is hardly any of them, whatever his caste, class or degree of Anglicisation, who has not had some of these experiences during his stay in England.

I

The always challenging, often bewildering, and at times maddening aspect of living in England is the almost total inscrutability of English character and society. I use the term 'inscrutable' advisedly, and not to return the adjective the English generally employ to describe us Orientals. The English reticence to talk about themselves renders them rather opaque to foreigners; the difficulty is aggravated by the fact that many of the extant accounts of English character have come either from antipathetic foreigners who cannot stand the 'slow-moving', 'lethargic', 'arrogant' and 'narcissistic' English, or from over-enthusiastic foreigners who become, in Namier's words, 'passionately attached' to English institutions and take it upon themselves to provide the English with an ideology of their national culture, urging them to preserve what they regard as priceless English heritage against alien cultural influence.[1]

Since the English would not talk about themselves,[2] perhaps they cannot without seeming un-English, and since foreigners' accounts are too patently partisan to be of value, the English remain inscrutable to outsiders who continue to weave their own pet theories about them. What follows[3] is one such account, based on the belief that the ideal of self-containment, and the concern with spatiality, insecurity and social subtlety which it generates, perhaps offers a more reliable clue than most to English identity. Members of a vibrant and intelligent society naturally have different ideals concerning how they should live. But these ideals can and do conflict, and therefore every society needs a more general ideal in terms of which to arbitrate between them and decide which of them it should encourage and how. Further, it is a common experience that in every society ideals of good life compete for the loyalty of its members, and that one or more of them, assisted by historical, economic and social forces, acquires dominance. In England it is the ideal of self-containment that has enjoyed dominance for the past few hundred years.

Self-containment (and other members of this family of ideals such as self-sufficiency, self-possession and self-mastery) is, of course, a familiar ideal in every liberal society. However, for a variety of reasons England has taken individualism much further than most other liberal societies and has given it a rather peculiar orientation. Individualism is taken to imply that each individual is his own 'master', and wields absolute sovereignty over himself which he is in no circumstances to compromise. He should 'mind his own business', 'stand on his own feet', receive no 'favours' except when unavoidable, and 'return' them at the first available opportunity. This is indeed how manliness is defined, so that he who depends on others is not regarded a man in the full sense of the term. Only children, it is said, depend on others. Even as an Englishman will not depend on others, he does not want others to depend on him. In depending on him they prove their lack of manliness, and he cannot therefore respect them or accept them as his equal. He even feels that in helping those who need his help he encourages their unmanliness, and therefore does them profound harm. Unlike in traditional societies like India and China where the capacity to offer affection and friendship without their being formally solicited, and to receive favours without feeling burdened or weighed down is considered a sign of emotional maturity and moral adulthood, in England it generally signifies moral and psychological under-development. The English concern with self-sufficiency, further, is extended to emotional areas of life as well. It is considered un-manly to betray an emotion, whether in public or in private. To do so, it is said, is to 'make an exhibition' of oneself, to show that one is weak and unmanly, that one is not self-contained. Even in critical situations the Englishman is expected to appear cool and unflapp-able, a man in full possession of himself. As I argue later an indi-vidual striving to be possessed *of* himself is in constant danger of ending up being possessed *by* himself, and that while one is highly admirable, the other is pathological and neurotic.

Prima facie the degree of self-containment cherished by the Englishman would seem extremely difficult, even impossible, to achieve, certainly to a foreigner who cannot imagine how anyone can avoid feeling deeply upset and wanting to cry, or feeling un-controllably angry and wanting to blow up. Deeply felt emotions must surely break through the restrictive barriers imposed by the ego and express themselves in ways disapproved of by the ordinary conventions of civilised life.

The apparently impossible English ideal of self-containment would therefore seem attainable only under two conditions. First, the individual should possess such enormous discipline and will-power that he can keep all his emotions under control. Second, his emotions should not be too powerful, since the weaker they are, the easier it is to control them. To put the point differently the ideal of self-containment requires a very strong self-control, or weak emotions, or both, and it is precisely these characteristics that English society seems to cultivate.

The endearing Epicureanism or, rather hedonism, of the English conceals, and indeed is founded on, a very powerful stoic impulse in the English character. Stoicism is cultivated and reinforced in a number of ways. From his childhood onwards the Englishman is required to discipline his emotions and to 'behave himself'. His temperamental 'outbursts' are discouraged by means of ridicule, social disapproval and punishment. One of the dominant images regulating parents' attitude to their children is that of the gardener pruning a plant; the child, it is feared, will grow misshapen or not grow at all if not properly moulded. Geoffrey Gorer is probably right in saying that English is the only European language which uses the same word *nursery* to refer to the place where both children and plants are reared.[4] Character, it is generally believed, is a matter of developing will-power, and development of will-power requires concentration, regulation of moods, and disciplining and mastering of feelings. A child would therefore be made to go through dull and boring routines because this is considered a desirable discipline, and would from time to time be made to endure small and avoidable privations on the ground that it is good for him to learn to do without things. It is suggestive that the withdrawing and stopping of privileges[5] is the most common punishment meted out to children in England. They are forbidden their favourite toys or pastimes or pocket money or food, or are put to bed early or are locked up in a room. The child is allowed to enjoy his pleasures but is made to feel that they are 'privileges' granted him by his parents, and are conditional on his continued good behaviour. Pleasure therefore appears to him not as a right but as a gift, and self-discipline is inseparably associated with its enjoyment. The image of the ideal man presented to the child is that of a man who enjoys pleasures but is not their 'slave', a man who can let his hair down but can collect himself at will; in short, a man whose will-power ensures him a complete mastery over himself. It is its ability to ground hedonism on Stoicism, and to make enjoyment of pleasure contingent on the cultivation of Stoic will-power, that probably explains the enormous hold the myth that the Englishman is at his best when 'his back is against the wall' has over English imagination. By reassuring him that when troubles come he has only to summon up his vast resources of will and energy, the myth leaves him free to enjoy life without any anxiety for the future. At the same time, almost as a price for granting him the licence to pursue pleasures with a clear conscience, the myth sternly exacts from him great sacrifices in times of crisis and requires him to keep his will-power in full trim for such occasions.[6]

The enormous emphasis on will-power, on self-mastery, on suppression of public and even private manifestation of emotions cannot but weaken the power of emotions. Of course, because a group of people does not express its emotions, it does not follow that it does not feel them with as much intensity as those who manifest them on every conceivable occasion. There is also a danger involved in talking about emotions as if they were an abstract homogeneous mass, since a group of people may not feel emotional about one set of issues but may feel deeply emotional about others. Despite these and other qualifications to which a comparison of the emotional life of different communities is necessarily subject, it would not be grossly inaccurate to say that the emotional life of the Western man, and more particularly of the Englishman, lacks the depth and intensity of, e.g., the Asian or the African. A number of factors are responsible for this difference.

Life is generally so organised in the West that emotion has an extremely limited role to play. Relations between individuals here are not generally direct and immediate but mediated by a complex body of rules and conventions. Rules necessarily create space and distance between men, whereas it is the very nature of emotion to negate distance. The greater the role of rules and conventions, the greater is the emphasis on distance between individuals governed by them, and therefore the lesser is the role of emotions. When there are definite conventions concerning how one individual is to conduct himself towards another, a deviation from them is naturally frowned upon and generally achieves nothing. If I want a civil servant or a businessman or a politician or a lecturer to do something, I am expected to proceed in a way clearly laid down; appealing to his emotions by crying, entreating or outlining my problems and miseries to him is not only of no avail but is generally counterproductive. When social life is seen as a cluster of roles and each individual considers it his duty to be guided by impersonal rules, emotions naturally appear arbitrary, irrational and out of place.

Not only in the civil but also in private life, emotions have come to play a limited role in the West, largely because of the dominant individualistic ethos. If my life is 'my' life and I am free to live it as I consider most conducive to my interest, my relations with others are naturally based on my calculations of where my interests lie. Friendship, marriage, etc. therefore appear more like alliances than

THE SPECTRE OF SELF-CONSCIOUSNESS 47

an intimate fusion of two persons, and can be dissolved when they appear to have become a liability. If a husband and wife cannot get on with each other, they accept that their relationship prevents them from living the way they want to live, and decide to separate. If one party were to appeal to the other's emotion or to urge him or her to make a sacrifice of his or her interest, it would be regarded as exerting an undue emotional pressure and will be strongly resisted. Or, again, if a spouse dies or business collapses, one simply comes to terms with it and, after a brief interval, resumes the thread of life as if these events had never occurred. Reflecting, ruminating, brooding over the significance and meaning of such events slows the tempo of life and is regarded as wasteful. The English proverb that there is no use crying over spilt milk sums up this attitude very well. To someone accustomed to a different approach to life, crying over spilt milk, brooding over events long past, assimilating their significance, and allowing them to mould one's consciousness and change one's pattern of life, is precisely what gives life a dimension of depth.

A highly industrialised, professionalised and individualistic society then leaves little room for emotions. They have no obvious role to play. They do not further an individual's objectives and even positively hinder his realisation of them. Although the weakening of emotions is a common phenomenon in all Western societies, in England it has gone much further for reasons too complex to disentangle. Expressions of emotions are frowned upon here far more than in most other societies. They are taken to betray unmanliness, and are therefore considered signs of weakness. It is difficult to see how the powerful restraints imposed on the expression of emotions could over a time fail to influence the structure and intensity of emotions themselves.[7] Emotions, like ideas, thrive on being displayed. If certain ideas are never expressed, people generally lose the ability to think them. Not seeing them publicly expressed, they feel timid and unsure about them and come to regard them as abnormal and perverse, and would therefore tend to push them out of their mind. In the same way a man is likely to feel, in the absence of its public manifestations, that his experience of an emotion may be morbid, perverse, exaggerated, unwarranted, abnormal. He is therefore likely to suppress not only the *expression* but also the *experience* of it. He would be constantly on his guard against the emotion and would want to nip it in the bud and to avoid situations where he is likely to experience it.[8]

Intense emotion, further, implies that one is willing and prepared to let emotions temporarily take over one's entire being, that one is

not averse to being swept off one's feet. But this is something against
which the Englishman constantly fights. His concern to remain in
full possession of himself is generally taken to mean that he should
never allow his behaviour to be guided by anything other than a
careful consideration of consequences. Cool calculation and Stoic
self-control have so much become a part of his character that his
deepest instincts revolt against his being swept off his feet even for
a short period. Since English emotions have a powerful restraining
element built into them, one would suspect that they rarely reach
their 'natural' intensity.

One index to a nation's emotionality is its response to death, an
event rightly surrounded in all human communities by intense
emotional experiences. In this context some of Geoffrey Gorer's
findings on the English attitude to death are revealing. He reports[9]
that in England as a whole less than a fifth of the people questioned
had given up any of their *leisure* activities after the death of a close
relative, and that in the Midlands and western half of the country,
the figure fell to little more than one in ten. Such abstentions,
further, were 'most uncommon' after the death of a brother or a
sister, and were practised chiefly in the case of the death of a parent
and, to a slightly lesser extent, of a husband or wife. Gorer found,
further, that only less than four per cent of the people cut down on
their *social* life after the death of a close relative; the overwhelming
majority of them continued to entertain or visit friends and their
clubs as if nothing had happened. To an outsider it seems remarkable that even the death of a father or a mother or a wife or a brother
does not seem to make a shattering impact on an Englishman.

Although the Englishman's emotion generally lacks intensity
and does not influence his life in a way that it does that of other
peoples, his life is not a de-emotionalised rationalist artifact. He
has a capacity for emotions which, although not as developed as in
other societies, is nevertheless there. But as he is fearful of
emotions and as he has not been able to integrate them into his way
of life, his emotions have a shyness and tentativeness about them.
Not only does he not flaunt them as, for example, Indians do, but he
does not even admit them to himself. They are confined either to
the political realm where he can freely display them without seeming odd, or to the private realm where he can appear odd without
being noticed. In the political realm his emotions centre around
pageantry, ceremonies, parliamentary rituals and events surrounding the monarchy. It is not so much the person of the monarch
as the ceremonies surrounding him or her that generally seem to
evoke an emotional response from the Englishman. In the private

realm it is striking how much of his emotional energy is expended on animals and hobbies. Children are no doubt shown considerable affection, but not always of the kind shown to animals. The Englishman does not generally feel inhibited in pampering a cat or in taking her in his lap in the presence of visitors, but would feel odd in doing this to his children. It is therefore hardly surprising that sometimes maltreated animals earn greater publicity than battered babies, as happened not very long ago.[10]

When English emotions have a human orientation they are often attached to dead men from whom there is no danger of reciprocity and involvement. The Englishman's nostalgia for the great men of the past and the affection with which he talks about them is striking. He will talk about Disraeli, Peel, Gladstone, Lloyd George or Churchill with such intimate knowledge and emotion that an outsider might suspect that they were his long-standing friends or neighbours who died only yesterday. When English emotions lack objects, they sometimes take rather strange forms. A large part of the nation would get upset about an unfortunate panda who will not mate; or about a bird which will not return to its cage in a zoo; or about a boy deservedly punished for a crime in a foreign country; or about a child who has become a subject of dispute between her separated parents.[11] Where no such objects are available, they tend to be manufactured. Trivial incidents are presented as signalling mortal threats to the English way of life; small 'affairs' get blown up into crises in international relations; and quarterly statements of trade figures become occasions for national rejoicing or mourning as the case may be. One wonders if the English would dissipate their emotions on relatively unimportant objects and lose all sense of perspective if their interpersonal life was characterised by greater warmth, trust and affection.

Because of his preoccupation with self-sufficiency, the Englishman wants to be left alone to regulate his life and environment as he pleases. His concern therefore is to carve out a portion of space which is his own and which he can stop others from trespassing upon. In other words, his personal ideal of self-containment requires the principle of spatiality to regulate his relations with other members of his society. This principle is applied to physical, social and private realms and leads to an intricate pattern of clearly demarcated physical, social and private spaces.

In the *physical* realm the principle of spatiality takes two forms. First, it leads to a desire to own a portion of clearly demarcated land which he can call his own and within which he is free to do what he likes without 'let or hindrance'. That is, it leads to a desire to own a house of one's own and to demarcate it from others by a fence and a gate.[12] The house with its fence is clearly marked off from its surroundings, so that everyone knows where it begins and ends. In clearly signifying to its occupant the extent of his jurisdiction, it provides him a measure of his physical extension. Second, the Englishman's concern with physical separation takes the familiar and, to an outsider, perplexing form of avoiding all physical contact with his fellow men. Indians embrace or shake hands with each other when they meet: Russians generally hug one another; and most Europeans too shake hands. The English generally avoid all physical contact. Indeed if an experienced medical observer is not mistaken, the English experience 'guilt feelings' on touching others and display 'unusual reaction' on being touched by them. In his view the aversion to physical contact is so intense that it could even be called 'the No-Touching Epidemic'—An English Disease'.[13]

In the social *realm* the principle of spatiality expresses itself as a demand for a clear demarcation of the area of conduct that is entirely his own and over which he has complete sovereignty. In other words it is expressed as a demand to know what his rights are, a demand to know what is his own 'business' and what is others'.

The third area to which the principle of spatiality is applied is that of *internal* autonomy, or what one might call the realm of the mind and soul. The Englishman's concern here is rather complex. He does not want his inner life to be probed and known; he does not want his grip over himself to be loosened; and he does not want his delicately maintained peace of mind to be disturbed either. All this means that he does not wish to be bothered with others' problems and anxieties. By 'touching' him they might bring him into close human contact with other men, and this he is desperately anxious to avoid. Hence his constant concern to prevent any emotional ties from developing between himself and others. Emotional involvement reduces the space between the men involved, and therefore appears a threat to someone who defines his identity in spatial terms.

Each of the three realms is safeguarded by a highly complicated system of legal and social conventions. The physical space is protected by requiring that nobody should call on him without his prior permission and appointment, and by relying on the law to safeguard its integrity. The social space is protected largely by law. Anybody who interferes with his rights is threatened with a solicitor's writ, which performs almost the same function as a club or a spear does in non-Western societies. Where the rights involved are not legal but conventional in nature and do not allow legal redress, the Englishman relies on a complicated mechanism. When in a civil service or a business firm or a university or a political party he feels that he is not given his due, he asserts his rights with characteristic tenacity, and displays considerable aggression that threatens the peace and harmony of the organisation. Where this fails, he relies on 'contacts' and 'alliances' that he would have struck up in anticipation of such situations. He might have 'obliged' people in the past who will now be expected to 'return' his favours. Motivated by actual or potential threats to their self-interest, even his bitterest enemies will join hands with him. If in spite of all this he cannot succeed he will make it clear to those involved that he has sustained an injury which he will one day want to avenge; and since it is generally recognised that he means business, either he gets his way, or those involved promise to make amends in future in some form acceptable to him.

As for the protection of what I have called his private and inner space, the Englishman relies on the subtle and fascinating device of imposing a psychological barrier between himself and others behind which he can retire to preserve his inner self. The Englishman has developed a most remarkable skill, almost unique in human history, in distancing himself from others. He is quick to detect a remark or a question that appears to him probing, and knows how to dodge or resist it. He might pretend that he has not heard it; or he might get up, suddenly remembering another engagement; or he might become silent and uncommunicative; or he might skilfully change the subject; or he might throw a fierce and contemptuous stare that freezes the questioner. When, in a party or in an informal social setting, he becomes suspicious that he might be being carried away, or being inveigled into opening himself up, he may almost instinctively and without any conscious thought, become formal and laconic, to the utter chagrin and bewilderment of foreigners who little realise that his coiling up as it were is an attempt to regain his bearings, to regain his possession of himself, and to fortify his inner core that he suspects is in danger of being besieged. Almost like elastic he will stretch up to a point, but will then suddenly spring back to his original condition for fear that he will snap if stretched any farther.

Not only does he know when to pause for respite and how to retain a firm hold over himself; he is also extremely skilful both at preventing physical contact from escalating into a mental contact and at avoiding unexpected or unwanted mental and emotional contacts. Consider, for example, the way conversation proceeds between two neighbours across a garden wall. It has almost always a predictable direction—the weather, the holidays, the garden, the weeds, the flowers, etc. There are almost endlessly rehearsed series of questions and answers that rarely contain anything new, and reveal little about the personality of the participants. It is as if the participants play a purely formal role for a few moments and then withdraw into their inner citadel. If one of the participants accidentally or intentionally introduced a personal element and started talking about his problems, almost instinctively the other party would raise a barrier and skilfully suggest that it was about time each withdrew into his private world. Consider, for example, the contact-avoiding role played by essentially non-communicative expressions like 'Oh really', 'how interesting', 'well, you can't win all the time, can you' and 'you think so!' It is interesting that unlike in India, for example, where conversation between two neighbours or even strangers is generally personal in nature and the participants are related almost from the start in terms of shared personal experiences, the relationship in England is mediated and preceded by an impersonal discussion relating to sport, hobbies or politics. No doubt this sometimes leads to more intimate contact. As John Berger puts it, 'It is as though the speakers bend over the subject to examine it in precise detail until, bending over it, their heads touch. Their shared expertise becomes a symbol of shared experience'.[14] The point of interest, however, is that often the participants, afraid lest their heads should ever touch, pull them back in alarm precisely at the moment when the relationship begins to get interesting.

It is the preoccupation with self-containment that explains the rather acute sense of insecurity that English behaviour sometimes displays. The English have traditionally been taken to be a highly self-assured and self-confident people. Their self-discipline and willpower make them a reasonably self-possessed people capable of handling difficult situations. When they find that they cannot cope with a situation, their healthy scepticism and their capacity to coil up and wait prevent them from total disintegration so characteristic of Indians and several other peoples. Yet lurking behind this apparent self-confidence, and perhaps growing out of it, is a good deal of aggressiveness and insecurity. The Englishman cherishes his clearly demarcated portion of physical, social and private space, and is anxious to retain total mastery over it. He is alert lest anyone should interfere with what is his, or probe too deeply into his inner life; and he has developed sensitive antennae that help him to detect such interferences at long range. For reasons too complex to disengage, he is deeply distrustful of his fellow men. He expects them to want to get something out of him, to interfere with what is his own or to make unacceptable demands on him. Convinced that everyone is concerned to promote his own interest, he suspects that if they approach him this can only be because they want something from him. Hence perhaps the familiar remark to a visitor, "what can I do for you?" If someone gets genuinely fond of him and shows him warmth, he seems to get especially suspicious. He finds it difficult to understand why anyone should show him affection unless he thereby expects to gain something. The deep-seated suspicion of other men naturally makes him tense and insecure. He dare not relax in their presence less they should take advantage of him. His ideal of self-sufficiency, which he knows to be extremely difficult to realise, too makes him deeply fearful and anxious lest he should inadvertently display his inner feelings in public and appear weak. The Englishman is therefore most at home in an environment where privacy is highly cherished and perimeters of permissible interpersonal conduct are rigidly drawn. Predictably therefore he feels ill at ease in the company of foreigners or even of his working class compatriots whose preoccupation with self-containment is less pronounced than his. Finding it difficult to rely on conventions and subtle signals to ward off unacceptable intrusions, he becomes aggressive; and since aggressiveness is not a normal part of his life-style, his aggressiveness lacks coherence and direction, and is often extremely fierce and unrestrained. This may perhaps explain why the English who, when in England, are generally civil and self-possessed behave arrogantly and clumsily when abroad. The best in an Englishman comes out only when he is with his own people.

The concern with self-containment has naturally given rise to remarkable subtlety and sophistication in interpersonal relationship unknown in most other societies. English social life is infinitely graded, and each grade symbolised by a nuance of behaviour and language. Let us take the relationship between two individuals who meet as strangers and gradually become intimate friends. In India the transition from one end of the scale to the other is generally a matter of days and sometimes even of hours. The conversation is struck up almost immediately, and is from the very start of a relatively personal kind. Each is anxious to reveal himself, and within a few minutes he would have said pretty much everything about himself. Before long they would be patting each other on the back, exchanging addresses, and inviting each other for dinner or to come and stay with them. In England this would be unthinkable. There is a vast repertoire of impersonal and trivial talk which enables people to strike up a conversation without getting involved with each other or without revealing themselves in any meaningful way. It is a kind of cushion, a barrier, that creates a space, a distance, that enables each to 'place' and size up the other and to form some idea of what to expect of him, what types of demand he is likely to make, and how far the relationship should be allowed to develop.

Having sized up each other in this way each party is able to decide if the relationship should be allowed to develop to the next level where they could regard each other no longer as strangers but as acquaintances. The new level of relationship cannot be reached until both parties are willing, and a highly subtle and complex system of symbolic communication is developed to enable each to communicate his intentions without spelling them out at length. The other party interprets the signals, and signals back his intention. The relationship is now raised to a higher level. However, the second party may not share the first party's intention to add a new dimension to their relationship, and that would be humiliating to the latter. This is avoided by making the original signal tentative, oblique and provisional, by couching it in hypothetical language. Witness the expressions like 'perhaps you could let me know if . . .' or 'maybe you might like to look me up . . .'. One other way to avoid humiliation is to expect the mutually acknowledged superior to take the initiative and send out the original signal. This is unlikely not to be reciprocated, and even if it was, his acknowledged superiority would easily compensate for the rejection.

Once the parties have subtly conveyed their wish to raise their relationship to a new level, the relationship stays at that level until each has explored all the possibilities open at that level, sized each other up in a way done at the previous level, and decided whether the relationship should stay as it is, or be raised to a higher level of intimacy, or whether it should revert to the original level of strangeness. Each signals in the same tentative way as before, interprets signals that are sent back and the two parties reach an understanding.

In this way the relationship between two persons develops slowly, subtly, tentatively and voluntarily. It is not abrupt and is allowed to ripen at its own pace. It is only over a time that 'Dear Mr Smith' becomes 'Dear Smith', 'Dear John' and 'My dear John', and a letter comes to be signed 'yours faithfully' 'yours sincerely', 'yours' and 'yours ever'. The relationship is not developed obtrusively, by bold gestures of love and affection, but through an intricate system of communication and after careful exploration. There are infinite nuances of behaviour and language indicative of the degree of intimacy between the parties concerned, and the amount of liberty each is allowed to take with respect to the other. A word used in a certain way or at a certain time signals to the listener that the speaker has redefined their relationship and is now proposing to invoke a different form of social etiquette and protocol appropriate to their new level of relationship. Further, the interpersonal relationship is always tentative, and can be terminated at any time by either party arbitrarily. At no stage does either party allow itself to be saddled with an accumulated burden of obligations and favours; they are 'returned', an English expression with no counterpart in any of the Indian languages, at the next available opportunity, and therefore each person remains relatively free, having 'discharged' the obligations charged by the other to his social and moral account. He therefore feels that he can terminate the relationship at any time with a clear conscience. Since, further, he contrives and generally manages not to get too deeply involved with the other, the break has few emotional consequences for him. The slow development of relationship has a pragmatic air about it; it allows for trial and error, for a constant verification of expectations, for a dignified retreat if the relationship threatens to turn out to be different to what one or both of the parties had hoped for. Finally, the relationship so struck up is a voluntary relationship. Each party has been 'sounded out' and has consented to it. There is no question here of a stranger unburdening his sorrows on an unwilling victim, or bamboozling or blackmailing him into a relationship of friendship, or so deeply involving him into his personal life that he cannot extricate himself without causing the other the gravest harm and humiliation.

The remarkable English national character sketched above has fostered a unique pattern of social life. Respect for each other's privacy is developed to a very high degree. Since rules by their very nature demarcate and protect areas of life, a spatially orientated society is a rule-governed society. This has made England one of the most law-abiding societies in the world. The Englishman's respect for law does not spring from fear; it is an organic expression of his very way of life. It also accounts for the Englishman's basic decency and sense of fairness. He knows that if he wants privacy and protection of his interests, so do others, and therefore he is prepared to respect others' basic rights. His preoccupation with a self-contained life also generates considerable sensitivity to others' feelings. He does not wish to burden others with his problems, and is therefore careful not to impose himself on them, nor to hurt their feelings nor to offend their sensitivities. Hence he will not introduce a subject of conversation without first making sure in his own subtle way that it is acceptable to them. It is not surprising that in a survey nearly 73 % of English men and 80 % of English women put down understanding and consideration for others as their, and their nation's, chief characteristics.[15]

Just as the Englishman does not wish to weary others with his problems, he emphatically does not want them to weary him with theirs. This makes his consideration for others somewhat negative. It springs from a desire not to hurt or offend, and not from a desire to help others or to share their problems. In other words what he generally prizes is consideration, and not concern, for others. His undoubted kindness therefore has a formal and passive air about it and does not generally rise to the level of compassion, as the recent thalidomide controversy showed. Even the Americans solved the problem of thalidomide children long before the English did and solved it on far more generous terms. It is also worth observing that an average Briton annually gives only £4.54 to charity compared to an American who gives £42.98, and that British companies on average give about a third of 1 % of their pre-tax profits compared to over 1 % given by their American counterparts.[16] While one must place against this the highly developed public spirit in England which is reflected in several areas of life like blood donation and personal helpfulness where the American record, as Richard Titmus has shown, is so shameful, it is still striking that the British performance should be so disappointing. Or take, again, the question of *apartheid* on whose inhumanity there is an almost universal moral consensus. Compared to the American record, the British record here is disappointing. While the American Congress has made several investigations and published scathing reports of the South African situation, and informed public opinion in America has taken a strong stand, the British Parliament 'can scarcely muster a single MP who has constantly questioned the realities of our South African involvement' and British agitation against *apartheid* has lacked 'coherence and effect'.[17] The widespread belief in Britain that she is 'the most humane and kind society in the world' represents only a part of social reality.

The Englishman's social morality then has a definite limit. In the collective, impersonal and institutionalised areas of social life, to which legal and political life belongs, English morality is high and probably higher than in any other society. The 'Watergate' incident is unthinkable in England. But in the sphere of interpersonal morality where men are directly related to one another, the maximum that English morality offers falls short of that offered by other societies. The Englishman's well-developed sense of decency and fairness is not often manifested in his relations with his working-class compatriots as the history of the industrial revolution shows, nor in his relations with the 'coloured' minority as the recent immigration acts, housing and job situation, and the 'sweat-shops' in the clothing industry have shown. In his interpersonal relationship, further, he is not as dependable as the myth of the Englishman's word being his bond suggests. If his word threatened to harm his interests, he will not generally hesitate to break it. What can truthfully be said about the Englishman's word is that, being quite skilful at handling his affairs, unlike an Indian (for example) he would not give his word if he felt that he might be unable to keep it. This means that it is not very often that he gives his word and for the most part only promises to 'think the matter over' or 'to do his best'. When he does give his word, however, he is more likely than not to keep it, especially if it does not involve any great sacrifice of his interest. The Englishman is far more human than his exaggerated self-image suggests.

II

Indian character and society presents a remarkable contrast to English character and society sketched above. The contrast begins in the family and is clearly reflected in the way the Indian child is brought up. As an Indian official put it to a visiting western psychologist, 'you bring up your children, we live with ours'.[18] There are no sharp age distinctions in India as in the West. The child mixes with adults as freely as adults do among themselves. He is not excluded from adult discussion; he walks in and out of adult company as he pleases, and often contributes to their discussions. It is quite a common practice for a father to take his child with him for a walk, or on his business and social calls, when he would generally talk to him about his business and family affairs. By the time he is about ten, the child would have picked up a good deal of knowledge about his ancestors, about his father's problems, values and worries, and about his family's financial and social standing. A boy of twelve or thirteen would generally know a good deal about his father's friends and business associates, and would know how to deal with them in his absence.

An Indian child is brought up in an atmosphere of considerable affection and rather mild discipline. His mother, uncles, aunts and elder brothers and sisters show him a great deal of indulgence; and although they may occasionally discipline him, he is never frightened of them. He gets constant attention from them and can always depend on their loyalty. Members of his family generally rely

on persuasion and threat of withdrawal of affection to secure conformity. His mother would cry or refuse to speak to him, and that
is usually enough. In extreme cases, she would threaten to report to
the father and this almost always works. Even the father does not
always rely on physical force but blends it with an appeal to the
child's love and respect for elders. This means that the Indian child
never really feels the impact of authority. His father is the only
person of whom he is in awe; but he is generally only one among
several figures of authority. The child, therefore, is not dependent
on his father in the way that he is in the West. He is not the only male
model he can or is required to emulate. He may take his grandfather,
uncle, neighbour, a dead ancestor, an elder brother or cousin as his
hero, and therefore he need not and sometimes does not identify
himself with his father. Further, from infancy the child is able to see
several males in action, and is therefore able to spot their strength
and weakness, and to take a critical attitude towards his father.
In short, although he has a special relationship to his father, the
latter does not enjoy the kind of importance he enjoys in the West.
(Freudian psychoanalysis must be drastically revised before it is
applied outside Western societies.)

All this has profound impact on the Indian's character and distinguishes him in some crucial respects from his English counterpart. Since he is not generally deprived of anything except what his
family cannot afford, he develops little aggressiveness and grows to
be a rather gentle sort of person. Since he is not constantly discip-
lined and since having a wide range of ideals from which to choose,
he is not subject to the rigorous demands of any one of them, he has
rather a weak superego. His morality is a morality of affection and
love, rather than of duty; and he can be morally influenced by
appealing to his emotions rather than to a stern sense of duty. As
we shall see later he makes enormous sacrifices that are far in
excess of his duty for a person he likes, but fails to meet even the
minimum demands of his duty if he does not feel warmth and
affection for him. In practice this means that he will literally die for
his family, relatives and friends, but will not feel any real concern
for strangers.

Since the Indian child grows up attached to several men and
identifies himself with a number of them, he does not identify himself enough with any one of them. What is important to him and
what holds his loyalty is not any one person but a complex of
persons who, collectively, constitute his family. This means that his
loyalty is to the family and not to his parents, and to the family
understood not as an historical entity that has existed for genera-

tions (this requires a sense of history which an Indian does not have) but as a group of men related to him by blood. As he grows up in a large circle of relatives, and is used to strangers visiting him or being visited by him, he has no fear of strangers. He can take all manner of men in his stride and does not feel uneasy or nervous in their presence.

Having grown up within a close and generally affectionate family, the family remains his model of interpersonal relationship and is his basic point of reference for understanding all other social organisations. He therefore finds it exceedingly difficult to cope with relationships that he cannot translate in familial terms. Predictably he understands political life in familial terms. India is referred to as *Bhārat-mātā* (mother India). Gandhi was and is referred to as *Rāshtra-pitā* (father of the nation). Nehru was referred to as *chā-chā* Nehru (uncle Nehru). The president of India is described as *Rāshtra-pati* (husband of the nation). Fellow Indians are referred to as brothers and sisters. It is worth noting that every public speaker in India addresses his audience as brothers and sisters. Familial terms are not mere metaphors but moral and epistemological categories; they reflect a deep-seated urge in the Indian to turn the nation into a family, and they provide him a conceptual framework in terms of which to comprehend complex political relationships and order his political perceptions.

Having been brought up in a sheltered and protective atmosphere, the Indian grows up expecting the world to be a hospitable and friendly place. When he finds that it is not, he grows suspicious and becomes cynical in the extreme. This might explain the inconsistency many commentators have noticed in the Indian—he is warm, generous and self-sacrificing, but also rather aloof and devious. The best in him comes out in the environment that resembles the family, an environment characterised by trust, goodwill and lack of strong and rigid discipline. Here he will ignore his personal interest, stop at no sacrifices for those he likes, and will generally err on the side of fanatical devotion and loyalty. However, once he becomes suspicious that his loyalty and sacrifices are not being reciprocated or are being misused and exploited, he becomes fearful, nervous, and insecure. It is not a situation to which he is used and therefore he loses his bearings and guidelines. He will try to turn his relationship into one resembling a family by making passionate professions of loyalty and affection to those involved and by proposing, explicitly or implicitly, that they look upon each other as brothers. If he is unable to define their relationship along familial lines he is lost and will tend to break it off. It is no longer a source of security to him, and it requires him to calculate and plan all his moves, which he finds not only tiring but also a perversion of what in his view all interpersonal relationships should be like. Self-consciousness in human relationships is painful to him. He likes to express his feelings freely and uninhibitedly, without having to worry that he will be misunderstood or that what he says will be held against him. Lacking the English and, for that matter, Western, ability to sustain different degrees of intimacy in different types of relationship, he swings between the two extremes of deep involvement and total withdrawal. People for him are either friends for whom he should make infinite sacrifices, or total strangers with whom he has no relationship of any kind. Total withdrawal may involve sacrifice of his interest, but he will not care. He will close himself in and develop amazing emotional toughness that is almost stoic in its magnitude and intensity. The well-known extremes of the Indian's character—his soft, indeed, liquid emotionality as well as his granitic emotional toughness, his extreme dependence on others as well as his equally extreme rejection of the world—that have so bewildered and maddened foreigners, are both inseparably connected and have a common origin.

What is called his deviousness is really a result of the Indian's failure to integrate his optimism and cynicism, or rather his failure to come to terms with the fact that not all relationships can be translated into familial terms. Optimistic at heart he takes the initiative in defining his relations with others in familial terms, and expects them to reciprocate in similar vein. He therefore promises to do things for them even at the cost of his own interest and shows great generosity, but others may find this an embarrassing and even unnecessary imposition, and may not see why they should reciprocate in the same vein. The Indian is then bewildered and thrown onto the defensive. He has already promised a number of things which he knows he should do, but realising that they will not be reciprocated, he does not want to do them. The result is a frantic and desperate attempt to redefine his commitment, to 'clarify' what he really meant; in a word, deviousness, a sneaky retreat from the full rigour of an unrequited act of unilateral goodwill.

His upbringing is also reflected in his attitude to his work. He seeks to transform his place of work into a familial setting and to create a hierarchical and informal pattern of relationships corresponding to that obtaining in the family. Accustomed to being looked after, and unaccustomed to fighting for his rights, his tendency is to expect his superiors to look after his interest. He expects them to give him his due without his having to fight for it. He is, of course, quite shrewd and knows what is his due and when it is being denied him. In situations where he thinks he is being unjustly treated he is extremely ill at ease. It shatters his illusion that he is a member of a family. He would therefore tend to suffer an injury rather than avenge it. On balance he finds this more gratifying. When he has to stand up for what he thinks is his due, he would generally tend to appeal to others' duties rather than to his rights, just as he would do in his family. He would vouchsafe his genuine affection[19] for his colleagues, friends and superiors in the hope of evoking a familial response. If this does not work, he either withdraws into himself or puts up an uncharacteristic fight. But as the fight forces him into an awareness that he is an independent locus of rights as *against* other such independent loci, and creates in him a feeling of loneliness and isolation, he is desperate to accept any form of compromise. Quite often a mere expression of affection and concern by others is enough to induce him to terminate his struggle. As the fight for his interest appears to him undignified, he would generally tend to couch it in moral terms and present it as a fight for a principle. Except in cases of sheer hypocrisy, the Indian moralising that so irks foreigners is really only an expression of the Indian's nervousness in the pursuit of his interest. This comes out most clearly in the life of Gandhi who put up a fierce fight against the British for denying India her due, but who almost always felt extremely uneasy and nervous at this 'individualistic' assertion of his rights and settled for whatever concessions were offered to him.

As self-containment is not his ideal, the English concern with spatial demarcation of life is alien to the Indian. In India there is little preoccupation with enclosed physical space. Few people own their houses. Often this is because they cannot afford it, but not entirely. When they do own houses this is generally not because that will give them privacy but because this is an investment that can never be 'stolen' as my grandfather always put it. Houses, further, rarely have fences, and gates are rarer still, so that one could walk across people's front 'gardens' with ease. Houses do have front doors but they are never shut during the day except in urban apartments. Houses do not have curtains or drapes, and are so structured that one can survey almost all the rooms at a glance. As with physical space, social space too is not generally demarcated and privately appropriated. The emphasis is always on duties rather than on rights, as is seen in the Hindu doctrine of *dharma* and in the fact that Sanskrit and many major Indian languages have no words corresponding to the English words claim and right. As we have seen an Indian generally feels guilty when he has to assert his rights and prefers to rely on reminding others of their duties than of his rights. This comes out very clearly in the expression that is used both in England and India. In England when a man who feels that he has been denied his right says to another that 'he will regret it', he is implying threat or reprisal. In India the expression means that the other person will be overwhelmed by remorse and guilt. As with physical and social space the Indian has very little regard for internal private space. His self is transparent and open, and there is little that he is concerned to hide. His urge to reveal himself is insatiable and has at times ridiculous and embarrassing results. Ask him almost any question, and he will answer it. If he has done something silly, he will good-humouredly admit it and at times even cry about it openly. If what he has done is good, he enjoys talking about it. In either case he does not mind exposure; indeed, he enjoys it. It makes him feel that he is being noticed, that he is visible to others, that others are interested in him. His exposure might lead others to ridicule him, but he finds that more gratifying than not being noticed at all. For the most part, though, he expects that others will show him sympathy and take an interest in his affairs. Using the analogy employed earlier he is like elastic that will keep stretching even when it is in danger of snapping. His repertoire for dodging awkward questions is extremely limited and usually rather crude. For the most part he will either shout back at his opponent exhorting him on what questions to ask, or tell a lie without feeling guilty about it in any way at all.

III

If the outlines of Indian and English character and society sketched above are correct, the two differ in some crucial respects. One is communitarian, the other is individualistic; one strives to turn all relationships into those resembling a family, the other spurns such intentions and draws a firm boundary between familial and non-familial relationships; one is averse to rules and to spatial structuring of life, the other is essentially spatial and rule-governed; one is warm, the other is cool; one displays emotions in public even to the extent of marked self-indulgence, the other represses such displays and verges on turning life into a rationalist artifact; one is optimistic to the point of foolhardiness, the other is suspicious to the point of cynicism; one is inconsistent and swings between the extremes of nobility and indifference, the other is consistent but rarely reaches the heights of compassion and total self-abnegation; one is so pre-occupied with social relationship that it has failed to find a place for individuality, the other has explored the depths of individuality but has in the process become morbidly self-obsessed; one feels profoundly nervous in the presence of the self, the other feels equally uneasy in the presence of the other.[20] When therefore an Indian finds himself living in England his life predictably becomes a saga of unresolved tensions and contradictions.

An Indian's life in England passes through several clearly-defined stages. When he is new to the country his ignorance of its customs and mores naturally induces him to seek the company of his already settled compatriots. He accepts their residential seniority and superiority and therefore the relationship lasts a while. As he gains in confidence he resents their patronising attitude and finds it far more gratifying to weary his apparently inquisitive English friends with lucid accounts of the customs and practices of his country than to listen to the adventures and frustrations of his senior compatriots. He thinks that he has come to England to understand the English, to 'get something out of' England, and therefore often avoids Indians like the plague. He is also desperately keen to leave behind English friends whose names and pictures he could flaunt when back in India and for whom he could give letters of introduction to his Indian friends. He is also haunted by a sense of insecurity in England, and feels that he might at any time fall foul of the law and be deported, and would then need his English friends and acquaintances to stand up for him. But as he asserts his independence and acquires new interests, his compatriots in turn begin to demand that he should reciprocate their past favours. The more he tries to get away from them, the more they try to bind him; and the more they do so, the more he revolts against their demands. The break is inevitable.

The Indian fails to evolve meaningful relationships with his compatriots for a variety of reasons. *Prima facie* one would have thought that with them at least he shared a common background of sympathies and experiences, and that living abroad would generally draw them closer. The fact, however, is the opposite. In my experience this is true not only of middle-class Indians but also of working-class Indians whose apparent comradeship conceals deep tensions and conflicts.[21]

The obvious but by no means most important reason is that Indians carry with them their stereotyped prejudices wherever they go; and this limits their circle of friends. Bengalis consider all non-Bengalis uncultured and have generally no interest in them. Their fanatical attachment to their language makes them feel that they cannot communicate 'meaningfully' with those unable to speak their language and therefore they generally avoid them. Non-Bengalis for their part dismiss Bengalis as parochial, interested only in Tagore and Satyajit Ray, and rather excitable and unpredictable, and therefore avoid them in turn. Punjabis find all 'rice-eating' non-Punjabis small, mean and calculative, and shun their company. Gujaratis find Punjabis crude and blunt, and feel that they have historical scores to settle with Maharashtrians, and therefore avoid both. The mutual antipathy of these communities goes too deep to allow the flower of friendship to blossom.

Within each community there are further causes of tension. Caste is, of course, one of the most important. The first encounter between two Indians is almost invariably an inquisition in which each party probes into the social background and antecedents of the other, and collects all the information he needs to 'place' him in some definite category. The relationship generally is rarely between two concrete individuals but between two categories. In some sense this is, of course, true of all human relationships; but caste makes it worse for want of a general consensus on how the two categories are to be related. Let me give an example. I met a fellow Indian at a party. Within a few minutes he was asking me all sorts of predictable questions about how long I had been in England, how many children I had, how often I had been to India, what I thought of the English, how much money I had accumulated, whether I agreed that Indian economy will not prosper without a heavy dose of capitalism, etc. My answers did not help him to 'place' me, so he asked me what my caste was. Annoyed by this silly question I replied that I was an untouchable. He was clearly not convinced and evidently reasoned that I *must* be a high-caste Hindu to have had the courage and audacity to pretend to be an untouchable. He did not pursue the discussion further, and we eventually became good friends. A few years later he made the discovery that I was not a high-caste Hindu as he had imagined but a middle-caste Hindu. His behaviour soon began to change. He had now been able to 'place' me; and since he thought, mistakenly, that his caste was higher than mine, he could no longer accept me as his equal. He unilaterally redefined our pattern of relationship, and thought that I should recognise his social superiority, which I could not do, not only because caste was not for me a determinant of human relationship, but also because in my view, which his wife shared, our respective castes were socially equal. Predictably we broke up.

Apart from the caste, language and provincial rivalries, there are other far more important factors that militate against any meaningful relationship among middle-class Indians. It is generally the case that every Indian who is in England is usually somebody in India. He may be the only one, or at any rate one of the very few, from his caste to have set foot outside India. When he left India scores of people must have come to see him off, and showered him with gifts and good wishes. Indeed it is not uncommon among Indians to compare the number of people who had come to see them off and/or who will come to receive them on their return. This means two things. First, the Indian in England, being an important personage in his caste, is rather a vain man and has an acute sense of self-importance which he strives to assert on all conceivable occasions. However, when everyone is engaged in this exercise, no one is willing to put up with another's self-display, and this generates tensions and rivalries that render meaningful social life impossible. Second, the Indian in England is acutely aware of those in his caste and in the neighbourhood who had come to see him off and who, so his parents keep reminding him, are always inquiring after his progress. He is therefore more concerned with what they think of him than with what his English and Indian friends in England do. He will write letters to a remote relative or to a well-known figure in his caste who may be totally uninterested in him, but not to a friend in England. A friend once told me that a common acquaintance of ours had distributed offprints of his article among the illiterate members of his caste in India and could not spare a copy for his literate friends here! To put it differently, the Indian in England is often like an actor performing before an audience nearly six thousand miles away. It is their clapping that matters to him and it is their adulation that gratifies his ego. It is difficult to see how such actors can generate a meaningful community. A pathetic situation arises when two actors share a common audience, as when two Indians come from the same village or caste. The rivalry between them is deadly; each sends home reports derogatory to the other, and is in turn fed with reports about the other's family circumstances that he can use against him here in England. Every epistle becomes a deadly missile accurately fired across the seas to a human target several thousand miles away.

It is interesting to observe how Indians in England have evolved a new form of caste system. The basic division is between those Indians who come from India, and those who come from outside India, especially from the West Indies where ties with India are weaker. The division corresponds somewhat to that between Englishmen who have spent all their life in England and those who have returned from a long stint in a colony. Like the ex-colonial Englishmen the 'overseas' Indians are regarded as an inauthentic copy of the original. They generally cannot speak any of the Indian languages or speak it with a 'funny' accent. Their English is not of the kind that either the Indians or the English speak and is regarded as a hybrid of the two. Indians find them lacking in gentleness and humility; they also find them aggressive, rather showy and somewhat simple-minded in social matters. They tend to treat them as cultural half-castes, as men who express their shame at being Indians and yet whose very expression of shame and anti-Indian tirades reveal how inescapably Indian they remain. They find it annoying that these overseas Indians should take their Indian origin to give them a right to attack Indian character and society, and yet should refuse to acknowledge the implied obligation to identify themselves with India and offer a sympathetic appreciation of her problems and anxieties. The antipathy is of course not entirely one-sided. The 'overseas' Indians for their part dismiss the 'real' Indians as timid, unsophisticated, unhygienic, parochial, caste-ridden, sexually and socially repressed, and lacking in elementary self-respect and pride.

Among the 'real' Indians the new caste-system evolved in England takes intricate forms. At the top of the hierarchy come those who have settled in England for a long time and are usually men of substance. They generally know one another, though this does not make them friends, and treat new arrivals, who are echoes from their own past, with patronising kindness and disdain. They have generally left India for good, have very few ties with her, and reminisce about her with a mixture of muted pride and self-indulgent sadness. Below them is the caste of professional Indians who are duly classified into different subcastes according to the twin criteria of their duration of stay in England and the eminence of their professional status. Below them is the caste of students, patronised by the above two and constantly exhorted to go back to India where they are believed to be most needed. At the bottom are the outcastes, those working-class Indians allegedly living in ghettoes and constantly criticised by the above three for giving Indians a 'bad name'. There are no clear rules governing the relationship between these groups and this leads to great confusion and misunderstanding.

It is a common experience that people, uprooted from their native surroundings, find it difficult to evolve a meaningful pattern of relationship among themselves. Old patterns appear inapplicable and new ones have not yet been evolved. This is especially so of middle-class Indians. They are uncertain as to whether they should treat each other in the way Indians generally do at home, or whether they should adopt the 'modern' and 'civilised' practices of Englishmen. They sympathise with both, and therefore end up adopting the one or the other as it suits them; and this only creates confusion. Let me give a few examples. We once invited an Indian couple to dinner. They never turned up. When my wife rang them up, she was told that it was rather cold and they did not feel like getting out of the house. After all, she was told, we are all Indians and this is not an uncommon practice in India. A few months later when they invited us, we rang them up an hour before the time to ask if they would mind our not going, since it was cold and neither of us felt up to it. We got a long and angry lecture on how 'civilised' Indians should behave, how we had learnt nothing during our three years in England, etc., etc. Some years ago an important Indian politician visited a British university to talk to a group of Indian students. As was to be expected, the students behaved towards him with the deference and obsequiousness characteristic of such an encounter in India. The speaker remarked how pleased he was that his countrymen had still retained their 'traditional' values. But this was his undoing. It reminded his audience of the fact that they were now in England and should therefore treat their politicians with a mixture of scepticism and satirical humour as English students do. So they started asking awkward and critical questions and making good-humoured remarks, and in general took the man down a peg or two. The politician was gravely offended by this 'un-Indian' behaviour and the meeting ended on a very sour note. We shall see presently how Englishmen and Indians have not yet evolved a set of norms to regulate their behaviour. It is worth noting that Indians in England have not yet evolved norms to regulate their interpersonal behaviour either. An Indian is therefore forced to treat each encounter with a fellow Indian as unique. He feels he has to remain sensitive to his every mood, puzzle out the insinuations of his every remark, and decide in each context whether he is playing the social game the Indian or the English way. A relationship that calls for such an enormous amount of emotional and intellectual energy, he is reluctantly compelled to conclude, is hardly worth the effort.

Dissatisfied with his compatriots, the Indian turns to Englishmen. They are, he thinks, fairly straightforward and free from common Indian prejudices and stereotypes and should therefore offer him sincere and warm friendship. He invites them home, shows them characteristic warmth and unsolicited generosity and goes out of his way to be nice and friendly to them. The somewhat embarrassed and flattered Englishman responds with as much warmth as he can muster, which by Indian standards is disappointingly meagre. The relationship lasts a while but contains seeds of its own destruction. A year or two in England could not have given the Indian that instinctive understanding of English life that is so vital for any meaningful relationship. As for his English friends, they too have little insight into the workings of the Indian mind. Not unexpectedly, well-meaning gestures and remarks of one party unwittingly offend and hurt the other. To take two examples: an Indian friend of mine had an English friend whose daughter was hospitalised for a fortnight. The Indian, feeling that only a 'friend in need is a friend indeed', regularly rang up the hospital to enquire after the girl's progress. His English friend thought this an unwarranted interference with his private life, and said so to the Indian in his familiar subtle but firm manner. The Indian was deeply hurt. A friend of mine was in bed for a few days with a bad attack of influenza. He expected his English friends to call on him to see how he was. This is a very common practice in India and he knew that he would have called on them if they were similarly bed-ridden. None of his friends visited him. He thought this the 'height of selfishness' and never spoke to them again. One can relate scores of such instances of misunderstanding that clearly militate against lasting and meaningful relationships.

There are also other reasons why an Indian's relations with Englishmen often remain disappointingly superficial. I referred earlier to the subtle and complex way in which an Englishman establishes relations with others. The relatively simple-minded Indian, unfamiliar with English signals, naturally gets lost. Since he does not understand the signals, he does not know how to respond to them. His difficulty is increased by the fact that the same signal is used at different levels of relationship to convey different degrees of intimacy. Take, for example, the common courteous remark like 'do look me up when you are next in London'. It could be made to a stranger to whom one wishes to be polite. Or it could be made to a person to whom one is fairly close. Foreigners recount countless stories of how they were asked by an English friend to 'look him up', but who studiously avoided them when they tried to do so. Sometimes most amusing and even tragic incidents occur. A Nigerian was once asked by an English academic, whom he had got to know quite well, to look him up when he was next in Oxford. A few weeks later the Nigerian had to go to Oxford for a conference. Thinking that his English friend would be offended if he ever came to know that he was in Oxford but had not bothered to call on him, the Nigerian wrote to him saying he was going to be in Oxford on such and such a day and inquiring what time would suit him. He got no reply. Thinking that perhaps his letter had not reached his English friend or that he was too busy to reply he rang him up when he was in Oxford. The professor's secretary said that he was not going in to college that day, so he rang his home, whereupon he was told by his wife, after she had duly identified who he was, that her husband had gone to the college. The gentleman concerned did not pursue the matter further, as he had by now realised the situation. To add to his sense of humiliation he received a formally cordial note from the professor the next day saying how sorry he was to have missed him and asking him to look him up the next time he was in Oxford! The Nigerian academic thought this a classic case of English 'hypocrisy' and even 'lying'. Perhaps it was; perhaps the professor, realising his 'friend's' failure to understand the purely symbolic significance of his original invitation, was simply trying to protect himself from what he thought was an escalation of their relationship to a level unacceptable to him.

Even if he can interpret signals aright, the Indian often finds the slow development of relationships most trying and frustrating. This is partly because he is not used to such an intricate and delicate system. Partly it is because such a relationship takes years to ripen, and is of no help to him in his first few months in England when he most needs a helping hand, and partly it is because he feels— wrongly—that a relationship that is cool and cautious in its origin must remain cool and superficial in its outcome. However, there are also deeper reasons why he feels frustrated by the English-man's mode of establishing relationships. He finds it very difficult to understand why an Englishman cannot instinctively take to some-one and strike off a warm relationship with him without prolonged screening and hesitation. He cannot see why the Englishman should remain excessively cautious and diffident, unwilling to plunge into the whirlpool of human relationships and abandon himself to its vicissitudes without making absolutely sure that nothing will ever go wrong. To the Indian this approach eliminates all surprises and excitement from life and makes it dull and boring.

Even when he can come to terms with English caution, the Indian suspects that he is being 'screened', scrutinised and sub-jected to a degrading social apprenticeship before being admitted into a meaningful relationship. Indeed, he apprehends that the 'screening' to which he is subjected is designed subtly to shape and mould him, and that the offer of friendship is used as an instrument to remove his native angularities and rawness and to turn him into a brown or black Englishman. In other words, 'screening' strikes him as brainwashing, and he feels that surrender of identity is the price he is required to pay for the Englishman's friendship. Even this price he might be prepared to pay if the eventual relationship promised to offer him what he is looking for, but he often concludes that it does not. He seeks security, but feels that his relationship with an Englishman is fundamentally insecure. His constant complaint is that the Englishman is too concerned with avoiding deep emotional involvement and preserving his inner quiet to be capable of offering warm and affectionate friendship. Friendship, to an Indian, is an extension of familial relationship. A friend, as is commonly said in India, is like a brother. The Indian's idea of a friend is one who will ring him up for no other reason than to find out how he is getting on, who is concerned about his well-being, whom he can fully trust, with whom he has no conflict of interest, to whom he can turn when in trouble without being apologetic, whose family he knows well, etc., etc. This does not seem to him to be the self-contained Englishman's idea of a friend, at any rate not in his relationship with the 'coloured' peoples. The Indian therefore concludes that his relationship with Englishmen has definite limits and that there is a maximum beyond which it simply will not go; and since this maximum does not meet even his minimum demands, he wonders if it is worth his while to expend his time and emotional energy and to suffer what he regards as a humiliating social probation for the sake of an insecure and shallow relationship.

It is when he realises the difficulties involved in establishing meaningful relationships with both Indians and Englishmen that the Indian experiences utter loneliness, a shattering sense of void, and is forced to come to terms with his predicament in all its tragic aspects. He generally responds to this situation in one of three ways. He might withdraw into the company of his compatriots, and spend his time condemning and hating the English. He might continue to switch from one English friend to another, perfect the art of flattering their ego by denouncing his compatriots, imitate English ways, marry an English girl and buy the best house in his area—desperately hoping that all this will gain him acceptance one day. Or, he might become a loner, hating and avoiding both the English and the Indians, withdrawing into his empty inner citadel and feeding on self-pity. Such Indians often go mad. I have no statistics, but can recall at least a dozen who have met this tragic fate. None of these three forms of response presents an edifying picture of human existence. Realising this some reflective Indians try out the fourth and the only human alternative open to them: to develop a character and style of life embodying the best that England and India have to offer. They know that living in England gives them a unique opportunity to compare and contrast English and Indian character and society and to evolve a form of life that incorporates the best of both. Speaking personally, the more I have reflected on English life, the more I have come to cherish Indian emphasis on duties as opposed to rights, on gentleness as opposed to assertiveness, on suffering as opposed to avenging an injury, on genuine warmth and affection as opposed to formal and impersonal cordiality, on sacrifice and loyalty as opposed to self-interest, and on the family as opposed to the individual. At the same time I have come to admire and envy many aspects of English life that are woefully missing in my own; for example, its understanding and consideration for others' feelings, respect for each other's privacy, caution in developing relationships, reluctance to weary others with one's problems, respect for rules, moderation and self-restraint, economy of expression, love of nature, sense of history, and tenderness to women and to animals. A number of Indians I know feel the same way, although their appreciation of specific values differs.

A reflective Indian then is presented with a challenge and an opportunity. There is much in his traditional heritage that he wishes to expunge, although, equally, there is much that he wishes to preserve. He realises that his values and life-style are partial and limited, and that if he could absorb what is valuable in English culture, he would make his life richer and fuller, indeed, that he would be able to live a higher, more universal, level of existence. He wonders if he can learn not to burden others with his problems without turning self-containment into an absolute value; if he can learn to protect his privacy without becoming too exclusive and secretive; to show warmth without becoming obtrusive; to develop his individuality without losing a sense of concern and commitment to his fellow men; to suffer an injury and forgive without encouraging others to take him for granted; to be cautious in developing relationships without becoming morbidly self-protective or losing all taste for the unpredictable. His concern, in other words, becomes nothing less than continual self-recreation. This is in no way unique to him. There are a number of Englishmen who, perturbed by their society's emphasis on egoism, social isolation, coolness and self-interested calculation, are engaged in similar experiments. An Indian who is lucky enough to encounter these men and to earn their trust and friendship is supremely blessed.

But an Indian engaged in recreating his identity is faced with a number of problems of which we have space to mention only one. It is a very important problem and has received little attention. It concerns the way an Indian brings up his children.[22] Naturally he wants to bring them up so that they too can acquire the best that both Indian and English cultures have to offer. He has come to accept a certain type of life as his ideal, and he feels it his duty to raise his children accordingly. But this is not easy. He has not in his own life integrated the two different components of his ideal, and is therefore never sure precisely how to help his children achieve it. This makes his behaviour towards his children uncertain, tentative, groping, lacking a firm sense of direction. There are also other factors that complicate his situation. He is never certain that he will be able harmoniously to integrate what he admires in English life with what he cherishes in his own tradition. For all he knows, he might remain an unintegrated amalgam of two different life-styles, and then like Nehru, who once said that his life in England had made him an essentially homeless man, missing India when he was in England and England when he was in India, he will be a misfit in India even as he is a misfit in England and remain condemned to a life of permanent homelessness. The tragedy of his predicament is that even if he were to succeed in integrating the two life-styles, he would still remain a homeless man, in that neither society can fulfil all the strivings and urges of his being. He therefore dreads the prospect of returning to India for good, and yet he cannot contemplate with equanimity the idea of spending the rest of his life in England. The moment he decides that he will never go back to India or that he will go back next year, he knows that he will have abandoned a part of his being and made his life poorer. He dare not therefore take an irrevocable decision, and tends to drift along hoping that time will somehow, some day, resolve his dilemma. While the 'open future' may be necessary to preserve his sanity, it deprives him of any clear guidelines in his approach to his children. Were he to return to India, his children will be misfits if they had not learnt and (given that English is being increasingly replaced as a medium of instruction in India) mastered their mother tongue, and acquired some of the Indian sensitivities and cultural habits sketched earlier. He thinks that he should therefore prepare them for their eventual return. Then learning and acquiring these imposes an extra physical and emotional burden on his children which might impair their school performance, turn them into cultural schizophrenics and burden them with the soul-wrecking problems of personal identity which they are too immature to resolve.

To take a personal example, we have found it exceedingly difficult to give our children a reasonable degree of competence in their mother tongue. Teaching them to speak it is no problem, but there were no books that one could give them to read and therefore their language is largely colloquial. We taught them the script after months of hard work, only to find that they had forgotten it within six months for lack of practice. The agony of cultivating some of the cherished Indian values has been even more acute. One evening my eleven-year-old son returned from school saying that a good friend of his was not well and had not gone to school that day. Our immediate reaction was to ask him to ring him up and inquire how he was getting on. He remarked that this was not the done thing, to which we rejoined that this was a common practice among Indians, that it was not an evil practice and that there was no harm in occasionally introducing innovations in one's relations with others. He agreed, rang his friend, and was pleasantly surprised at the warmth of the response.

But there were other situations where the outcome was not always so happy. My son once quarrelled with a friend. He came home very angry, resolved never to speak to him again. Falling back on my own upbringing, I suggested that his friend might have blown up because he, my son, might have inadvertently hurt his feelings, and that he should therefore have a frank chat with him. He did so and the result was disastrous. His friend, not being used to such things, interpreted this as a sign of the weakness and 'loneliness' of a 'coloured' child. My son felt a fool and doubted my judgement and capacity to guide and advise him. A few days later another occasion arose. A boy had called him 'coloured' and 'nigger', and had asked why he did not go back to his own country. He replied in the same vein calling him a 'pale-faced whitey', etc. I told him that he had reduced himself to the level of that boy and that he should have treated him with a mixture of understanding and disdain. He saw some sense in the advice, tried it out later in a similar situation, and was ridiculed for not fighting back. Cases like these tended to undermine his confidence in me and made me doubt the wisdom of exposing him to values different to those to which his peers were familiar. This worried me greatly.

Reluctantly I left him alone to work out his own pattern of behaviour: but that was no use either. The pattern of behaviour he had acquired in the school began to spill over into his relations with his brothers. He would fight for his rights and interests as he would in the school; he would show little understanding and charity towards his younger brothers; he would feel possessive about his things; and so on. What was more, all this began adversely to affect his relations to his parents. The language of contract began to be introduced and he would do an errand only if he was paid for it. The language of sovereignty came to be used, and he asserted his *right* to use *his* money as *he* pleased. All this was disturbing, not so much because it was wrong, which I thought it was, but because it introduced an alien universe of discourse and redefined our relationships in a way that was utterly foreign to my conception of a family. I began to feel, further, that I was losing control over an intimate area of my life, and that the surrounding society was subtly forcing me, through the instrumentality of a young and immature child, to adapt to a way of life to which I was only partially sympathetic. I often wonder if our way of bringing up our children may not some day spell disaster for them. Nothing can be more humiliating and shattering than not to know how to raise one's children.

IV

Having discussed at some length the existential and emotional problems an Indian faces in England, I should like to consider briefly the problems he encounters in his intellectual life.

The academic life of an Indian student presents a rather stark contrast to that of his English counterpart. He rarely gets the kind of attention an English student does.[23] To take a personal example, I never wrote an essay or a tutorial paper or even attended a tutorial during four years as an undergraduate at the most prestigious Jesuit college in Bombay nor during two further years as a graduate student at a leading post-graduate institute. If one was lucky one saw a great deal of one's lecturers[24]. One was invited to their homes, to go out on daily walks with them, and to drop into their offices whenever one wanted to. This gave one opportunities to learn a great deal of one's subject and compensated for the absence of institutional supervision. But one had to be exceptionally good and lucky to enjoy this privilege, and even then one's education was entirely confined to oral discussions and never involved any written work. As for the vast majority of students they spend almost all their time preparing for examination, the success at which is vital for sheer survival. They prepare notes from standard commentaries and memorise them several times over until they feel able to regurgitate them faithfully. Even though I specialised in politics, I cannot remember ever reading Plato's *Republic* or Aristotle's *Politics* or Hobbes' *Leviathan* or Hegel's *Philosophy of Right*. The only 'text' I read was J. S. Mill's *On Liberty*, and that was by sheer accident.

An Indian who comes to England as an undergraduate faces relatively few problems. Along with his English counterparts he is subjected to the familiar academic routine of tutorials, seminars and essays, and is able to acquire the capacity to think systematically and critically and to write clearly and economically. His tutor has no inhibitions in telling him that he is a fool, if he is one, or that he is lazy, or that his performance is below standard, or that his written work is muddled and confused. He generally lives in a university hall of residence and this gives him an opportunity to mix with his peers informally and pick up a great deal of general knowledge about his subject.

The Indian who comes to England to do post-graduate work is in a much less happy position. His ability to regurgitate his 'knowledge' of the subject hides from him the basic fact that his 'knowledge' is unforgivably shallow and superficial. After all, he is not likely to have read the basic texts and the relevant commentaries, nor to have read them with any care. Further, his oral fluency hides from him the fact that he has never really learnt to write. His intellectual tradition, which is largely oral and places little emphasis on writing, has equipped him to communicate his ideas in direct, face-to-face conversations, but not through the impersonal medium of the written word. Because the Indian is usually good at articulating himself orally, he is prone to the illusion that he can wield the written word with equal ease. He writes as he speaks, and therefore his writing is often repetitive and somewhat verbose, and lacks coherence and organisation. He may not even know how to organise paragraphs or employ punctuation marks. The tragedy is that he often does not realise this until he actually begins to produce written work during the last few months of his stay in England. It had never even occurred to him that writing is very different from talking, that the written work must stand alone, unassisted by profuse gestures and gesticulations or a string of synonyms which may be nice to listen to, but tedious to read. His supervisor, who might be his own age, would generally have been too polite to tell him that he could benefit from lessons in written English, or too lazy to demand and check his written work. Not surprisingly some Indians never manage to get the degree. Unable to return home and unwilling to stay on, they live a nightmare existence. What makes their predicament really tragic and unbearable is the fact that it is not a result of any lack of native intelligence on their part. They know that they are competent and even bright, and in no way intellectually inferior to their English peers, and that it is their lack of scholarship and the technical ability to wield the medium of the written word that is responsible for their unsatisfactory performance— something they know they could overcome if only they had the money, which most of them do not have, to stay a few more years in England.

If an Indian is lucky and tenacious enough to survive the initial intellectual ordeal, he would normally wish to spend a few years teaching in an English university. This brings him more money than in India; hopefully, it secures him a better job on his return; and, above all, it gives him a propitious environment in which to further develop and deploy his intellectual skills. Once he is settled in an English university, his intellectual life is generally not very different from that of his English colleagues. Professional socialisation generally sees to that. Yet it would be most surprising if his Indian background did not give a distinctive direction, at least a tone, to his academic life. His Indian background is likely to cut him off from several types of intellectual inquiry. Let me take the example of my own discipline, political theory. Never having learnt Greek or Latin makes it impossible for the Indian to do any scholarly research on people who have written in these languages. He also generally lacks proficiency in any of the modern European languages. For the most part therefore he remains confined to the study of English political thought. Even here his not having been born a Christian renders certain men or sorts of problems rather opaque to him. It is difficult for a non-Christian really to understand Hobbes's anxieties and preoccupations in the third and fourth book of his *Leviathan*, or to comprehend the anxieties and concerns of Hooker, or to see the significance of sectarian conflict in the English civil war, or to grasp the religious inspiration and evangelical zeal of British Idealists. Not that the Indian cannot study these men and movements and say something interesting about them, but that he has a persistent feeling that he has not really and truly understood them in their innermost details. A similar difficulty arises at another level as well. If one does not understand the unspoken conventions of English society and the deep anxieties, fears and aspirations of the Englishman, the whole area of intellectual biography is virtually denied to him. I once thought of writing an intellectual biography of Jeremy Bentham. The deeper I dug, the more I felt that I was constantly in danger of misinterpreting the motives and behaviour of the key figures. What precisely precipitated Bentham's estrangement from James Mill? How can one account for his several silly eccentricities? Why did Lord Brougham not show greater loyalty to him? Why was John Bowring so unfair to J. S. Mill? If these men were Indians, I could make fairly accurate guesses about their motives. But under the circumstances, I would have no clue to the range of motives that might possibly have influenced them. One is therefore constrained to concentrate on abstract ideas and issues, which, unlike concrete historical thinkers, raise no intricate problems of interpretation. Even here, the more abstract a problem, the greater one's feeling of confidence, and therefore the greater its attraction.

However, this raises other difficulties. The more abstract a problem, the less is its relevance to real life, and this is profoundly disturbing to someone who cannot avoid feeling uneasy at living a comfortable and privileged life when millions of his countrymen live a wretched sub-human existence. Rightly or wrongly one is haunted by their faces—a starving and emaciated child and his helpless and pathetic parents, a son sadly watching the life of his mother slowly ebbing away, millions sleeping on pavements under heavy rains, political prisoners punished for no other reason than that they had the courage to fight for a just society. These are the people whose misery and toil made possible a society from whose heritage one benefited. The question as to what one has done for them cannot but haunt a man with even a minimal sense of gratitude. To know that one has contributed nothing to their material well-being is painful and extremely difficult to live with. However, one can at least come to terms with it by, say, pledging a part of one's salary to worth-while causes. But to know that the sufferings, anxieties and aspirations of these men do not even form a part of one's intellectual concern, that one is not offering them the highest gift which is within one's power to give—one's time, thoughts and intellectual skill and energy—is shattering and paralysing. Concern with abstract problems then appears inhuman, even irresponsible. Yet these problems have their own powerful appeal, reinforced constantly by professional pressures and internalised norms of what is and what is not academic scholarship. So the unhappy mind, racked by conflicting sympathies, keeps shifting from one type of problem to another, uneasy with either alone, and therefore unable to give it its fullest attention and energy.

There is one other aspect of an Indian intellectual's life in England to which I would like to draw attention. It concerns the nature of the English language. More than ever I did while in India, I have become increasingly conscious of how English, like any other language, is suited to conceptualise a particular way of experiencing the world. Not that someone with different experiences cannot use it to describe them, but rather that he feels that it expresses only a part of what he wishes to say or that some of its words and idioms are not acceptable to him. Let me explain. In India there are three different ways one can address a person. If he is younger or inferior or very dear, one addresses him one way; if he is one's peer or a relative stranger, one addresses him differently; and, finally, if he is one's superior or a man of high standing and distinction, one employs yet another mode of address. English language, on the other hand, employs the universal 'you' to describe all three. Ever since I learnt to speak English I have felt disturbed by this egalitarianism. Not that I am unsympathetic to social equality. Far from it. Rather is it that this linguistic egalitarianism seems totally incongruent with the general hierarchical ethos of Indian society. I remember feeling acutely uneasy at having to address my headmaster in the same way in which I addressed our servant. I felt that I was not showing him proper respect and regard, that there was something false about my way of addressing him. Nearly all my fellow-students apparently felt the same way, and almost unconsciously and universally we devised a way to overcome what then struck us as the impertinent egalitarianism of the English language by adding 'sir' and 'headmaster' after 'you'. 'Would you, sir' or 'would you, headmaster, be taking your lecture today?' seemed more satisfying, more true, than the mere 'would you'. 'Sir' was not a sign of obsequiousness, or a title of courtesy, but added a definite meaning and sense to the pronoun 'you', and brought it into harmony not only with the way we would have addressed him in any of the Indian languages but also with our deep emotional concern to distinguish our relationship with him from that with, say, our peers or our servants.

It seems to me, further, that English as it is spoken in England[25] is far more anthropomorphic than any other language known to me. There is no part of the human body, excepting one, which it does not invoke. Head, foot, arm, eye, face, ear, chest, breast, bottom, tooth, leg and stomach, to name but a few, appear in endless and rather amusing combinations. Consider for example, the expressions like the head of a hammer, eye of the needle, ears of the corn, nose of the plane, neck of the womb or of bottle, brow of a hill, face of a mountain, stomach an insult, belly of the batting, underbelly of Europe, hands of the clock, making a clean breast of something, getting a matter off one's chest, heart of the country, arteries of the nation, legs of a chair, weak-kneed argument, spine of a book, foot of a hill, and bottom of a street. English also abounds in expressions that appear rather violent to someone not used to them from childhood onwards. Consider, for example, expressions like getting one's teeth into an argument, or the introduction to a book having a bite, or chewing over and digesting a point, or breaking the back of a problem, or an animal eating its head off. Speaking personally, I have never been able, even after years in England, to ask a student to get his teeth into an argument without actually clenching my teeth. My father was deeply offended when I told him that the vegetable he had so much enjoyed in an Indian restaurant in London was called 'lady's finger'. He could not understand why the English should use such a 'cannibalistic' term. The sexuality of several English expressions also strikes foreigners, especially women, as rather odd. Take, for example, the words like seduce, intercourse, abortive, rape, impotent and virginity. A Ceylonese girl threw away a book in disgust when the author remarked in the introduction that he was concerned to seduce his reader with a particular thesis. I learnt to use the word impotence in a human context and even now find myself haunted by the saddening image of a sexually pitiable middle-aged gentleman every time I hear or read of a Vice-chancellor or a government minister being impotent to handle a situation of crisis. There are countless Indian students and writers who eschew the term social intercourse,[26] and blush at expressions involving the words like rape, impotence, prostitute, virginity and abortive.

To be sure no language is imaginable without metaphors. The point, however, is that metaphors are not linguistic accidents, especially when they reveal a certain pattern as in the examples already given. Metaphors basically signify an attempt to highlight certain types of similarity between the objects concerned, and the similarity a linguistic community perceives and the importance it assigns to it is not accidental but presupposes a certain type of *weltanschauung*. It could at least be argued, for example, that the various expressions listed above indicate a desire to anthropomorphise the material world, a desire to relieve its strangeness and perhaps to deny its otherness by imposing upon it terms whose reference, whatever it may originally have been, is now recognised to be primarily human. One might even wonder if they do not reflect anthropomorphic narcissism which has played so vital a role in removing pre-modern inhibitions to the ruthless exploitation of nature. Whatever the explanation, it is obvious that in allowing words to travel freely between the two realms, one denies the distinction between the living organism and the material world. To a person like myself whose *weltanschauung* draws a fairly firm ontological boundary[27] between the two realms, and whose language generally has a separate vocabulary for each, these metaphorical expressions are disturbing. They represent an attempt both to cheapen the dignity of the species and to violate the being of the material world. Indeed, by confusing his perception of the world, they destroy his intellectual and emotional signposts and disorientate him. He feels extremely nervous and insecure in their presence; and every encounter with them shakes him to the very depths of his being. Personally, having been conditioned into a fairly clear separation between the sentient and the natural world, and having had a rather gentle and (alas) puritanical background, many of the expressions that I have called anthropomorphic, violent, and sexual, outraged my sensibilities for years; and not only could I not use them myself but also reading a piece where they were freely used became a most painful and terrifying experience to me. I felt that my inner world was besieged and assaulted on all sides. Only as I became Anglicised after several years of stay in England did the emotional resistance to them weaken, but it has not entirely disappeared. Even now after nearly thirteen years in England I cannot persuade myself to use some of these expressions; and when I do employ others, I feel strange, nervous and highly self-conscious.

The point I am making is this. What appears natural and straightforward to a native speaker may appear vulgar, odd, offensive and violent to outsiders, who cannot therefore help avoiding certain expressions. This inevitably limits their vocabulary, their 'range of descriptions', and forces them to use circumlocutions or to invent new modes of expression which native speakers may find odd and clumsy. Learning a language is not simply a question of learning grammar and vocabulary, it involves learning to see the world the way a linguistic community is accustomed to seeing it. If therefore one sees the world differently, one finds oneself having to do battle with words in order both to prevent one's character from being shaped by the communal character reflected in the language, and to express one's own distinctive character and experiences. One might even feel constrained to 'violate' the established canons of syntax and style. An Indian used to colourful garments and spicy food might like his language to be colourful and ornate, and might hold different standards of good style. Being relatively simple-minded and a great talker, he might feel that a good style is one where men write as they talk, and that a measure of repetitiveness and verbosity rather than economy are its desirable qualities. This raises an important question. Even as different societies have different notions of what is elegant in dress and food, there is no *a priori* reason why there should be one uniform standard of style, or why cultural pluralism should not be extended to language as well. After all how can a man feel at home in the world if he is alienated from the language itself? A complaint has increasingly been voiced that immigrant children find it difficult to 'master' English. If what has been said above is correct, the answer to the complaint is that 'Indian' English, for example, is not 'English' English insufficiently mastered by Indians, but English that has been Indianised to suit Indian attitudes, experiences and forms of thought. It is not a 'corrupt' version of a supposed 'real' English, but a distinct 'language-game' with its own distinctive syntax and canons of style, and as valid and authentic as the so-called standard English. Much of the silly resentment against English in India, and even among some immigrant circles here, based on the feeling that it is a 'white master's language' would lose its point if Indians (and others) were able, without any feeling of guilt, to 'Indianise' English as freely as they wished, consistent with the minimal demands of clarity and intelligibility.

V

The Indian in England is haunted by the spectre of self-consciousness. For all but a few brief moments, almost everything conspires to remind him of his difference from the society around him. He wears his origin on his face, and this heightens his identifiability. Then there is the problem of communication, written as well as oral. Not only his accent but also his choice of words, formulation and organisation of sentences, reluctance to use certain forms of expression and the inevitable recourse to circumlocutions emphasise that he speaks and writes differently from others. Others' conversations and writings often contain allusions that elude him, jokes that do not amuse and even offend him, assumptions that he cannot share, and implications that at times seem to him outrageous. Even something as prosaic as reading a newspaper first thing in the morning might start off his day rather badly. There is often little coverage of the parts of the world with which he identifies himself emotionally, and what is reported is sometimes so ill-informed and one-sided that it may disgust and sicken him. In times of crisis the feeling of being an outsider becomes especially heightened, as he is forced to realise how much he is out of sympathy with the national sentiment. In his relations with his friends, colleagues, and neighbours he is never quite sure if he is behaving properly. An odd remark, and he might be misunderstood and lose a friend. A spontaneous gesture or laughter, and he might be ridiculed or considered awkward, or he might hurt someone's feelings. He must therefore consciously calculate how his actions will affect others; and this makes his behaviour deliberate, self-conscious, serious, and ponderous. What is more, he can never be sure that his calculations will be correct. Therefore, for the most part he tends to remain reticent, never taking the initiative lest it should backfire, and remains content to listen and follow, to laugh and nod and smile when others do. There is no area of social and personal life where he can trust his instincts. Everything he does has a sad air of tentativeness and uncertainty about it, and therefore fills him with anxiety and unease. The curse of self-consciousness paralyses his life and threatens to turn him into a human artifact.

To avoid embarrassment and acute self-consciousness, he generally tends to conform to established conventions in his relations with his friends, colleagues and strangers. Since he does not fully accept these conventions, there is an air of falsity and inauthenticity about his behaviour, and he knows this. Lest this falsity should create a 'lie in the soul', he tries constantly to reassure himself that he is only 'playing' a role which he may abandon at will, but he knows that the roles he plays can easily take deep roots and become a second and eventually even a first nature, and so profoundly alter his being. Hence the frantic effort to separate the self from its roles, and the perpetual struggle to insulate it from getting corrupted and shaped by them. Roles, however, are an individual's primary links with society, and therefore his constant attempt to distance himself from his roles ultimately means that the Indian is trying to dissociate himself from the wider society. This deprives him of anchorage in, and any real contact with, the outside society; and predictably he finds himself living a life that lacks any firm assurance of its reality, a kind of twilight existence in which he is never entirely sure if he is mad or sane, silly or wise, foolish or profound.[28]

NOTES

1. Foreigners' fascination with English character goes back several hundred years and has yielded an amazing crop of compliments and condemnations. Sorbiere, a French visitor in Charles II's reign, thought that 'the English may be easily brought to anything, provided you fill their bellies, let them have freedom of speech, and do not bear too hard upon their lazy temper'. Count Hermann Keyserling observed, 'whenever I meet one of this people I am shocked by the dearth of their talents and the limitation of their horizon. . . . Even the more eminent Englishmen can hardly be taken seriously as intellectuals. They are like animals furnished with a number of unerring instincts, but otherwise blind and incapable. They all think, feel and act alike; there are no surprises in the inner lives of any of them.' He went on, 'They represent, as they are, the perfect realisation of their possibilities; they are completely what they might have been.' He found the Englishman a 'thoroughly integral unity', something he owes 'to Puritanism, a Yoga or culture of concentration no less intensive than that of India'. Cf. W. H. Auden's attack on 'the suffocating insular coziness' and intellectual 'laziness' of the English in his *Forewords and Afterwords* (Faber, London, 1973). For the remarks on English character quoted above, see the chapter entitled 'The soul of England' in William Ralph Inge, *England* (E. Benn, London, 1926). See also Wilhelm Dibelius, *England* (Cape, London, 1930) and George Santayana's *Soliloquies in England* (Constable, London, 1922). Santayana contended that the Englishman was constitutionally incapable of becoming a Roman Catholic or a saint; 'with freedom and reserve and experiment in his blood, to go over to Rome is an essential suicide. . .; an Englishman might become a saint, but only by becoming a foreigner'.

2. Some recent accounts of English life, like those by David Frost and Peter Grosvenor, are too slight to be of much value to a social philosopher. Geoffrey Gorer is an exception. See below.

3. The following analysis of English character has benefited from my discussions with Professors Ian Cunnison, C. H. Dodd and Preston King, and with Drs Gordon Hutton, Ivar Oxaal, and R. N. Berki. I have also benefited from the comments made by Mr Geoffrey Gorer and Mr Philip Mason on the draft version of the paper.

4. *Exploring English character*, London, 1955, p. 163.

5. *Ibid.*, pp. 186 ff.

6. To avoid misunderstanding I am not suggesting that the myth gives an inaccurate account of English character. I am only interested in elucidating how it has acquired such power and appeal.

7. Santayana is right to observe in his *Soliloquies in England* that constant repression of an emotion could easily kill it, so that over generations a nation might lose the capacity to experience it.

8. I would like to argue that no emotion is natural to man. Emotions are ultimately based on the agent's *Weltanschauung*—his estimation of objects and activities, the degree and kind of importance he attaches to them, etc., and hence cultural in origin.

9. *Death, Grief and Mourning in Contemporary Britain* (London, 1965), pp. 51 f.

10. Muralt's seventeenth century work entitled *Lettres sur les Anglais* makes a similar point quite well. The English, he thought, hated cruelty so much that

royal proclamations required the fish and ducks to be fed properly, and yet they would allow prisoners in their gaols to die of hunger. 'The great cruelty of the English', he remarked, 'lies in permitting evil rather than doing it'.

11. All these are examples from the recent past.

12. Dean Inge remarks, the Englishman 'is quite willing not to be able to look out of his windows upon the street, if only he can prevent other people from looking in' (*England, op. cit.*, p. 68).

13. Dr P. F. N. Heylings, Personal View (*British Medical Journal*, April 14, 1973). Some of his recommendations are worth quoting: 'Every Briton should learn to touch the people he loves and knows every day. We should shake hands more easily, embrace and welcome each other more readily. Little children should sit on older people's knees. Teachers and parents should smack their children with their hands instead of sending them to bed or standing them in a corner. . . . Every nurse should comb more heads and rub more bottoms, more vigorously than ever before. For the more timid, touching can be done with the sound of the voice and the look on one's face'.

14. *A Fortunate Man*, Allen Lane, The Penguin Press, London, 1967, p. 93.

15. Gorer, *Exploring English Character, op. cit.*, p. 280.

16. *A Wells collection of 1971 U.K. Charitable Giving Reports*, The Wells Group. Reported in the *Guardian*, March 16, 1973.

17. Peter Walsher, 'South Africa: cutting the Profits of Starvation', *Sunday Times*, March 18, 1973.

18. Quoted in Rajni Kothari, *India*, Little Brown & Co., 1970, p. 271.

19. Surprising as it may seem, this comes out in the behaviour of highly sensitive and reflective Indians as well. Naipaul's *An Area of Darkness* (Andre Deutsch, London, 1964) is an interesting example of this. Consider the way he reasoned when he was overcharged by his hotel manager. 'I was being overcharged. I was bitterly disappointed. I had known them for four months; *I had declared my affection for them*; I had done what I could for the hotel; I had given them a party . . . I jumped up . . . and heard myself shouting . . . "This is *not good*, Mr Butt . . . do you know what you have done? You have *hurt* me"'. (p.166). A European, especially, an Englishman, would not have allowed himself to get so deeply involved with the hotel in this way. He would not have transformed a purely business relationship into one of affection; and nor would he have talked of being 'hurt', expecting thereby to appeal to his manager's moral emotion. He would have kept the relationship at an impersonal level and would have haggled and used the threat to go elsewhere to exert commercial pressure. It is worth observing how Naipaul also got so deeply involved with Aziz and how he struggled to own his being. Describing the moment of their parting, Naipaul remarks 'I could not be sure that he had ever been *mine*' (p. 192). Consider also the way he allowed the Sikh to take over and dominate his being (pp. 238 ff). Not only does Naipaul reveal basically Indian demands and sensitivities, his account of India, surprising as it may seem to those who have dismissed it as anti-India, errs, if that is the right word, in being excessively pro-Indian. On p. 219 he describes Indian sculpture as 'worth all the sculpture of the rest of the world', and on p. 257 he remarks 'Out of all its squalor and human decay . . . India produced so many people of grace and beauty . . ., permitted a unique human development to so many. Nowhere were people so heightened, rounded and individualistic; nowhere did they offer themselves so fully and with such assurance. To know Indians was to take a delight in people as people; every encounter was an adventure. I did not want India to sink; the mere thought was painful.'

20. The two differ in countless other trivial and important respects as well. Sunday for an Englishman is a day of rest; for an Indian it is a day of socialising, to be spent outside his house. The English, and Western, idea of a holiday has no place in India; if one did take a holiday in India it would take the form of going and staying with a friend or a relative. The ideas of beauty differ too. The Indian prefers his woman plump and white, is fascinated by her eyes and cannot see why anyone should find anything attractive in her legs. Naipaul (in *An Area of Darkness*, *op. cit.*, p. 75) remarks that Indians use only the left hand in love-making, but I have found no evidence for this. Most Hindus fast once a fortnight on grounds of both health and religion. Unlike Western food which is served one dish at a time, Indian food is served all at once. Indians parade death; the English suppress it and surprisingly have no norms to regulate their conduct towards the bereaved. See *Death, Grief and Mourning in Contemporary Britain* (*op. cit.*, pp. 14f).

21. For some interesting examples and their perceptive analysis, see Michael Banton, *White and Coloured* (Cape, London, 1959, pp. 123ff). See also Ursula Sharma, *Rampal and his Family* (Collins, London, 1971, pp. 85ff) for an account of the way an Indian falls out with his compatriots.

22. I am not suggesting that this problem is unique to Indians or to 'coloured' people in general. Many Jewish and East European parents feel it no less acutely.

23. To avoid misunderstanding I am here thinking of India of the early fifties. The situation has, of course, changed for the better since.

24. What I owe to two of my teachers, Professor G. N. Mathrani and Dr Miss Usha Mehta, is beyond words.

25. English as it is spoken in India is in many respects different from the way it is spoken in England. Many of the points made below do not therefore apply to it.

26. A Ghanaian student of mine, on the other hand, found these expressions especially pleasing, and would not only use the term 'intercourse' on all conceivable occasions but would also pronounce it with special force and almost as 'e . . . n . . . t . . . er-course'. He liked the sound of the word and enjoyed playing with it. Every time he spoke it, his face would light up, and show signs of gratification and even a sense of release, as if he was experiencing the activity expressed by the term. I sometimes wondered if this was linguistic copulation.

27. The boundary, to be sure, is not absolutely rigid and is gradually disappearing. Incidentally I have sometimes wondered if Marx's project of humanising nature entails that nature should be referred to only in anthropomorphic terms in order for man to feel fully at home in it.

28. This essay has greatly benefited from my long discussions with Pramila.

4 A Child and a Stranger: On Growing Out of English Culture

KRISHAN KUMAR

There are all too many intellectual aids to these very self-conscious reflections. How tempting to reach out for concepts like 'marginality', 'rootlessness', 'alienation', 'cultural schizophrenia'. How nice to dwell on the cool dissections of Sartre's 'Anti-Semite and Jew'; or to revel in the passionate pages of Baldwin, Cleaver, Fanon, on being a black man in a white man's civilisation. Most seductive of all I have found the writings of V. S. Naipaul—the novels and the personal statements—which show individuals, and Naipaul himself, 'in a free state': aliens between cultures, with no social anchorages, no significant environment against which to shape out a confident and hopeful identity. There are plainer reasons for looking to Naipaul. Like him, I am a West Indian Indian. Like him, I have spent the greater part of my life in this country. There, unfortunately, the resemblance stops. How strong the inclination to seek in the strength and subtleties of his thought and expression the articulations of my own position.

It would be silly for me to say that these various treatments have no relevance to my own situation, no bearing on the way I see myself. I have learned a lot about myself from them, and am sure their influences are at work, in one form or another, in much of what I shall have to say, but yet they do not seem to me to be in any sense points of departure. I cannot see in them a concern with what seems to me the distinctiveness of my own experience, and unlike Naipaul, I do not feel that 'I'm only passing through'. Indeed, it was only comparatively late in life that I had any real consciousness of having *arrived from* somewhere—somewhere outside England. This may set this contribution a little apart from the others in this symposium. Most of the other contributors have, I imagine, come to England already possessing solid experience of other family systems, other cultures, perhaps other religions. The perspective of 'culture-contact', of adjustment and

accommodation, of rejection and withdrawal, perhaps of quiz-
zical detachment—this perspective is all set up for them. It
probably will not take them very far, but at least it is a beginning.
I cannot start from there. The story of my 'contact' with English
life and culture follows, in a sense, a reverse direction. I have had
to *grow into* the perspective of the outsider. The discovery of
myself as an Indian in England came only as part of the ordinary
process of discovery of one's self, the attainment of self-
consciousness that is the usual consequence of growing up in any
particular society.

My oddity in this respect is I think one of time, rather than of
type. When we settled in London in 1951 there were very few
Indians here and they were mostly students, employees of the
Indian High Commission, a few businessmen, writers, and professionals. Most of them really were simply 'passing through', as
were other Africans and West Indians. Or, if they thought of
staying, they often did so for cultural and artistic reasons. Their
Anglicised education made them look towards, yearn rather, for
England. However perplexed, disillusioned or dampened by their
experiences of the 'Mother Country', as self-conscious intellectuals
and artists they could not live anywhere else. England was for them
the source of all things, the originating and total reality, of which
their societies seemed fragmentary and impoverished imitations.
Their situation, while socially marginal, was not necessarily
uncomfortable. An Indian writer of those years, Victor Anant,
could write of having 'lived smugly and comfortably on the
borderline, battening on the profits that derive from playing the
role of cultural schizophrenic'. At any rate, their niche was a
relatively clear one. Based largely in London, unencumbered by
families, and the social obligations springing from these, they were
the professional outsiders. It was their duty to be introspective
and analytical about their responses to English culture, and to the
fact of their exile from their own. It was their privilege to offer
the objective, unflattering verdicts on the questions of the day:
the ramshackle apparatus of the new 'Welfare State'; Britain's
pretensions to be an independent nuclear power; the decompo-
sition of Empire, and the cynical adventurism of Suez; the tear-
away hedonism of the Macmillan years; the hyprocrisy of British
sexual morals. (This is a rough selection of their own terms.)
At the end of the fifties, a symposium in book form was commissioned, in many ways like the present one. The contributors
were 'gifted exiles', most from Commonwealth countries. The
title of the symposium was *Alienation*; and the contributors,

although some grumbled a little at the ponderousness of the theme imposed on them, did not seem to think that it was an especially questionable description of their experience.

My experience of those years was very different. For one thing, we were here as a family. Not a whole family, admittedly, our father remained in Trinidad, and while staying in touch has not re-joined us in the more than twenty years that we have been here. Still, we were a large family, and a young one. I was, at nine years, the middle child of six children, of whom the eldest was still only twelve. Immediately the ordinary problems of family living engulfed us or at least my mother. We had to find schools for those old enough to attend them. My mother, unsure of firm financial support from her husband, took a job at the Indian High Commission. There had then to be nurseries for the youngest. There were various welfare agencies to be sought out. There was, at every moment, the whole intricate process of learning the environment—the streets and shops, the buses and tubes, the families of friends met and made at school.

Looking back, there was a surprising aspect to this process. I had had after all nine years of early learning in a non-English environment. Why then did my new experiences have so unmistakably a 'grounded' quality about them—as if forming the primary, most elementary layers of consciousness, unaffected by anything that had gone before? It was as if all earlier experience had been annulled—not forgotten, exactly, but simply and unconsciously defined as irrelevant, and so not offering any resistance to the full absorption of the new influences. Certain accidental background factors may have helped to create this situation of openness. We had, as a family, been unusually exposed to 'non-Indian' influences for a long time. My father had spent his boyhood in London, attending both school and university there. He had lived alone with his mother, with no other family around and few Indian friends and contacts. English became his 'natural' language, the language he always used both with his wife and his children. Returning to India in his early twenties, he got on neither with British India nor his newly-wedded wife's family, and took himself off to the West Indies, to Trinidad, his wife following soon after. There the family they produced continued this somewhat untypical pattern. There were, of course many Indian families in Trinidad but they lived mainly in the interior, or in San Fernando. We lived in Port-of-Spain, and were therefore further insulated from Indian family life, religion, language. English was the only language we knew; our father was indifferent to Indian customs;

our friends were our West Indian neighbours and their children. Our situation in London completed this history of 'imperfect socialisation'. We lived at first with my father's mother in her house at Chalk Farm. An Indian influence? No, she was more suspicious and contemptuous of Indians than any non-Indian I have ever met, and constantly warned us to beware of Indians and their knavish ways. Finally there was the state of the family itself: lacking a father to give it direction, headed by a mother with the Herculean task of coping with six young children in a strange environment, and composed of children with sufficient curiosity and capability of communication to make their own diverse lives with the English friends they encountered in the school and the streets.

I do not think this peculiar history is the whole explanation of the sponge-like receptivity towards English culture which we showed. As I shall suggest in a moment, there seems to me a sense in which such receptivity may well be becoming typical of British-born children of recent immigrant families, despite the stronger insulation afforded by those families compared with ours. In any case, peculiar or not, I have to set it down as the fundamental point of departure for these reflections on my reactions to English culture. I knew we were West Indian Indians. I was even very fully aware of the specific fact of our Indian-ness: just before coming to London we had spent two very happy years with my mother's family in India. But this seemed abstract, bureaucratic information, the sort of thing required for filling in application forms for passports and the like. In concrete, day-to-day terms, I was quite simply not aware of any differences between my experiences and those of the English people I mixed with. I was learning the culture from within, as if one newly born to it. Whatever the reactions of others towards me as an Indian—and there must have been some—I either did not perceive them as such or buried them deeply in the unconscious. I was fully 'exposed' to all the complicated influences of the mass media—in those days, especially the radio, comics, films and the popular news-papers. I learned from these, perhaps more directly than English children, the various 'tones' of the culture: the accents of speech, the gestures and intonations of behaviour, the conventionalised attitudes towards those of other classes, and of other cultures. The last must have involved me in what now seems a particularly striking form of self-deception. One memory sticks out especially grotesquely. While intellectuals and 'outsiders' hammered British intervention in Suez, and while this was also the attitude of the

families of most of my English friends, I could find in myself a
response to the jingoistic appeal of a headline in the *Sketch*:
'It's D-Day Again—The Bombers Go In!'. That will teach those
wogs a lesson. A curious response, perhaps, but no more curious
than the analogous testimonies of Jews, Negroes, women, and
ex-members of the working class. Anyway, at the time I saw no
contradiction, and even secretly distrusted the *New Statesman*-like
parrotings of the left-wing families I mixed with. And, perhaps
most important for a boy of fourteen, there were no other primary,
face-to-face influences to offset the predominantly nationalist cast
of the culture diffused by the main social institutions. Apart from
my grandmother, whose effect was purely negative, we had no
relatives outside the immediate nuclear family living in England.
Our mother had a few Indian friends, but they impinged hardly
at all on family life, and were mostly treated by us with the polite
detachment reserved for people from remote regions. The North
London grammar school I went to had at most half a dozen other
Indians in the whole seven years I was there. In fact until I went
up to Cambridge at the age of nineteen I did not have a single
Indian friend. At Cambridge for the first time I met Indians of
my age and interests, and for the first time reflected seriously on
myself as an Indian. The fact that they had mostly come to Cambridge direct from India, from colleges and universities there,
while I had been brought up in England, and had got to Cambridge
through the English educational system—this created its own
ambivalences in our relationships. But they supplied an essential
component for my understanding of myself, and of my relation
to English life.

I have said that, while my situation may be rather different
from that of many of the contributors to this symposium, it could
well be typical for a considerable number of black British in
the future. I should like to touch on this just very briefly, for it
assumes a number of things about British society that may well
not be borne out by future developments. But let us take the situation of the Indians, Pakistanis, West Indians, and perhaps others,
born in this country to parents who formed part of the mass
immigration of the early sixties. No doubt the route for most of
these children is depressingly clear and straight: out of school at
fifteen, and into the bottom, most insecure layers of the labour
force. No doubt, too, particularly in the case of the Asians, the
family structure will act to prevent a total loss of ethnic identity,
and so mitigate the stress of the encounter between a totally
anglicised black person and a society that treats him as black before

British. Still, the educational system does offer the means for a certain limited amount of social mobility and intellectual development; and the family controls only a relatively narrow area of socialisation in a society where occupational opportunities, education, and general cultural patterns are so dominated by centralised agencies. Granted this, it is not a remote possibility that quite a large number of young blacks will go through substantially the same sequence that for a number of accidental reasons I have gone through earlier—'prematurely', as it were. That is, they will either not perceive or they will reject the latent identity offered them by the fact of their family's alien origin or the colour of their skin. They will grow up thinking of themselves as English, and will probably explore and internalise the cardinal elements of English culture more intensely than their white co-nationals. They will think initially of a wide range of professional careers, not just the technical, 'neutral' ones like accountancy or electronics, but the ones touching more nearly the central values of the society: the law, the civil service, the City finance corporations, politics, the cultural bureaucracies. They will find, a little to their surprise, that they in fact make a number of largely unconscious decisions which mean that they end up in the culturally more marginal occupations. They will sense, too, critical difficulties over social areas such as marriage, family, and community. If they have not done so already, this will be the time for reflection; perhaps, for some of them, for action.

Let us, here, remain contemplative. The first point seems to be to interrogate the autobiography briefly sketched earlier. It is true that I was not conscious of following a line of development, intellectual or social, different from that of my English friends. Looking back I can see that a quite distinctive pattern was imposed on that development. Certain choices were made, certain predilections established, certain avenues closed off. The influences in all this worked obscurely, and largely below the threshold of consciousness; but they made for a pattern that had a coherence more than that simply of the individual personality. It was the coherence of a generality, of a type: a type of one who thinks himself English but is not, and is not so regarded by others: and who comes to see this.

Intellectual interests presumably feed upon the emotional and experiential residues of an individual's life, and so can be good indicators of the underlying shape of that experience. I found myself, at school, greatly attracted to the study of history. But it was history written with a special slant, with an eye for the comparative generalisation and the structural features of a society's history. Later on I was to discover Marx and Weber, and to call this interest 'sociological'. At the time I liked Acton and Namier (I still do). With their European interests and affiliations, I was particularly drawn to their emphasis on the distinctiveness of the English tradition. I found it easy to sympathise with their obvious preference for the English style of 'political culture' over the Continental variety. England, it seemed, had had Common Law, which had protected individual liberty against the pretensions of Crown and State; the Continental political tradition was bedevilled by the reception of Roman law, and the consequent subservience of the individual to the State. England had been a naval power, and had, since the time of Cromwell, abominated standing armies; unlike the Continental states, she had as a result avoided the threat posed to public liberty by the presence of an ever-ready agency for use by the executive power. England had evolved a territorial nationality, as opposed to an ethnic or linguistic nationality, and so had escaped the fanaticism of the nationalist movements that swept Europe and the rest of the world in the nineteenth and twentieth centuries. A passage in Namier's essay 'Nationality and Liberty', re-read many times since, struck an especially responsive chord: it evoked a response to the totality of English culture.

'For men rooted in the soil there is, as a rule, a hierarchy of allegiances: to their village community or estate, to their "country" —for them the nation is of a naturally federal structure. Traditional beliefs and hereditary ties persist; class and the way of living determine alignments; things are individual and concrete in the village or the small, old-fashioned town. But in the great modern cities men grow anonymous, become ciphers, and are regimented; thinking becomes more abstract and is forced into generalisations; inherited beliefs are shaken and old ties are broken; there is a void, uncertainty, and hidden fear which man tries to master by rational thought. He starts by proudly asserting the rights of the abstract average individual freed from the bondage of tradition, and then integrates him into the crowd, a collective personality, which unloads itself in mass movements. The mass is the refuge of the uprooted individual and the disintegration of spiritual values is as potent a process as the splitting of the atom: it releases demonic forces which bursts all dams. . . . Liberty is the fruit of slow growth in a stable society; is based on respect for the rights of the individual, deeply embedded in the life and habits of the community; is in its origin an aristocratic idea: of the self-conscious individual, certain of himself and his position, and therefore perfectly at ease. It spreads when every man's house becomes "his castle": yet he must have a house and be safely rooted.' (Shades of Mr Biswas!)

It was not very long before I came to see this barely concealed paean to the English political tradition as a seriously distorting piece of special pleading; and when I later encountered similar positions in other varieties of 'philosophic conservatism'—as, for instance, in the writings of Michael Oakeshott—I had already been sufficiently exposed to alternative interpretations of that tradition to be less impressed. Even so, I felt, and still feel, that any form of radical social philosophy has to come to terms with, to incorporate somehow, the ideas and sentiments informing that passage. At any rate, the significance of that early reverence for English culture seems clear. Whether one interprets it generously as the informed appreciation of the great strengths of the English tradition, or, less kindly, as the aping of the English gentleman, I was following a path well marked and trodden by generations of cultural 'outsiders'. I was willing myself to be more English than the English; simply, perhaps, to be more self-consciously English than the English. It was the pattern of the culturally converted, akin to, and with the intensity of, the religiously converted. I have always thought it best exemplified in the life of Benjamin Disraeli, a Jew formally Christianised only at the age of thirteen, but, in André Maurois' words, 'brought up as an Englishman, shaped by Englishmen, shaped by English thought, surrounded by English friends, and passionately attached to England'. Namier himself was of course also a Jew, from Poland, who became 'passionately attached' to English institutions, yet who remained, according to a Balliol contemporary, 'all his life outside the English social system' and was indeed denied a Fellowship at All Souls because of his race. There are numerous examples at the present time, of distinguished émigrés who seem to have conceived it as their mission to tender to their hosts a coherent philosophy of the English tradition; to point up the distinctiveness of English development, to urge upon the largely unreflecting English the need to defend the priceless store they have so unwittingly garnered, now threatened by seductive but wrong-headed ideas and practices from other cultural traditions. The line started externally, as it were, by Montesquieu and de Tocqueville, is continued internally by Karl Popper, Isaiah Berlin, F. von Hayek, as well as Namier; indeed by the whole set of 'White' émigrés so persuasively identified by Perry Anderson as key ideologues of English national culture.

In passing, is it not significant that a volume of commemorative essays in honour of Michael Oakeshott should have been edited by two non-English academics, Bhikhu Parekh and Preston King? There seems at least a *prima facie* case here of 'elective affinity'.

My pursuit of the quintessentially English took other, sometimes more devious, forms. There was the preference for the countryside over the coast; later, even over the towns. Countryside seems somehow closer to a society's culture, more impinged upon by it and therefore more expressive of its ways; seas and coasts are much the same everywhere. Even here I was drawn to a special type, the type of southern English countryside that has somehow picked up strong associations with the dominant culture: the Cotswolds, the Sussex downs, the lush green acres of Dorset. (Of course there is no mystery why these associations are there—one is pointing to the domains of the squirearchy that has diffused its social ideals pretty widely throughout the culture.) When it came to thinking of university, the same influences were powerfully at work: Oxford and Cambridge were the institutions to aim for, there simply were no others. The prestige of these places was an important factor, no doubt; but I think there was even more importantly some sense that there I would be put in touch with the core values, the generative energies, of that elusive English culture that was everywhere but could not quite be fully grasped. Later still I found myself inhabiting an ancient, pre-industrial cathedral city, cultivating a pseudo-*Gemeinschaft* existence in a quiet cul-de-sac near the cathedral, and within visible and striking distance of the countryside. False consciousness seemed incapable of further extravagant invention.

The culture I was so busily burrowing into was, of course, heavily class-based: the culture of the traditional English middle and upper middle classes. That was inevitable. It is really the only culture made available to the foreigner to come to terms with, if he wishes to do more in this society than continue the patterns of his ethnic group. Even if he is born and brought up in England the culture of the working-class will remain largely impenetrable. There is more to this than simply the famous insularity and xenophobia of the English working class, noted by Orwell. ('In all countries the poor are more national than the rich, but the English working class are outstanding in their abhorrence of foreign habits'.) It has also to do with another characteristic noted by Orwell, the *privateness* of English life. He saw this illustrated in the English addiction to hobbies and spare-time occupations, and commented: 'All the culture that is most truly native centres round things which even when they are communal are not official—the pub, the football match, the back garden, the fireside and the "nice cup of tea".' While this privateness is a feature of English cultural life as a whole, it is especially marked in working-class life, as Orwell's list of activities suggests. They are activities you have to grow up in, from within. There are no recipes for learning how to act in them. There are rituals and quasi-specialised, quasi-technical vocabularies surrounding the areas of the family, work, hobbies, sex, animals, cars, foreigners: with easy transitions from one area to another, following a determinate but quite unpredictable logic, like the wild merriment and blasphemy that can follow a deeply-felt funeral; and always concrete, never abstract, so that there are no rules for learning them.

There is a further aspect of these 'sub-institutional' activities that reinforces the foreigner's exclusion from working class life. That is the *inarticulateness* which both surrounds these activities and finally is transcended by them, but the manner of its transcendence makes admission to working-class culture appear as difficult as entry into a masonic society. I cannot resist quoting at length John Berger's fine account of this (the passage occurs in his book, with Jean Mohr, about a country doctor, *A Fortunate Man*):

'The inarticulateness of the English is the subject of many jokes and is often explained in terms of puritanism, shyness as a national characteristic, etc. This tends to obscure a more serious development. There are large sections of the English working and middle class who are inarticulate as the result of wholescale cultural deprivation. They are deprived of the means of translating what they know into thoughts which they can think. They have no examples to follow in which words clarify experience. Their spoken proverbial traditions have long been destroyed: and, although they are literate in the strictly technical sense, they have not had the opportunity of discovering the existence of a written cultural heritage.

Yet it is more than a question of literature. Any general culture acts as a mirror which enables the individual to recognise himself— or at least to recognise those parts of himself which are socially permissible. The culturally deprived have far fewer ways of recognising themselves. A great deal of their experience—especially emotional and introspective experience—has to remain *unnamed* for them. Their chief means of self-expression is consequently through action: this is one of the reasons why the English have so many "do-it-yourself" hobbies. The garden or the work bench becomes the nearest they have to a means of satisfactory introspection.

The easiest—and sometimes the only possible—form of conversation is that which concerns or describes action: that is to say action considered as technique or as procedure. It is then not the experience of the speakers which is discussed but the nature of an entirely exterior mechanism or event—a motor car engine, a football match, a draining system or the workings of some committee. Such subjects, which preclude anything directly personal, supply the content of most of the conversations being carried on by men over twenty-five at any given moment in England today. . . .

Yet there is warmth in such conversation and friendships can be made and sustained by it. The very intricacy of the subjects seems to bring the speakers close together. It is as though the speakers bend over the subject to examine it in precise detail, until, bending over it, their heads touch. Their shared expertise becomes a symbol of shared experience.'

Can it be wondered at that the foreigner feels excluded from this intricate, tortuous process of communication and communion? That he pursues instead the more visible, articulated, and graspable qualities of the national culture? Michael Banton, impressed by what he takes to be the more explicit, external, forms of sanctions and social control in working-class culture, supposes therefore that it is more accessible and thus that 'it is easier for the stranger to gain social acceptance in the lower social categories' than in the higher. But this is surely to take too behaviouristic a view of culture. The working class are for the most part kindly and tolerant towards foreigners, but they are so the less they are, or seem to be becoming, English. The best foreigners are those who, however long they stay in England, look as if they wish to retain their foreignness.

The English middle and upper class have managed with astonishing success to identify their culture with the national culture. (For a comparable case one has to look at something like the diffusion of the Brahminical ideal throughout Indian society.) To an extent they have even got significant sections of their own working class to accept their definition of cultural goals and ideals. Certainly to a foreigner, their culture *is* English culture: an easily recognisable compound of faces—the Queen, Duke, Winston Churchill; places—London and parts of the southern counties;

speech and accent—that of the southern middle class; institutions—
the monarchy, the two-party system, the City, the public schools,
Oxbridge, the armed forces, the BBC, *The Times*. Of course,
nothing in this conventional recital indicates the sheer complexity
of middle-class culture, the difficulty of learning actually to live it.
English middle-class life gives nothing to its working-class counterpart in its inwardness, its labyrinthine patterns of custom and
convention. Like most aspects of English culture, it is heavily
dependent on implicit norms and tacit modes of instruction—more
so than in cultures which are less homogeneous. Deviance is
punished by sanctions which are extremely indirect, which have
to be known therefore to be recognised as such and the appropriate
piece of behaviour reformed. The pitfalls attending those 'outsiders' who do not, for instance, fully understand the curious
cut-throat logic of the English gentleman's commercial practices,
can be seen in the career of the publisher Robert Maxwell, an
ex-Czech pilot turned English gentleman.

However, in at least two ways the situation is different from that
relating to working-class culture. First, there do exist some quite
obvious articulations of middle-class life and values, and in those
places where foreigners, especially from Commonwealth countries,
are most likely to have encountered them. Middle-class assumptions and pictures of the world have been diffused through countless agencies, ranging from children's stories, English films right
up to the 'sixties, middle-class stereotypes like the Major Thomson
stories, and the sort of English novelists read abroad (my mother,
who took an English degree in India, seems to have read largely
John Galsworthy. Other favourites include John Buchan and
P. G. Wodehouse). So there is at least superficially something for
the Anglicised immigrant to model himself on, some rough sort
of map to guide him through the thickets of English culture.
Second, and as an immensely successful mechanism of self-
preservation, the English middle-class have facilitated entry to
their ranks for those who can perform certain strict but relatively
simply recognised routines. A newcomer, whether from another
class or another country, found it almost impossible to gain
acceptance in his own lifetime, however wealthy he became. But
let him use this wealth so that his children lived in the right places,
mixed with the right people, went to the public schools and Oxbridge: and there was no problem about their being admitted to
the charmed circles. The procedure had worked more or less
successfully for Scots, Welsh, and Irish (though largely Anglo-
Irish); it had worked for Flemings, Huguenots, and Jews (by no

D

means completely for the last). Would it work for the latest arrivals, whose skins were black?

We do not yet know. There has not been time, but if I am to continue using my own experience as some indication of what is in store for others likely to be in my situation, I should like to express some doubts. It is not a matter of overt rejection and discrimination—and one has really to be thankful for this, for the writings of American blacks make terrifyingly clear the intense self-hatred and self-destructiveness generated in those so subjected. So far as things go at the moment in this country, the educated black, brought up here, does not have to deal with the brutal facts of that problem. Rather, he has to face the subtler patterning of choices, the half-conscious but steady process by which he 'writes off' central areas of social, cultural, economic and political life; relegating himself, apparently voluntarily, to the margin of the society's existence. We are back here perhaps, in the end and by a rather circuitous route, to Naipaul's men 'in a free state'. To talk of 'the role of the black intellectual' is to miss the point that for the educated black the *only* role available to him is that of intellectual.

Take the area of work. A sort of filtering process operates in your mind, a species of natural selection by which you eliminate all occupations other than those you sense compatible with the possibilities of your social position. I had done well at school, and was expected to go on to some career in the professions. While interested in my work, I cannot say I was possessed by the fervent desire to dedicate the rest of my life to the world of scholarship or of ideas, but that was the position I finally arrived at—I might almost say, drove myself into. My father, for instance, wanted me to be a lawyer, and I have no doubt I could have made a living as one. I knew, however, without ever having presented it consciously to myself, that my ethnic origin would debar me from really succeeding in it, would severely limit the extent to which I might develop any talents I possessed. The Law is a traditional, established profession. Its technical, expert, aspect is simply the tip of the iceberg. Basically it is an elaborate system of patron-client relationships in which, therefore, beyond the level of the solicitor's clerk social contacts and social relationships are of overwhelming importance. How could I, an Indian, however anglicised, hope to penetrate this intricate web of relationships, so heavily infused with considerations of class, culture, family background, kinship and friendship networks? (One answer to this presumably would be to 'go ethnic'—to seek one's clients in a constituency of those with like ethnic origin, just as lawyers like D. N. Pritt have formed constituencies out of left-wing and anti-colonial cases. But for reasons I have mentioned earlier this course could not suggest itself at the time.)

Similar considerations applied to other careers in areas where central decisions are made about economic and political affairs: in the Civil Service, private commerce and industry, the political parties (one does not even remotely consider that bastion of the national culture, the armed forces). In each case I was aware, often obscurely, of the innumerable face-to-face situations, personal encounters, occasions of social contact, which would be crucial for the matter in hand: whether it was negotiating with private interest groups, clinching a sale, or appearing before the selection committee of a constituency party. They would be situations where the criteria for efficiency and success would be so diffuse as to handicap seriously any participant not able to deploy his resources of 'impression management' to the full. In these situations the fact of one's ethnicity would have a marked 'interference effect', interposing itself as a mask that could obliterate all other relevancies in the situation. So, at any rate, I imagined, thereby mentally closing off the avenues that led into the centre of the society's activities.

There is then this feeling of powerlessness, on the most intuitive sort of survey of the social environment. Some mysterious agency seems to have taken away most of the options. At least its influence is mainly subconscious, so that one is not faced with the pain of actual choices on the basis of the sort of analysis just made. But certain choices unfortunately have to be made later, in the full glare of self-consciousness. The decision to marry, and to have children, belong here; and they become very difficult decisions. My English friends assume, as a matter of course, that they will marry and raise families. They have parents to help them with the children; grand-parents, aunts, uncles, and cousins dotted around the country, whom they can visit and expect help from in various ways; a whole network of in-laws that, however remotely connected, can be expected in some measure to act in a supportive way when necessary. English family life, far from becoming 'nucleated' as sociologists once supposed, remains among both the working and middle class astonishingly dependent on extended kinship ties. These ties offer points of the most intimate contact with the culture. They link their members back through the generations with the work and life of the national past; in the present they act as taken-for-granted points of stability in the social structure, islands of familiarity in an environment that has a tendency to fluctuate and convulse.

What if one lacks those ties? For someone with my sort of biography, marrying an Englishwoman would be a more natural step than seeking an Indian girl with whom I shared almost nothing of the binding experiences of childhood and adolescence. The children would be brought up here—where else? What then would be the consequences? Probably my wife would be torn from the greater part of her family network. I would have next to none. The children would be left to grow up in an unsupported void. Even my very slight experience of an extended family pattern makes me aware of how important it is, and how intolerable the free-floating nuclear family would be. More generally, I cannot visualise, cannot sketch out with any degree of clarity or confidence, the sort of relationship such a family would make with its environment. I am afraid of bringing into this society children of a mixed marriage, since the society has not given me confidence that it has the capacity to make them feel secure. I fear for their happiness, and do not want the burden of dealing with their unhappiness.

Yet to decide against a family is to push oneself even further over to the margin of the culture. So much of English social life seems to turn on relationships formed through families. It is not simply that a good deal of social life *is* family life: relatives visiting other relatives, children being sent off to stay with a sister here, an uncle there, whole groups of families going on holiday together. There is also the point that many non-family relationships are made through family. Children are especially important in this. The common problems of mothers with young children bring them together over such matters as baby-sitting, and in such places as creches and nurseries. The friendships made by children in the neighbourhood and at school bring different sets of parents together, initiating and perhaps cementing friendships at the parallel adult level. Here once again the sub-institutional nature of much English life is noticeable. Structured encounters between adults in clubs and societies seem of secondary importance in creating the bulk of relationships—compared, say, to the United States. So to be a non-participant at the informal level is, in a real sense, to forgo participation at any level of social life.

It seems that the black person, socialised and educated in English society, must come to consider himself as a 'participant-observer' rather than as an actor in that society. He has known much of the culture from inside, has grown up with it; at the same time his room to manoeuvre within it seems severely limited. He is driven therefore to make a livelihood out of the peculiarities of his condition. Himself made conscious of self and society, he undertakes to be a student of society. I am not saying that he necessarily becomes an intellectual in the sense of the nineteenth century Russian intelligentsia, or the Frankfurt school of Marxists. His exclusion from the central regions of social life is based on 'ascriptive' criteria: the fact of his race, or colour. He gravitates then to those regions where more universalistic criteria prevail, based on clearly defined qualifications, or the ability to manipulate symbols in the impersonal medium of writing. His is the world of the academy, of journalism, of 'creative writing' in all its forms, perhaps also of the communications industry. His materials are abstractions, ideas, language, and other forms of the symbolic universe. He may settle for the more ordinary routines of the academic life, cultivating an area especially in the non-human sciences, like mathematics or physics, or in a special period of history or literature. Or, more self-consciously, he may strive to be a student of the culture as a whole, especially English culture, since his own experiences force upon him an awareness of the shaping force of different cultural complexes. What distinguished his choice in either case is its fundamental detachment from the everyday life of the society, the arena of face-to-face encounters and of decisions negotiated in public places.

Even in this ethereal world of intellectual pursuits the constraining effect of the cultural reality persists. I had moved, after Cambridge, and as a purely bureaucratic step, from history to sociology, thereby as it were generalising and intellectualising my earlier emotional involvement with the distinctive aspects of English culture. Once again the direction of movement seemed determined. Most English sociologists do what they are pleased to call 'empirical research': going out into people's homes with questionnaires on class and family, or living for a while in close contact with a particular community or subculture. This sort of research I have never seriously contemplated, preferring instead the area of sociological theory, and of comparative, historically-based analyses of social and cultural structures, in the Weberian tradition. I think I can give good theoretical reasons for this preference; but for the moment the personal ones seem more relevant. The fact is that, as things stand, for an Indian to undertake research that involved direct, face-to-face contact with the subjects under study, would be to introduce a distorting factor far in excess of that normally present in such personally conducted research. Knowing that the respondents were probably reacting to me as an Indian as much as to me as a researcher, I simply would not know how to assess their responses. The parallel here with women researchers seems to me very close. Why in Europe and the United States are there so many more distinguished women anthropologists than women sociologists? Surely it is, at least partly, because women can get close to the totality of a culture only in non-European areas, where the fact of their sex is subordinated to the more salient fact of their status as white/ European/scientist? At home their research must be restricted to the family and other areas of traditional female involvement; in most other areas their sexual status acts with a heavy 'interference effect'.

So, too, I can do field research in other cultures; or, here, cultivate my own garden and go into race relations, but if I wish to study English society as a whole, I must find other intellectual tools. As I have suggested, this may be no great loss. One of the advantages of being pushed into the peripheral areas of the subject (the sociology of literature, of culture) is that one encounters approaches not being developed in the central areas. Looking for a way into the understanding of English culture, one very soon comes across the rich but still largely unworked vein represented by the contributions of George Orwell, Geoffrey Gorer, Tom Harrison, Richard Hoggart, and Raymond Williams. The last two are particularly interesting, from the point of view of the present concern. Both Hoggart and Williams have used with great sensitivity their experiences of a working-class background, and their movement beyond that class culture, as a way into the analysis of English culture as a whole. The early experience is not rejected or ignored; it is, as the Hegelians might say, dialectically transcended. The result is the most satisfying approach so far: a combination of the knowledge gained from the most primary, intuitive experience of the culture, together with the distancing perspective provided by a highly self-conscious passage through the different strata of that culture.

I started off this essay with some remarks about possible models for these reflections; here, at the end, I want to return to this. The perspective of 'the stranger', or 'the immigrant', or 'the outsider' seems useful if one is talking about a situation where an individual with one set of cultural assumptions encounters a whole culture with a different set of assumptions. I have suggested that my own situation is not really like this. It is perhaps best described as one of heavy cultural overlap: a syndrome where the ordinary, unselfconscious process of growing up in a culture is startled, as it

were, into a different mould by an awareness that one is perceived
and treated as an alien, with the physical and cultural features of
'other' cultures. And I have found it more illuminating to see this
pattern as akin to a movement from one class to another *within* a
culture, than as a movement from one culture to another. There
are some obvious differences, of course, but I have been repeatedly
struck by a certain basic sense of familiarity in episodes related
by British intellectuals who have travelled socially through the
culture. There is the same feeling, not so much of cultural confrontation or disruption—the continuity is too strong—but rather
of cultural disenchantment, a sort of personal distancing from the
culture. In his absorbing semi-autobiographical novel, *Border
Country*, Raymond Williams tells of the return of a university
lecturer to the small Welsh village where he was born and brought
up, as part of a railway signalman's family. The man, Matthew
Price, describes his feelings on returning as that of someone at
once 'both a child and a stranger': and I can find no better title for
this piece than that.

5 Alien Gods

A. SIVANANDAN

Wherever colonisation is a fact, the indigenous
culture begins to rot. And among the ruins
something begins to be born which is not a
culture but a kind of sub-culture which is
condemned to exist on the margin allowed by
an European culture. This then becomes the
province of a few men, the elite, who find
themselves placed in the most artificial
conditions, deprived of any revivifying contact
with the masses of the people.

Aime Cesaire[1]

On the margin of European culture, and alienated from his own,
the 'coloured' intellectual is an artefact of colonial history, marginal man par excellence. He is a creature of two worlds, and of
none. Thrown up by a specific history, he remains stranded on its
shores even as it recedes; and what he comes into is not so much a
twilight world, as a world of false shadows and false light.

At the height of colonial rule, he is the servitor of those in power,
offering up his people in return for crumbs of privilege; at its end,
he turns servant of the people, negotiating their independence
even as he attains to power. Outwardly, he favours that part of
him which is turned towards his native land. He puts on the garb of
nationalism, vows a return to tradition. He helps design a national
flag, compose a People's Anthem. He puts up with the beat of the
tom-tom and the ritual of the circumcision ceremony. Although,
privately, he lives in the manner of his masters, affecting their
style and their values, assuming their privileges and status. For a
while he succeeds in holding these two worlds together, the outer
and the inner, deriving the best of both. But the forces of nationalism on the one hand and the virus of colonial privilege on the other,
drive him once more into the margin of existence. In despair he
turns himself to Europe. With something like belonging, he looks
towards the Cathedral at Chartres and Windsor Castle, Giam-
bologna and Donizetti and Shakespeare and Verlaine, snowdrops
and roses. He must be done, once and for all, with the waywardness

and uncouth manners of his people, released from their endemic ignorance, delivered from witchcraft and voodoo, from the heat and the chattering mynah bird, from the incessant beat of the tom-tom. He must return to the country of his mind.

However, even as the 'coloured' intellectual enters the mother country, he is entered into another world where his colour, and not his intellect or his status, begins to define his life—he is entered into another relationship with himself. The porter (unless he is black), the immigration officer (who is never anything but white), the customs official, the policeman of whom he seeks directions, the cabman who takes him to his lodgings, and the landlady who takes him in at a price—none of them leave him in any doubt that he is not merely not welcome in their country, but should in fact be going back to where he came from. That indeed is their only curiosity, their only interest; where he comes from, which particular jungle, Asian, African or Caribbean.

There was a time when he had been received warmly, but he was at Oxford then and his country was still a colony. Perhaps equality was something that the British honoured in the abstract. Or perhaps his 'equality' was something that was precisely defined and set within the enclave of Empire. He had a place somewhere in the imperial class structure, but within British society itself there seemed no place for him. Not even his upper-class affectations, his BBC accent, his well-pressed suit and college tie afford him a niche in the carefully defined inequalities of British life. He feels himself not just an outsider or different, but invested, as it were, with a separate inequality; outside and inferior at the same time.

At that point, his self-assurance which had sat on him 'like a silk hat on a Bradford millionaire'[2] takes a cruel blow. But he still has his intellect, his expertise, his qualifications to fall back on. He redeems his self-respect with another look at his Oxford diploma (to achieve which he had put his culture in pawn): but his applications for employment remain unanswered, his letters of introduction unattended. It only needs the employment officer's rejection of his qualifications, white though they be, to dispel at last his intellectual pretensions.

The certainty finally dawns on him that his colour is the only measure of his worth, the sole criterion of his being. Whatever his claims to white culture and white values, whatever his adherence to white norms, he is first and last a no-good nigger, a bleeding wog or just plain black bastard. His colour is the only reality allowed him; but a reality, which, to survive, he must learn to cope with. Once more he is caught between two worlds: accepting his colour and rejecting it, or accepting it only to reject it—still aping the white man (though now with conscious effort at survival), playing the white man's game (though now aware that he changes the rules so as to keep on winning), even forcing the white man to concede a victory or two (out of his hideous patronage, his grotesque paternalism). He accepts that it is their country and not his, rationalises their grievances against him, acknowledges the chip on his shoulder (which he knows is really a beam in their eye), and, ironically, by virtue of staying in his place, moves up a position or two—in the area, invariably of race relations.[3] For it is here that his skilled ambivalence finds the greatest scope, his colour the greatest demand. Once more he comes into his own—as servitor of those in power, a buffer between them and his people, a shock-absorber of 'coloured discontent'—in fact a 'coloured' intellectual.

But this is an untenable position. As the racial 'scene' gets worse, and racism comes to reside in the very institutions of white society, the contradictions inherent in the marginal situation of the 'coloured' intellectual begin to manifest themselves. As a 'coloured' he is outside white society, in his intellectual functions he is outside black. For if, as Sartre has pointed out, 'that which defines an intellectual . . . is the profound contradiction between the universality which bourgeois society is obliged to allow his scholarship, and the restricted ideological and political domain in which he is forced to apply it'[4], there is for the 'coloured' intellectual no role in an 'ideological and political domain', shot through and through with racism, which is not fundamentally antipathetic to his colour and all that it implies. For that very reason, his contradiction, in contrast to that of his white counterpart, is perceived not just intellectually or abstractly, but in his very existence. It is for him, a living, palpitating reality, demanding resolution.

Equally, the universality allowed his scholarship is, in the divided world of a racist society, different to that of the white intellectual. It is a less universal universality, as it were, and subsumed to the universality of white scholarship, but it is precisely because it is a universality which is particular to colour that it is already keened to the sense of oppression. So that when Sartre tells us that the intellectual, in grasping his contradictions, puts himself on the side of the oppressed ('because, in principle, universality is on that side'),[5] it is clear that the 'coloured' intellectual, at the moment of grasping his contradictions, *becomes* the oppressed—is reconciled to himself and his people, or rather, to himself in his people.[6]

To put it differently. Although the intellectual *qua* intellectual can, in 'grasping his contradiction', take the *position* of the oppressed, he cannot, by virtue of his class (invariably petty-bourgeois) achieve an instinctual understanding of oppression. The 'coloured' man, on the other hand, has by virtue of his colour, an *instinct* of oppression, unaffected by his class, though muted by it. So that the 'coloured' intellectual, in resolving his contradiction as an intellectual, resolves also his existential contradiction. In coming to consciousness of the oppressed, he 'takes conscience of himself',[7] in taking conscience of himself, he comes to consciousness of the oppressed. The fact of his intellect which had alienated him from his people now puts him on their side, the fact of his colour which had connected him with his people, restores him finally to their ranks. At that moment of reconciliation between instinct and position, between the existential and the intellectual, between the subjective and objective realities of his oppression, he is delivered from his marginality and stands revealed as neither 'coloured' nor 'intellectual', but BLACK.[8]

He accepts now the full burden of his colour. With Cesaire, he cries:

> I accept . . . I accept . . . entirely, without reservation . . .
> my race which no ablution of hyssop mingled with
>   lilies can ever purify
> my race gnawed by blemishes
> my race ripe grapes from drunken feet
> my queen of spit and leprosies
> my queen of whips and scrofulae
> my queen of squamae and chlosmae
> (O royalty whom I have loved in the far gardens of
>   spring lit by chestnut candles!)
> I accept. I accept.[9]

And accepting, he seeks to define. But black, he discovers, finds definition not in its own right but as the opposite of white.[10] Hence in order to define himself, he must first define the white man. To do so on the white man's terms would lead him back to self-denigration, and yet the only tools of intellection available to him are white tools—white language, white education, white systems of thought—the very things that alienate him from himself. Whatever tools are native to him lie beyond his consciousness somewhere, condemned to desuetude by white centuries. But to use white tools to uncover the white man so that he (the black) may at last find definition requires that the tools themselves are altered in their use. In the process, the whole of white civilisation comes into question, black culture is reassessed and the very fabric of bourgeois society threatened.

Take language for instance. A man's whole world, as Fanon points out, is 'expressed and implied by his language':[11] it is a way of thinking, of feeling, of being. It is identity. It is, in Valery's grand phrase, 'the god gone astray in the flesh'.[12] But the language of the colonised man is another man's language. In fact it is his oppressor's and must, of its very nature, be inimical to him—to his people and his gods. Worse, it creates alien gods. Alien gods 'gone astray in the flesh'—white gods in black flesh—a canker in the rose. No, that is not quite right, for white gods, like roses, are beautiful things, it is the black that is cancerous. So one should say a 'rose in the canker'. But that is not quite right either—neither in its imagery nor in what it is intended to express. How does one say it then? How does one express the holiness of the heart's disaffection (*pace* Keats) and the 'truth of the imagination' in a language that is false to one? How does one communicate the burden of one's humanity in a language that dehumanises one in the very act of communication?

Two languages, then, one for the coloniser and another for the colonised, and yet within the same language? How to reconcile this ambivalence? A patois perhaps: a spontaneous organic rendering of the masters' language to the throb of native sensibilities—some last grasp at identity, at wholeness, at private communion with his fellows.

But dialect betrays class he is told. The 'pidgin-nigger-talker' is an ignorant man. Only common people speak pidgin. Conversely, when the white man speaks it, it is only to show the native how common he really is. It is a way of 'classifying him, imprisoning him, primitivising him[13]—or so the white man believes. For to the native, the freeing of his speech from the master's tongue is also what frees him from his master.

What if the native has a language completely his own, a literature even? Compared to English (or French) though his language is held to be dead, his literature *passé*. They have no place in a modern, industrialised world. They are for yesterday's people. Progress is English, education is English, the good things in life (in the world the coloniser made) are English, the way to the top (and white civilisation leaves the native in no doubt that that is the purpose of life) is English. His teachers see to it that he speaks it in school, his parents that he speaks it at home—even though they are rejected by their children for their own ignorance of *the* tongue.

If the coloniser's language creates an 'existential deviation'[14] in the native, white literature drives him further from himself. It disorientates him from his surroundings: the heat, the vegetation,

the rhythm of the world around him. Already, in childhood, he
writes school essays on 'the season of mists and mellow fruitful-
ness'. He learns of good and just government from Rhodes and
Hastings and Morgan. In the works of the great historian Thomas
Carlyle, he finds that 'poor black Quashee . . . a swift supple fellow,
a merry-hearted, grinning, dancing, singing, affectionate kind of
creature . . .' could indeed be made into a 'handsome glossy thing'
with a 'pennyworth of oil', but 'the tacit prayer he makes (unconsciously he, poor blockhead) to you and to me and to all the
world who are wiser than himself is, "compel me"'—to work.[15]
In the writings of the greatest playwright in the world, he discovers
that he is Caliban and Othello and Aaron, in the testaments of
'the most civilised religion' that he is for ever cursed to slavery.
With William Blake, the great revolutionary poet and painter,
mystic and savant, he is led to believe that:

> My mother bore me in the southern wild
> And I am black, but O! my soul is white;
> White as an angel is the English child,
> But I am black, as if bereav'd of light.[16]

Yet, this is the man who wrote *The Tyger*, and the little black boy,
who knows all about tigers and understands the great truth of
Blake's poem, is lost in wonderment at the man's profound imagination. What then of the other Blake? Was it only animals he could
imagine himself into? Did he who wrote *The Tyger* write *The
Little Black Boy*?

It is not just the literature of the language, however, that ensnares
the native into 'whititude', but its grammar, its syntax, its vocabulary. They are all part of the trap. Only by destroying the trap
can he escape it. 'He has', as Genet puts it, 'only one recourse: to
accept this language but to corrupt it so skilfully that the white
men are caught in his trap'.[17] He must blacken the language,
suffuse it with his own darkness, and liberate it from the presence
of the oppressor.

In the process, he changes radically the use of words, word-order
—sounds, rhythm, imagery—even grammar. For he recognises
with Laing that even 'syntax and vocabulary are political acts that
define and circumscribe the manner in which facts are experienced,
[and] indeed . . . create the facts that are studied'.[18] In effect he
brings to the language the authority of his particular experience
and alters thereby the experience of the language itself. He frees
it of its racial oppressiveness (black *is* beautiful), invests it with
'the universality inherent in the human condition'.[19] He writes:

As there are hyena-men and panther-men
so I shall be a Jew man
a Kaffir man
a Hindu-from-Calcutta man
a man-from-Harlem-who-hasn't-got-the-vote.[20]

The discovery of black identity had equated the 'coloured' intellectual with himself, the definition of it equates him with all men. But it is still a definition arrived at by negating a negative, by rejecting what is not, and however positive that rejection, it does not by itself make for a positive identity. For that reason, it tends to be self-conscious and overblown. It equates the black man to other men on an existential (and intellectual) level, rather than on a political one.

But to 'positivise' his identity, the black man must rediscover himself—in Africa and Asia—not in a phrenetic search for lost roots, but in an attempt to discover living tradition and values. He must find, that is, a historical sense, 'which is a sense of the timeless as well as the temporal, and of the timeless and temporal together'[21] and which 'involves a perception not only of the pastness of the past, but of its presence'.[22] Some of that past he still carries within him, has forged out of it a culture of his own. But it is a more conscious presence of that past, a sense of the timeless and temporal at once, that he now seeks to discover, and in discovering where he came from he realises more fully where he is at, and where, in fact, he is going to.

He discovers, for instance, that in Africa and Asia there still remains, despite centuries of white rule, an attitude towards learning which is simply a matter of curiosity, a quest for understanding—an understanding of not just the 'metalled ways' on which the world moves, but of oneself, one's people, others whose life styles are alien to one's own—an understanding of both the inscape and fabric of life. Knowledge is not a goal in itself, but a path to wisdom: it bestows not privilege so much as duty, not power so much as responsibility. It brings with it a desire to learn even as one teaches, to teach even as one learns. It is used not to compete with one's fellow beings for some unending standard of life, but to achieve for them, as for oneself, a higher quality of life.

'We excel,' declares the African, 'neither in mysticism nor in science and technology, but in the field of human relations. . . . By loving our parents, our brothers, our sisters, cousins, aunts, uncles, nephews and nieces, and by regarding them as members of our families, we cultivate the habit of loving lavishly, of exuding

human warmth, of compassion, and of giving and helping. . . .
Once so conditioned, one behaves in this way not only to one's
family, but also to the clan, the tribe, the nation, and to humanity
as a whole.'[23]

Chisiza is here speaking of the unconfined nature of love in
African (and Asian) societies (not, as a thousand sociologists
would have us believe, of the 'extended family system'), in marked
contrast to Western societies where the love between a man and a
woman (and their children) is sufficient unto itself, seldom opening
them out, albeit through each other, to a multitude of loves. The
heart needs the practice of love as much as the mind its thought.

The practical expression of these values is no better illustrated
than in the socialist policies of Nyerere's Tanzania. It is a socialism
particular to African conditions, based on African tradition,
requiring an African (Swahili) word to define it. Ujamaa literally
means 'familyhood'. 'It brings to the mind of our people the idea
of mutual involvement in the family as we know it',[24] and this
idea of the family is the sustaining principle of Tanzanian society.
It stresses co-operative endeavour rather than individual advancement. It requires respect for the traditional knowledge and wisdom
of one's elders, illiterate though they be, no less than for academic
learning. But the business of the educated is not to fly away from
the rest of society on the wings of their skills, but to turn those
skills to the service of their people, and the higher their qualifications, the greater their duty to serve. 'Intellectual arrogance',
the Mwalimu has declared, 'has no place in a society of equal
citizens'.[25]

The intellectual, that is, has no special privilege in such a society.
He is as much an organic part of the nation as anyone else. His
scholarship makes him no more than other people and his functions
serve no interest but theirs. There is no dichotomy here between
status and function. Hence he is not presented with the conflict,
between the universal and the particular of which Sartre speaks
and in that sense he is not an intellectual but everyman.

The same values obtain in the societies of Asia, sustained not so
much by the governments of the day, as in the folklore and tradition
of their peoples. The same sense of 'familyhood', of the need to
be confirmed by one's fellow man, the notion of duty as opposed
to privilege, the preoccupation with truth rather than fact and a
concept of life directed to the achievement of unity in diversity,
characterise the Indian ethos. One has only to look at Gandhi's
revolution to see how in incorporating, in its theory and its practice,
the traditions of his people, a 'half-naked fakir' was able to forge a

weapon that took on the whole might of the British empire and beat it. Or one turns to the early literature and art of India and finds there that the poet is less important than his poem, the artist more anonymous than his art. As Benjamin Rowland remarks, 'Indian art is more the history of a society and its needs than the history of individual artists.'[26] The artist, like any other individual, intellectual or otherwise, belongs to the community, not the community to him, and what he conveys is not so much his personal experience of truth as the collective vision of a society of which he is part, expressed not in terms private to him and his peers, but in familiar language—or in symbols, the common language of truth.

In Western society, on the other hand, art creates its own coterie. It is the province of the specially initiated, carrying with it a language and a life-style of its own, even creating its own society. It sets up cohorts of interpreters and counter-interpreters, middlemen, known to the trade as CRITICS, who in disembowelling his art show themselves more powerful, more creative than the artist. It is they who tell the mass of the people how they should experience art. The more rarified it is, more removed from the experience of the common people, the greater is the artist's claim to ART and the critic's claim to authority. Did but the artist speak directly to the people and from them, the critic would become irrelevant, and the artist symbiotic with his society.

It is not merely in the field of art, however, that Western society shows itself fragmented, inorganic and expert-oriented: but the fact that it does so in the noblest of man's activities is an indication of the alienation that such a society engenders in all areas of life. In contrast to the traditions of Afro-Asian countries, European civilisation appears to be destructive of human love and cynical of human life, and nowhere do these traits manifest themselves more clearly than in the attitude towards children and the treatment of the old. Children are not viewed as a challenge to one's growth, the measure of one's possibilities, but as a people apart, another generation, with other values, other standards, other aspirations. At best one keeps pace with them, puts on the habit of youth, feigns interest in their interests, but seldom if ever comprehends them. Lacking openness and generosity of spirit, the ability to live dangerously with each other, the relationship between child and adult is rarely an organic one. The adult occupies the world of the child far more than the child occupies the world of the adult. In the result, the fancy and innocence of children are crabbed and soured by adulthood even before they are ready to beget choice.

Is it any wonder then that this tradition of indifference should pass on back to the old from their children? But it is a tradition that is endemic to a society given to ceaseless competition and ruthless rivalry—where even education is impregnated with the violence of divisiveness, and violence itself stems not from passion (an aspect of the personal), but from cold and calculated reason (an aspect of the impersonal). When to get and to spend is more virtuous than to be and to become, even lovers cannot abandon themselves to each other, but must work out the debit and credit of emotion, a veritable balance-sheet of love. Distrust and selfishness and hypocrisy in personal relationships, and plain cruelty and self-aggrandisement in the art of government are the practice of such a society, however elevating its principles. Government itself is the art of keeping power from the people under the guise of the people's will. And the working people themselves are inveigled into acquiescence of the power structure by another set of middlemen: the union bosses.

In the face of all this, the black man in a white society—the black man, that is, who has 'taken conscience of himself', established at last a positive identity—comes to see the need for radical change in both the values and structure of that society. But even the revolutionary ideologies that envisage such a change are unable to take into their perspective the nature of his particular oppression and its implications for revolutionary strategy. White radicals continue to maintain that colour oppression is no more than an aspect of class oppression, that colour discrimination is only another aspect of working-class exploitation, that the capitalist system is the common enemy of the white worker and black alike. Hence they require that the colour line be subsumed to the class line and are satisfied that the strategies worked out for the white proletariat serve equally the interests of the black. The black struggle, therefore, should merge with and find direction from the larger struggle of the working class as a whole. Without white numbers, anyhow, the black struggle on its own would be unavailing.

What these radicals fail to realise is that the black man, by virtue of his particular oppression, is closer to his bourgeois brother (by colour) than to his white comrade. Indeed his white comrade is a party to his oppression. He too benefits from the exploitation of the black man, however indirectly, and tends to hold the black worker to areas of work which he himself does not wish to do, and from areas of work to which he himself aspires, irrespective of skill. In effect, the black workers constitute that section of the working class which is at the very bottom of society, and is distinguished by its colour. Conversely, the attitude of racial superiority on the part of white workers relegates their black comrades to the bottom of society. In the event, they come to constitute a class apart, an under-class: the sub-proletariat: and the common denominator of capitalist oppression is not sufficient to bind them together in a common purpose.

A common understanding of racial oppression, on the other hand, ranges the black worker on the side of the black bourgeois against their common enemy: the white man, worker and bourgeois alike.

In terms of analysis, what the white Marxists fail to grasp is that the slave and colonial exploitation of the black peoples of the world was so total and devastating—and so systematic in its devastation—as to make mock of working-class exploitation. Admittedly, the economic aspects of colonial exploitation may find analogy in white working-class history. But the cultural and psychological dimensions of black oppression are quite unparalleled. For, in their attempt to rationalise and justify to their other conscience 'the robbery, enslavement, and continued exploitation of their coloured victims all over the globe',[27] the conquistadores of Europe set up such a mighty edifice of racial and cultural superiority, replete with its own theology of goodness, that the natives were utterly disoriented and dehumanised. Torn from their past, reified in the present, caught for ever in the prison of their skins, accepting the white man's definition of themselves as 'the quintessence of evil . . . representing not only the absence of values but the negation of values . . . the corrosive element disfiguring all that has to do with beauty or morality',[28] violated and sundered in every aspect of their being, it is a wonder that, like lemmings, they did not throw themselves in the sea. If the white workers' lot at the hands of capitalism was alienation, the blacks underwent complete deracination, and it is this factor which makes black oppression qualitatively different from the oppression of the white working class.

The inability of white marxists to accept the full import of such an analysis on the part of black people may be alleged to the continuing paternalism of a culture of which they themselves are victims. (Marxism, after all, was formulated in an European context and must, on its own showing, be Europocentric.) Or it may be that to understand fully the burden of blackness, they require the imagination and feeling systematically denied them by their culture. But more to the point is that, in their preoccupation with the economic factors of capitalist oppression, they have ignored the importance of its existential consequences, in effect its consequences to culture. The whole structure of white racism is built no doubt on economic exploitation, but it is cemented with white culture. In other words, the racism inherent in white society is *determined* economically, but *defined* culturally. Any revolutionary ideology that is relevant to the times must envisage not merely a change in the ownership of the means of production, but a definition of that ownership: who shall own, whites only or blacks as well? It must envisage, that is, a fundamental change in the concepts of man and society contained in white culture—it must envisage a revolutionary culture. For, as Gramsci has said, revolutionary theory requires a revolutionary culture.

However, to revolutionise a culture, one needs first to make a radical assessment of it. That assessment, that revolutionary perspective, by virtue of his historical situation, is provided by the black man. For it is with the cultural manifestations of racism in his daily life that he must contend. Racial prejudice and discrimination, he recognises, are not a matter of individual attitudes, but the sickness of a whole society carried in its culture. His survival as a *black* man in white society requires that he constantly questions and challenges every aspect of white life even as he meets it. White speech, white schooling, white law, white work, white religion, white love, even white lies—they are all measured on the touchstone of his experience. He discovers, for instance, that white schools make for white superiority, that white law equals one law for the white and another for the black, that white work relegates him to the worst job irrespective of skill, that even white Jesus and white Marx who are supposed to save him are really not in the same street, so to speak, as black Gandhi and black Cabral. In his everyday life he fights the particulars of white cultural superiority, in his conceptual life he fights the ideology of white cultural hegemony. In the process he engenders not perhaps a revolutionary culture, but certainly a revolutionary practice within that culture.

For that practice to blossom into a revolutionary culture, however, requires the participation of the masses, not just the blacks. This does not mean, though, that any *ad hoc* coalition of forces would do. Coalitions, in fact, are what will not do. Integration, by any other name, has always spelt death—for the blacks. To integrate with the white masses before they have entered into the practice of cultural change would be to emasculate the black cultural revolution. Any integration at this stage would be a merging of the weaker into the stronger, the lesser into the greater. The weakness of the blacks stems from the smallness of their numbers, the 'less-ness' from the bourgeois cultural consciousness of the white working class. Before an organic fusion of forces can take place, two requirements need to be fulfilled. The blacks must through the consciousness of their colour, through the consciousness, that is, of that in which they perceive their oppression, arrive at a consciousness of class; and the white working class must in recovering its class instinct, its sense of oppression, both from technological alienation and a white-oriented culture, arrive at a consciousness of racial oppression.[29]

For the black man, however, the consciousness of class is instinctive to his consciousness of colour.[30] Even as he begins to throw away the shackles of his particular slavery, he sees that there are others beside him who are enslaved too. He sees that racism is only one dimension of oppression in a whole system of exploitation and racial discrimination, the particular tool of a whole exploitative creed. He sees also that the culture of competition, individualism and elitism that fostered his intellect and gave it a habitation and a name, is an accessory to the exploitation of the masses as a whole, and not merely of the blacks. He understands with Gramsci and George Jackson that 'all men are intellectuals'[31] or with Angela Davis that no one is. (If the term means anything it is only as a description of the work one does: the intellect is no more superior to the body than the soul to the intellect.) He realises with Fanon that 'the Negro problem does not resolve into the problem of Negroes living among white men, but rather of Negroes exploited, enslaved, despised by a colonialist, capitalist society that is only accidentally white'.[32] He acknowledges at last that inside every black man there is a working-class man wanting to get out.

In the words of Sartre, 'at a blow the subjective, existential, ethnic notion of blackness[33] passes, as Hegel would say, into the objective, positive, exact notion of the proletariat. . . . "The white symbolises capital as the Negro labour. . . . Beyond the black-skinned men of his race it is the struggle of the world proletariat that he sings"'.[34]

And he sings:

> I want to be of your race alone
> workers peasants of all lands
> . . . white worker in Detroit black peon in Alabama
> uncountable nation in capitalist slavery
> destiny ranges us shoulder to shoulder
> repudiating the ancient malediction of blood taboos

we roll among the ruins of our solitudes
If the flood is a frontier
we will strip the gully of its endless
covering flow
If the Sierra is a frontier
we will smash the jaws of the volcanoes
upholding the Cordilleras
and the plain will be the parade ground of the dawn
where we regroup our forces sundered
by the deceits of our masters
As the contradictions among the features
creates the harmony of the face
we proclaim the oneness of suffering
and the revolt
of all the peoples on all the face of the earth
　　and we mix the mortar of the age of brotherhood
　　out of the dust of idols.[35]

NOTES

1. Aime Cesaire, in his address to the Congress of Black Writers and Artists, Paris, 1956, reported in 'Princes and Powers', in James Baldwin, *Nobody Knows My Name*, Michael Joseph, London, 1961.

2. T. S. Eliot, 'The Waste Land' in *Collected Poems, 1909–62*, Faber & Faber, London, 1963.

3. The British media use the 'coloured intellectual', whatever his field of work, as white Africa uses the Chief: as a spokesman for his tribe.

4. Jean-Paul Sartre, 'Intellectuals and Revolution: Interview', in *Ramparts*, Vol. 9, No. 6, December 1970, pp. 52–5.

5. *Ibid.*

6. If this man manages to compromise, to hide from things; if he succeeds, by some kind of pretence, vacillation or balancing act, in not living that contradiction . . . I do not call him an intellectual; I consider him simply a functionary, a practical theoretician of the bourgeoisie.' Jean-Paul Sartre in *Intellectuals and Revolution.*

7. Jean-Paul Sartre, *Black Orpheus*, Presence Africaine, Paris, 1963.

8. Black is here used to symbolise the oppressed; white as the oppressor. Colonial oppression was uniform in its exploitation of the races (black, brown and yellow) making a distinction between them only in the interests of further exploitation—by playing one race against the other, and, within each race, one class against the other—generally the Indians against the blacks, the Chinese against the browns, and the coolies against the Indian and Chinese middle class. In time the latter came to occupy, in East Africa and Malaysia for example, a position akin to a comprador class. Whether it is this historical fact which today makes for their comprador role in British society is not, however, within the scope of this essay. But it is interesting to note how an intermediate colour came to be associated with an intermediate role.

9. Aime Cesaire, *Return to my Native Land*, Penguin, Harmondsworth, 1969.

10. 'Black: opposite to white.' *Concise Oxford Dictionary*. 'White: morally or spiritually pure or stainless, spotless, innocent. Free from malignity or evil intent, innocent, harmless esp., as opp. to something characterised as *black*.' *Shorter Oxford Dictionary*.

11. Frantz Fanon, *Black Skin: White Masks*, McGibbon & Kee, London, 1968.

12. Paul Valéry, quoted in Fanon, *op. cit.*

13. Fanon, *op. cit.*

14. *Ibid.*

15. Thomas Carlyle, 'Occasional Discourse on the Nigger Question', in *Latter Day Pamphlets*, Chapman & Hall, London, 1869.

16. William Blake, from 'Songs of Innocence', in *A selection of Poems and Letters*, edited by J. Bronowski, Penguin, Harmondsworth, 1958.

17. Jean Genet, Introduction to *Soledad Brother: the Prison Letters of George Jackson*, by George Jackson, Jonathan Cape, London, 1970.

18. R. D. Laing, *Politics of Experience and Bird of Paradise*, Penguin, Harmondsworth, 1970.

19. Fanon, *op. cit.*

20. Cesaire, *op. cit.*

21. T. S. Eliot, 'Tradition and the Individual Talent', in *The Sacred Wood: Essays on Poetry and Criticism*, Methuen, London, 1934.

22. *Ibid.*

23. Dunduzu Chisiza, 'The Outlook for Contemporary Africa', in *Journal of Modern African Studies*, Vol. No. 1, March 1963, pp. 25–38.

24. Julius K. Nyerere, *Uhura na Ujamaa: Freedom and Socialism: a Selection from Writings and Speeches, 1965–67*, Oxford University Press, Dar es Salaam, 1968.

25. *Ibid.*

26. Benjamin Rowland, *Art and Architecture of India: Hindu, Buddhist, Jain*, Penguin, Harmondsworth, 1970.

27. Paul A. Baran, and Paul M. Sweezy, *Monopoly Capital: an Essay on the American Economic and Social Order*, Penguin, Harmondsworth, 1968.

28. Frantz Fanon, *The Wretched of the Earth*, McGibbon & Kee, London, 1965.

29. Investigation into this aspect of the problem, however, is the business of white radicals and is not within the purview of this essay.

30. He may, of course, become frozen in a narrow cultural nationalism of his own in violent reaction to white culture.

31. Antonio Gramsci, 'The Formation of Intellectuals', in *The Modern Prince and Other Writings*, New York, International Publ., 1957.

32. Fanon, *Black Skin: White Masks, op. cit.*

33. 'Negritude' in the original French.

34. Sartre, *Black Orpheus, op. cit.*

35. Jacques Romain, quoted in Fanon, *Black Skin: White Masks, op. cit.*

6 All are Consumed

JOHN LA ROSE

To be called a black intellectual in Britain is to be trapped in the tangle of a peculiar drama. Lurking in the background is the ambiguity of place and time.

In this country there is the linguistic convention of calling Indians Indian, Pakistanis Pakistani, and now Bangladeshis Bangladeshi. Into this fairly definite categorisation has now entered the Kenyan and Ugandan Asian. I still find these last descriptions odd. It is as if, like the Americans in the United States, a people from a large corner of Asia had decided willy nilly to appropriate for themselves all of that vast Asian continent when they were landed on another, Africa.

Of all these groups who have erupted on to the quiet banks of the British Sunday it is the West Indian who willingly accepts a self-description of Black, with perhaps a few additions among other immigrant groups. The West Indian black has flung contempt on its back and stands poised over it. Just another mark of the dissolution of self-contempt inherent in any challenge to the colonised process.

The contempt of the coloniser for the colonised and the internalising of this contempt into self-contempt by the colonised are two related aspects of the same process. But if one enters more profoundly into an exploration of this complexity, one also discovers other attributions especially in historical situations like the West Indian. Here we have a catalogue of rebellions and revolts and partial victories in Jamaica, Surinam and Guyana; then the successful slave revolution in Haiti, and the confidence which this remarkable victory gave to the African slaves themselves, especially as this confidence grew out of the demonstrated capacity of the African slaves themselves to put an end to their own oppression.

Contempt stalked by fear erupted in a brutalisation and sadism conceived as the sole bulwark against the consequences of that corrosive fear. That was the white slave owner's dilemma. The self-contempt, never fixed or total but always subterranean and partial, saddled with a smouldering rage that often bucked and built huge fires; all this grown out of frustration and a profound desire for destruction and change. That was the black slave's problem.

When the term West Indian originated it was the Anglo-West Indian who claimed the honour of the description. I can think of four well-known West Indians—a film-writer, an art and literary critic, a drama critic and a theatrical director—whom no one in Britain thinks of as West Indian. If they are thought of at all, what defines them in the larger society, because they are white, is their occupational status. West Indians today are obviously the Afro-West Indians—the Black West Indians. It is we whom the British, with their unending taste for diplomacy, at first labelled coloured and mostly still do. Yet, both in the Caribbean and in Britain, the West Indian is an uncertain amalgamation. There is a Caribbean or West Indian consciousness and its growth, especially at present, is rapid for many reasons. However, compared with the attachment to a single-island consciousness, its place is marginal, though its potential is great in modern Caribbean society. In the Caribbean the term West Indian is all-embracing, for all the ethnicities which were transplanted there, while the naming of ethnic sub-divisions and other subtle nuances and gradations complete the contours of an intricate mosaic. From being simplistically all defined as Jamaican, suddenly, with the increasing sophistication of journalists about our affairs, we were all labelled West Indian. The media's gift for neologisms sets the seal on all this.

Samuel Selvon in his *Lonely Londoners* captured the media's hold on the people's imagination and linguistic conventions:

'But big headlines in the papers every day, and whatever the newspaper and the radio say in this country, that is the people Bible. Like one time when newspapers say that the West Indians think that the streets of London paved with gold a Jamaican fellar went to the income tax office to find out something and first thing the clerk tell him is "You people think the streets of London are paved with gold". Newspaper and radio rule this country.'[1]

Newspapers, radio and television have fixed us, in a certain way, in the imagination of the society regardless of what we really are. To be West Indian is to have been nurtured in an area of consciousness fixed in space and memory. George Lamming speaks of acres in his head out of which his creativity springs. Wilson Harris explores a remarkable 'series of subtle and nebulous links which are latent within him (the West Indian) the ground of old and new personalities'.[2]

To be black in Britain means being tied to those links. Certain erosions occur and new links are forged resting unfussily on the old. No black youngster born of West Indian, or even of black parents born in Britain, can be free of the West Indian connection; though there is now a widely held view among some British educationists, sociologists and journalists that these youngsters are completely British. For those who were born of West Indians here and those who, early transplanted from the Caribbean, grew up here, certain ties are less binding, but experience of blues dances, ska, rude bwoy and now reggae must clearly indicate that these links are not tenuous. Record shops packed with black youths on Saturdays sharpens one's awareness that there is a constant to-ing and fro-ing to the Caribbean and back, in imagination, in consciousness as well as in actual fact.

Every Christmas Day, Independence Day for the various Caribbean states and every Trinidad Carnival thousands of West Indians return home to the Caribbean for from four to six weeks, and their children too are now returning to the Caribbean, not to stay but to visit and return to Britain. In the last few years there has been a new and growing interchange involving family relations on vacation coming from the West Indies. The cost of accommodation for these visitors is no longer what it was, because accommodation and board can now be provided by friends and relatives here. This also means that fresh two-way transfusions are constantly at work in the black population. These and other factors might account for an observation I made in early 1970 and since, that the political and social temper of the blacks in Britain closely approximates to that of blacks in the Caribbean.

There are Africans in Britain and most Afro-Caribbean lower-class people are encountering one another and Africans for the first time. Interchange between Africans from the African continent and transplanted or overseas Africans has grown enormously from the contact in places of work, study and recreation. The mischief which missionaries implanted disappears and people take stock of one another without the mediation of the divisive word.

For most Africans, blackness is a term taken for granted, especially where their daily cultural life has not been severely assaulted by the pressure towards assimilation into the eurocentric society. Wole Soyinka's pithy statement about negritude (does a tiger need to proclaim its tigritude) pierced the soft underlay of the argument sustained by the useful but now exhausted negritude theorists. What has not been noted was that negritude was the valid recoil of assimilated, intermediate (petit bourgeois) and mediated groups in a movement for the partial recovery of their personality. Even though the colonial pressure was on the whole society to conform to the norms established for the assimilé group the possibility of such conformity by the whole population was remote and improbable. They could not be absorbed or the process of colonisation would have been unprofitable and self-defeating. The agony of negritude did not apply to the bulk of the population, either the Wolof or Susu speakers or the creole speakers who lived in their negritude, i.e. tigritude, like the proverbial fish in water and without need or desire to proclaim it.

Negritude in other words must be seen in some ways as a class reaction, a mediated class reaction indicating a self-assertion which was not only cultural but also political and economic. The unassimilated lower class, therefore, lived in their negritude and still do; while the negritude theorists contributed to a closer cultural alignment between themselves, a self-alienated assimilated group, and a largely unassimilated mass that held on to and modified ancestral traditions which frequently we are not consciously aware of; so we declare unthinkingly that nothing was left, 'an absence of ruins'.

It is this kind of process which is at work among a black population, overwhelmingly lower class, in fairly close contact with a more prosperous section among them. Both are driven into one another's arms by the circumstances and context of a racist society. Afro-Caribbeans and Africans find one another and painfully adjust.

What is the intellectual and his function given this framework of references and nuances? Edward Brathwaite argues[3] that the West Indian tradition is fractured by the absence from the Caribbean of a significant number of writers and artists—poets, novelists, playwrights, painters and sculptors. Whereas the academic intellectual tradition provides a certain continuity, especially since the University of the West Indies was established, the artistic-intellectual is fractured.

We—Brathwaite, Salkey, myself and others—established the Caribbean Artists Movement in Britain in December 1966. CAM organised two major conferences on the Caribbean arts, numerous public artistic events and discussions and gave a new impetus to West Indian and black creative activity. It introduced a new generation of artists and activists to an older generation. Its latest activity is the magazine *Savacou* based in the Caribbean. Two of its editors are in the Caribbean, one is in London. The impact of what CAM did carried over into the Caribbean and through various private discussions and contacts especially affected all the artists who were intimately involved with it. That is the other leg of Edward Brathwaite's fractured tradition.

The way these two traditions meet and mesh is through the published work of the writer, or, the exhibited painting or sculpture and the references which they set up. In the wake of Caribbean political nationalism of the forties, cultural nationalism—a kind of ornament it is true—found its props in the artists, the folk traditions and the writers. The work therefore has become more influential in the Caribbean, particularly in the last decade. Most of that work has been published in Britain. This is now changing in two directions. Publishing is increasing in the Caribbean itself and much more Caribbean work is being published in the United States.

It would appear therefore that the presence of this body of artists and writers here in Britain, though diminishing in some ways the strength of the West Indian intellectual tradition and its growth in the Caribbean, nevertheless retains its influence both in the Caribbean and in Britain and has been an important element in the founding and gradual emergence of a black intellectual tradition in this country.

Yet there is an omission in this argument which I must correct. It is what I have been calling the political activist-intellectual. In the United States the epitome of this type with his extraordinary historical, political and cultural sensibility was Malcolm X, and to a lesser extent George Jackson, Eldridge Cleaver and Stokely Carmichael. Cuba spawned the overwhelming figures of Fidel Castro and Che Guevara. These types become known or notorious because of a certain conjunction of events which highlight their presence but their presence is still there whether highlighted or not and their influence on the intellectual tradition is frequently more direct and immediate.

Their counterparts can be found in Britain today and the vicious police–immigrant relations is the sounding board of their intelligence. The ancestor of them all, I think, is Olaudah Ekweano (Equiano) who freed himself from the slave abomination and later campaigned to bring about its extinction. He will also be remembered for publicly exposing the paternalism involved in the organisation of the first repatriation of blacks from Britain to Sierra Leone. As yet in Britain there is no independent black academic tradition, nothing of the kind that Carter Woodson, W. E. B. Du Bois, Franklin Frazier, John Hope Franklin and others have established with great effort in the USA. And there appears to be little probability, perhaps through unconscious workings or deliberate manipulation, of its emergence in the near future as long as the education of the black student in the secondary school in this country continues to remain in the deplorable state which we have witnessed in the last two decades.[4]

An infinitesimal number of black students in Britain are entering universities, for example, or other institutions of higher learning. The black tradition of learning and experience has been renewed through the constant contact with black post-graduate students and academics, creative writers and artists and political activists coming from the Caribbean itself. Walter Rodney, to some extent, Bernard Coard and Edward Brathwaite are examples of this inter-penetration. The list of names can be lengthened. They and the handful of academics and professionals living here, in addition to the writers and artists, Samuel Selvon, Andrew Salkey, Wilson Harris, C. L. R. James, Ronald Moody and Aubrey Williams—again this list can be added to—and the new political activists are the basis of an intellectual response to this society and the particularity of our experience of it.

'The black intellectual is one of the few in our times who does not really have the liberty to pursue his narrow and selfish academic interest; the liberty to close his eyes to the problems of his people. The black intellectual bears a heavy burden, his own cross as well as that of his less fortunate brothers. Whatever his field of studies and specialisation he gropes around for help, for a collective solution of the major problems facing his people.'[5]

In some senses Mezu, whom I have quoted, is referring here to certain problems of group power and social class. As a group we blacks are generally in a depressed state compared with other groups and it is this concern, he thinks, which makes all blacks, whether intellectuals or not, involved.

Martin Carter, radical political activist that he was, shared this view in his poetry:

> This I have learnt:
> today a speck
> tomorrow a hero
> hero or monster
> all are consumed
> Like a jig
> shakes the loom
> like a web
> is spun the pattern
> all are involved
> all are consumed.

The poem moves from the political into the larger metaphysical and back.

This view can descend into *naiveté* if it does not strictly examine the reasons and circumstances for the coincidence of interests and divergence within the group. That intellectual privilege of which Mezu speaks can be both heartening and alarming. Heartening in that it allows for the time, the still centre which is required for any kind of serious creative activity. Alarming in the distancing it provides from other deprived and struggling human beings and absorption into a comfortable elitist position. This distancing has been the rule rather than the exception in most countries and in most countries with black majorities possessing whatever modicum of political and economic power. It has also been true for black intellectuals even in such countries as the United States.

James Baldwin entered a caveat concerning the artist, given the circumstances that Mezu outlines, having to carry the burden of the tribe, of being the spokesman for the tribe. The intellectual—artist, academic or activist—can only be true to his own awkward perceptions which frequently puncture and put off balance the accepted consensus. That is the main merit. We are shaken out of our complacencies and are shifted into new uncertain ground which later becomes the grounding for the newer orthodoxy.

There is nevertheless a dichotomy. It is between the usual complacent even comfortable position of the intellectual, in whatever society he exists and the new dangerous propositions which his ideas, by being perceptive or profound, suggest. Changes, when made and as they occur, involve us all in a drama of action and reaction, where intellectuals and others take sides according to the propagation or abandonment of interest, propagation or abandonment of ideas. In this, the intellectual counts as one—one for or one against—and change is as much directed against him as against the rest of the elite. 'All are consumed.'

It was Hartley, I think, who, in a book review I read many years ago, said that the British intellectual is generally of the right. In effect, he is both ideologist as well as agent of the status quo. The problem is serious. We have only touched the beginning.

NOTES

1. Samuel Selvon, *Lonely Londoners*, Longman, 1972, p. 8.
2. Wilson Harris, *Tradition The Writer And Society*, New Beacon Books, 1967, p. 28.

3. Edward Brathwaite, Lecture to Caribbean Artists Movement at the West Indian Students Centre, London, 1969, entitled 'Africa In The Caribbean'.

4. Bernard Coard, *How The West Indian Child Is Made Educationally Sub-Normal In The British School System*, New Beacon Books, 1971—for a general statement on this question.

5. S. Okechukwu Mezu, 'Towards A Progressive Pan Africana Studies And Research Programme', *Black Academy Review*, Vol. 1, No. 2, Summer, 1970, p. 74.

7 And One Khaki

P. CACHIA

Am I a 'non-white'? Before I was invited to contribute to this symposium, I had never seriously asked myself that question. Even now, when I have been faced with it, I can only say that I know I am somewhere near the borderline, but it is the borderline that I find most difficult to draw. Even after cautioning myself that in this area it is tempting to half-close one's eyes to what may threaten one's defensive illusions and rationalisations, I must say that I honestly do not think I care.

Here are the facts for what they are worth. My father was of pure Maltese descent, although born in Egypt. My mother is Russian but brought up mostly in Palestine. Like my father I was born in Egypt, and the law as it was then made me a British subject by birth. I have resided in Scotland uninterruptedly since 1948. My passport describes me as a 'Citizen of the United Kingdom and Colonies', but the newly coined term 'non-patrial' applies to me and to my children, although their mother is English and they were all born in Scotland.

Do these facts matter in the present context? They become known only to people well acquainted with me—and I suspect they have 'typed' me long before this. Not even my appearance would seem to be decisive: I am rather swarthy, but no more so than most South Europeans, or indeed than many whose 'patrial' status is undoubted. I do, however, have an unusual name that is difficult to place, and I teach an Oriental language: I suspect it is this combination that makes most people think of me as vaguely 'foreign'.

Vague indeed is my status; but vaguer still are the notions which purport to distinguish between white and non-white. A professional gentleman I met in Scotland once happened to remark that Liberace 'had a touch of the tar-brush'. 'But he's Italian,' remonstrated his daughter, hot at what she took to be an insult to an idol of hers. Quite unperturbed, he replied, 'That's what I mean'. I once asked a church group directly: 'Where do *you* draw the dividing line between white and non-white?' I had expected no clear answer and I got none, but it also quickly became clear that no one had asked himself the question before, and the discussion soon strayed to 'the queer ideas *some* people have'. Some, I was told, took it for granted that the 'coloured' began at the English Channel; and—since I was among Scots—some professed to be none too sure which side of the Channel was meant. . . .

I have also tested the reaction of many friends and acquaintances to the invitation extended to me to write of my experiences as a non-white. One was indignant on my behalf. One—a very close friend who genuinely saw, and knew that I saw, no stigma in the designation—was doubtful, and ended by confessing to having no criterion by which to settle the matter. All others asserted that they had never thought of me as anything but white; one of them was even uncomfortably emphatic that the 'non-white intellectual' label was *entirely* inapplicable to me. On the other hand, a few of these friends and acquaintances showed sufficient embarrassment to suggest that they would rather not have had the issue thrust upon them; and the invitation to take part in this symposium came at the suggestion of someone who, having known me for some years, had clearly formed the impression that I fitted its terms of reference.

Marginal as my qualifications may be, I hope that I may have something of relevance to contribute. To begin with, the very attempt to give such a symposium an intelligible title sets up one category of people in contradistinction to another—'non-white' as against 'white', or even as against 'British'—and possibly encourages polarisation; it is as well that the haziness of the demarcation line should be illustrated by my case. Even if my witness is largely negative—for I am not conscious of having suffered anything traumatic as a result of my indeterminate colouring—it may have some value in a discussion that seems to invite the airing of grievances. Finally and more positively, the experience I have to share is rather varied and unusual in that I was a member of a privileged minority before I became a relative outsider in British society, and I served in the ranks of the British Army during the Second World War before I entered the sheltered community of a British University. I am not merely sitting on the fence, therefore; I have been on both sides of it.

My father was in the service of the National Bank of Egypt, and most of his career was in the provinces, where eventually he held the position of 'Agent' or Branch Manager. Until I started attending University in Cairo at the age of seventeen, my life was spent in one provincial capital or another—small towns of about 30,000. But the society of which I was aware in my boyhood was scarcely a part of these 30,000.

The foreign communities that carved a place for themselves in Egypt in the nineteenth century and the first half of the twentieth deserve a serious sociological study. None has been attempted that I know of, so in trying to characterise them I must draw on distant memories and unsystematised impressions formed in childhood and adolescence, and mostly concerned not with the large concentrations of foreigners that existed in the large cities, but with the small pockets that were to be found in provincial towns.

In such a town in the 1930s, the State usually maintained a secondary school which employed five English teachers and four French ones. There might be another two or three Englishmen in senior positions in banks or with commercial concerns. Another dozen Europeans or so—mostly Greeks, Maltese, and Italians—were engaged in banking, in the hotel business and the cotton trade, or in the administration of the law; a few practised skilled crafts, such as motor engineering.

Small as their numbers were, these foreigners with their families did not form a fully integrated community. The English and the French were tacitly assumed to be a cut above the rest; they met and acknowledged the others at the one sports club and in places of public entertainment, but hardly ever exchanged visits with them. To some extent this distinction no doubt reflected the status of their countries as world powers; but it also in part derived quite naturally from the fact that they were almost invariably homebased—born and educated in their country of origin, and intending to end their days there after a remunerative career or tour of duty abroad. The others were permanent residents, and many were members of families long settled in the country: it was my great-grandfather who had emigrated to Egypt about 1860, and my father never saw Malta though he called himself Maltese and was of pure Maltese descent, for at least until his generation there was a strong tendency among the Maltese abroad to inter-marry. But the country in which they lived was to them little more than a location. They might like it and do well by it, but they developed no loyalty towards it. Intellectually, they gave their allegiance to an undefined and composite abstraction called Europe, by whose values they lived and in whose prestige they gloried. It is almost symbolical that one of the houses provided by the bank for its 'Agent' in the South of Egypt had such outlandish features as fireplaces and a sloping tiled roof; I never saw a fire lit in any of the fireplaces, and the sloping roof was so far from functional that on the one occasion in four years of occupation when we

E

had some heavy rain, it washed down the accumulated dust, overflowed the choked gutters, and left such a pattern of muddy streaks down the walls that the entire building had to be repainted!

Let it be said, however, that this motley collection of outsiders did have genuine if tenuous roots in the real Europe. The culture they drew on, maintained in their homes, and passed on to their children—the books they read in their leisure, the music they listened to by choice, their dress, their table manners—derived from Europe. Their common language was French, a French only slightly tainted with local idioms. The national groups did have distinctive traits and preferences, but all together they formed a fairly close and homogeneous archipelago within which social contacts multiplied, friendships developed, and marriages were made.

The sea of Egyptians in which this archipelago was set did little more than bathe its shores. There were of course daily contacts at many levels: the Europeans gave orders to Egyptian servants and shopkeepers, they received professional services from Egyptian doctors and teachers, they presented their petitions to Egyptian State officials: but social contacts were minimal. A few Egyptian social standards inevitably rubbed off on to the Europeans: their women had to behave in a somewhat restrained fashion in public if they were not to attract too much unwelcome attention, their men had to be discreet about their drinking; I myself acquired habits of deference to my elders which remained with me until I was old enough to realise that I was not going to get like treatment from my juniors. But otherwise the Europeans created their own social milieu from which Egyptians were not systematically debarred but into which they seldom penetrated. Cultural influences were largely one way, from European to Egyptian, for there had long been powerful forces urging Egyptians to imitate Europeans, whereas Europeans never felt they had anything to learn from the Egyptians. Indeed some who lived in big cities seemed extraordinarily ignorant of everyday realities in Egypt: a Greek girl born and bred in Alexandria and brought to a provincial town as a bride was astounded at seeing streets and houses—she had expected, she said, to find 'crocodiles running about'. The provincial Europeans were more familiar with the immediate environment, and most of them acquired a competence—though seldom a complete mastery—of spoken Arabic, but hardly ever did they learn to read and write the language, and the cultural heritage to which it is the key was a closed book to them. I myself first went to a Franciscan missionary school where no Arabic was taught, and where the History and Geography lessons dealt not with Egypt but with France, as it was for a French examination that the children were prepared. It was not until I was ten and my brother twelve that my father came to the conclusion that residents in Egypt ought to learn the national language, and even though it meant our starting primary schooling all over again, he sent us first to a private school nominally Italian but using Arabic as the teaching medium, then to an Egyptian State secondary school. In this he was completely out of step with virtually all his contemporaries, who reproved him roundly for his folly. My brother and I had only one non-Egyptian companion (an Italian) in primary school, and none at all in secondary.

Whenever I have discussed this situation with people who have no first-hand experience of anything similar, I have found it necessary to point out that there were understandable reasons other than unmitigated arrogance for the isolation maintained by these foreign communities. The clash in social values could be real and acute. A sports club once tried to organise a dance for its members. The European members brought their wives and daughters, and members of different families danced with one another. Egyptian members, all male, turned up unaccompanied, and claimed the right to dance with European girls. There soon was an altercation. The Europeans argued that since Egyptians considered it shameful for a woman to dance with a man unrelated to her, they were not approaching their womenfolk in a properly respectful frame of mind. The Egyptians retorted that since Europeans did not mind having their womenfolk partnered by strangers, they ought not to discriminate between these on grounds of nationality. Needless to say, the club never again tried to hold a dance.

There were other formidable barriers, not so emotively charged as the rationalised prejudices that surround sex possessiveness. European norms of cleanliness and hygiene are not self-evident in their validity, and in the thirties had not penetrated all provincial Egyptian families even when these fell within the same income bracket as most Europeans. A Coptic family living in a flat immediately below ours once sent us a daughter of the house to borrow tools as they wanted to put up new wall-paper to hide the traces of vermin. My mother—always plain-spoken—told the girl that there were more radical approaches to the problem, but the notion that any household might be free of bugs was a new one to her. When she was shown over our house and could see no trace of any, she merely said, 'Ah well! You Europeans have cold blood; the lice don't like it'. Prejudices there certainly were, but it was not necessarily narrow-mindedness that made a fond European mother tell her well-scrubbed child not to play with 'the natives'.

Looking back on those days, I realise also that the glass curtain that separated European from Egyptian was certainly hurtful to Egyptian pride, but it must also have taken its toll of the foreigners restricted to so small a community. This was not something that troubled me, for I was an introspective, bookish, almost self-sufficient child. I always had one or two very close friends, and I wanted no more. Since I went to Egyptian schools, virtually all the friends I made were Egyptians, and for a long time I saw nothing anomalous in that such friendships should be confined to school and playground. Then when I was fourteen, one such friend invited me to his house so that we might 'study together'. The practice was one which I abhorred, for what Egyptian schoolboys meant by 'studying together' was reading aloud and reciting to one another until one was sure that the lesson was not necessarily understood but memorised; I on the contrary had such a preference for quietness and solitude that I often got up at four in the morning to work while everyone else was asleep. Yet for his sake I agreed. My visit to him was quite the most scalding experience of my boyhood. For the boy who at school dressed like me, sat at a similar desk, played the same games and ate school dinners at a table where a teacher saw to it that European table manners were observed, had wasted no time in changing to a loose robe and skull-cap, and he took me into a mean room where the floor was beaten earth and the only furnishings were a pan of very greasy water and a wooden divan on which he squatted cross-legged. He must have been equally startled to see me still wearing a suit and adopting the postures which he associated with the restrictions and impositions of school life. I had come prepared to invite him back to my house. I felt that to let him see the comparative luxury in which I lived would be to widen further the chasm that had suddenly appeared between us. We remained friends at school, but we never again met outside.

Of course, far outweighing the trials of the 'poor little rich boy', and far more insidious, are the enticements of growing into a position of privilege. The mainspring of this privilege is no great mystery, but to say that we were the pawns or beneficiaries of imperialism is a little too crude and simplistic. Most Europeans did enjoy legal immunities (which incidentally were not the result of British domination but of the Capitulations signed long before by the Ottomans), but I cannot think of any occasion when this was of material advantage to the very respectable people I knew since they were not engaged in any commercial activities nor were they potential law-breakers; on the contrary, all it ever meant to us was that when my grandmother died and her very small estate had to be wound up, the formalities had to be carried out in accordance with English law and we had to have recourse to an English lawyer who commanded much higher fees than any Egyptian might have charged. We were not merely parasitical either. The influx of foreigners had begun before the British Occupation, when the need was felt in Egypt for modernisation in emulation of European powers. Foreign experts were imported, and there soon was a momentum of change that attracted fortune-seekers who had skills genuinely in demand: technical knowledge, proficiency in languages, understanding of foreign markets, and the like. These distinctive skills were passed on to succeeding generations through the homes they maintained and the schools they created or patronised, reputedly better than those run by the State. Also, of course, when the British became masters of the country, the advantage they had was greatly expanded and institutionalised, so that they prospered in their own enterprises, and when employed in any State or semi-State organisation the European was hardly ever under the direct orders of an Egyptian, and the Briton almost always answerable only to another Briton. Thus in the National Bank of Egypt, all Branch Managers between the wars were Europeans and all the higher officials, from Inspector to Governor, were Britons. Exceptions there were: the headmasters of State secondary schools were Egyptians, but how firmly they asserted their authority over English teachers I had no means of ascertaining. I recall, too, that late in the thirties or early in the forties an Egyptian was appointed Bank Inspector; he was a member of the royal family!

Inevitably, the Europeans associated their favoured position with, and indeed justified it by, an assumption of innate superiority. This was something one grew into long before one realised how one's self-interest was engaged. The naughty child was told 'not to behave like an Arab'. His parents and their friends lived more graciously than most Egyptians, were treated with more deference. People 'who knew what they were talking about' roundly asserted that 'Egyptians are all right as long as you tell them what to do', but that 'they can never run anything properly' and 'will never be able to govern themselves'. Very representative of the prevailing mentality was the amused condescension with which the vagaries of Egyptian behaviour were observed by Lord Edward Cecil[1] in

one generation, by Major Jarvis[2] in another. Neither, it must be
made clear, was attempting a serious, considered, rounded characterisation of Egyptians; both were light-heartedly setting down
their observations on human types of whom they had close first-
hand knowledge, and there is no denying the humour or even the
truth of many of their thumbnail sketches. But whereas a Marma-
duke Pickhall,[3] for example, could bring out differences in the
ways an Arab and a European might look at the same situation
and end up with conclusions uncomplimentary now to the one
and now to the other, Cecil and Jarvis never depict the native as
anything but some kind of a knave or fool. In a frothy little story
about an Arab nicknamed Willie who pretends to be cultivating
oleanders for their beauty until his baser motives are uncovered by
a visiting English personage, Major Jarvis can throw in such a
sweeping aside as: 'It was obvious that Willie was no ordinary
Arab, for never yet has this peculiar people shown the slightest
eye for beauty or desire for decoration.'[4]

It should perhaps be added that there was much in the local
scene to confirm the Europeans in their prejudice. Among Egyptian
intellectuals, the validity of values vaguely identified as "Western"
was virtually unquestioned. As late as in 1949, a leading writer
could say that it would be 'fatuous bigotry and dense ignorance to
pretend that we need not be the pupils of Europe, need not import
Western culture then digest it and assimilate it before we can make
a serious contribution to the advancement of human civilisation'.[5]
Acknowledgements were seldom so explicit, but Europeans were
constantly being offered what is reputed to be the sincerest form of
flattery. Egyptians of professional status almost invariably adopted
European dress and manners; teachers of Arabic, traditionally
trained at the Azhar, might retain kaftan and turban in primary
schools, but not if they were promoted to secondary schools.
Local Jews often claimed Italian nationality. Copts, perhaps
because their church is very exclusive, were somewhat reticent,
though they often gave their children European names (including
some that were anathema to nationalists, such as Kitchener). The
Christians of Lebanese origin went a long way indeed towards
identifying themselves with Europeans: they often spoke French
in preference to Arabic, and not only gave their children French
names but gallicised the pronunciation of their Arab surnames.
We even knew one gentleman who for years represented himself as
an Italian; but when Italy came into the war and he was not
interned, he suffered some weeks of embarrassment, then made
the best of a mixed-up world and began using an Egyptian Muslim

name. He offered no explanation, but it was apparent that he was only half Italian, and for years had borrowed his mother's nationality and maiden name.

The presence of European minorities in various parts of the Near East did provide the occasion for political interference in the days when the great powers were jockeying for position—a Maltese was involved in the Alexandria riots which led directly to the British Occupation of Egypt. This appears to be the reason why European governments were none too restrictive in granting the status of a subject or of a protected person to many who were at best distant relations. Once British authority was firmly entrenched, these minorities scarcely played any positive political role: they were too heterogeneous, and with the approach of the Second World War, European enmities were reflected among them. However, they did contribute to the general image of a dominant Europe and an Egypt apparently doomed to inferior status. With Egyptian national aspirations they scarcely had any sympathy. If anything, the growing vehemence of Egyptian nationalism, which looked upon them—not unjustly, but a little too indiscriminately— as cat's-paws of imperialism, made them feel that the continuance of British rule was necessary to their well-being and even to their safety. Amongst them, such groups as the Maltese had the strongest reasons for identifying with the occupier; yet the identi- fication was far from complete. The British provided so few schools (far fewer than the French) that it was only a minority of Maltese who learnt English; I myself first spoke French and Arabic, and when I began to study English in earnest it was mostly under American teachers. Nor was there any mistaking the difference between being British and being a Briton; a fellow- Maltese who tried to make up to the Britons, insisting on speaking of all alike as 'British subjects', drew from an Englishman the gibe that he was not so much a British subject as a British object!

Ironically, the main principles professed and taught at the time were those of liberalism. Today the call to revolution comes much more readily, and liberalism is often sneered at. One can see why; and yet there were, and are, situations in which the most hopeful prospects derive from an effort of the mind to understand, and an effort of the will to counter, forces of which one is oneself the target or even the beneficiary. Precept is not without power, and in my idealistic youth this liberalism allied itself to a fairly close acquaintance with the Egyptian point of view and a growing appreciation of Arab culture and made me resist (at the conscious level at least) the prejudices I had grown up with.

Before long, anyway, I had ceased to be a somewhat self-conscious top dog and been put into a pound in which my pedigree was at best suspect. The Second World War had broken out, hostilities had reached the borders of Egypt, and along with other British subjects there I was called up for military service.

An army is scarcely a citadel of liberalism, war scarcely produces conditions in which susceptibilities are spared, and a wartime army in particular, because hastily expanded, has a fair quota of what were termed 'temporary gentlemen', people hastily promoted to positions of greater authority than they were fit to use. I witnessed not a few instances of racial inequality involving coloured people—from the almost charming paternalism of white NCOs in Mauritian units to the institutionalised discrimination which put Indian officers in a different category from British ones on the ground that they held the Viceroy's, not the King's, commission; I was on a troopship where Indian officers had to mess with British WOs and sergeants. I noticed, incidentally, that British apartheid could be self-denying and perhaps awkwardly self-conscious rather than crudely aggressive. After hostilities were over and some trains had started to run in Italy, I had to make a 52-hour journey in a train where men were packed at least eight to a compartment—except in one compartment where two South African black privates had moved in early, and no one had either joined them or ordered them out. I moved in with them, and by using one of the luggage racks as well as the two long seats in the compartment, we were able to stretch out whenever we wanted, and travelled in greater comfort than anyone else.

But what of those not so clearly marked off by the pigmentation of their skin? The most I can say is that I have heard of humiliations—some petty, some not so petty—that they are purported to have suffered. A Maltese girl who met a British officer at a dance was only half-amused when, after she had told him her nationality, he exclaimed, 'That's funny. I had heard of Maltese dogs and Maltese cats before, but it had never occurred to me that there were Maltese people as well'. More serious (if true) is the assertion made to me by a fellow-Maltese that when he applied for a commission his CO bluntly told him that he would never support such an application from any Maltese because he himself had a brother in the ranks, and he could not bear the thought of his brother having to salute a Maltese.

I cannot testify whether such incidents were at all common or representative, for I was an interpreter attached to a unit where I was the only non-Briton, and for my part I cannot recall that

I was subjected to any indignity which I can ascribe to my nationality. It is true that I was nicknamed 'the Wog', but this was because in the bantering debates that took place round the cookhouse at meal-times I invariably put forward the Arabs' point of view. I was on excellent terms with the entire company, and made some firm and lasting friendships among its members—one of them was best man at my wedding many years later; I even attended a divisional reunion as late as in October 1971.

If I was more fortunate in my relationships than many others with a background similar to mine, I can offer two conjectures to account for the difference. One is that either by nature or by dint of early conditioning I have never been inclined to pass myself off as other than what I am, never been tempted, for example, to Anglicise my name; and because my background defies easy categorisation, I am more readily accepted (or rejected) as an individual. The other likely reason is that my war service was with a front-line unit. The pettinesses of army life are noticeably reduced among such bodies of men, no doubt because they have more elemental issues to face, a recognisable common purpose to pursue, and fewer personal ambitions to divide them. And though wars have little enough to commend them, it must be recognised that the comradeship of arms is no mere jingoist fiction.

For more than twenty years now my home has been in Scotland. From State agencies I have sensed no reluctance whatever to grant me my legal rights—within months of my arrival, although it was as a postgraduate student that I had come, I had been put on the electoral roll and had voted in a general election. Socially, because I remain a somewhat introverted person, my contacts have been made in rather restricted strata: the University, and a city church. In both I had the right to expect open-mindedness, and I have not been disappointed. Although the reputation of the church in this respect is a mixed one, I have not only made excellent friends within it but have held the highest elective offices that I was willing to take on; I have even been sole representative of Scottish Methodism at an international conference!

My self-imposed limitations in this respect leave a number of hypothetical questions unanswered. Would I have fitted comfortably into a village community? Would I be blackballed if I applied for membership of a golf club? I do not know: my academic interests will always keep me in a University town, and I am not yet old enough to take up golf. Observation suggests, however, that although being foreign may entail some disabilities, it does at least absolve one from the need to sport the right accent or the right school tie.

Also somewhat conjectural are the career prospects of a non-Briton in Britain. When I lived in Egypt, it was taken for granted that in a British-run administration the non-Briton stood fair chances of promotion in the lower echelons, but never to the top. In the army, I got to be a sergeant but was never commissioned, although I do not take this to be conclusive evidence of a bias, for although University graduates were the exception rather than the rule in the ranks, they were not unknown; nor do I pretend that I had either high ambitions or notable aptitudes as a soldier. When considering long-term careers, however, I was well aware that some would be blind alleys for me. If I had wanted to be a diplomat, for example, I could scarcely have expected to reach a position of responsibility—my background would have looked a good deal less reliable than that of a Kim Philby. It is as well that my inclination has been for University teaching, for there I have had satisfaction at many levels. Whether here also the way for the non-Briton is open only up to the second highest rung, it is impossible to determine objectively. My field is one where, as may be expected, not a few non-Britons are employed; not one has so far reached professorial rank.[6] Also, Chairs of Arabic are very few, and more than one highly esteemed British Arabist has ended his teaching days without the formal accolade of a professorship.

For my part I readily admit that in no other part of the world—not Egypt, where nationalism has developed understandably strong anti-bodies, nor Malta, which lacks the resources to develop out-of-the-way academic subjects—is it likely that I might have achieved a more favourable balance of self-fulfilment over frustration.

So far, I have tried to confine myself to providing data for the symposium—candid recollections of things I have experienced or had opportunity to observe at close quarters. Let me now, while recognising that I have no specialist competence to do so, offer some broad generalisations for discussion.

Swift was scarcely exaggerating when he spoke of parties divided on whether eggs should be cracked at the broad or the thin end. Human beings are capable of polarisation over any recognisable difference, be it ever so trivial or adventitious. I had a prize illustration of this very recently. My son had to undergo extensive surgery a few months ago, and after a period of intensive care he was moved to a new hospital ward. Immediately, a patient of about fifteen went up to his bed and asked, 'How many scars

have you got?' 'Five'. 'How many stitches?' 'Eighty-four.' The
boy turned away snapping, 'I don't believe you,' and thereafter
made no attempt to conceal his animosity. It seems that until
then he had boasted of the traces left upon him by four successive
operations, and my son had outdone him in a single one!

And to be aware of a permanent difference between one's own
group and another is almost always associated with an assumption
of superiority. I know of no language where the word for 'foreigner'
is not tinged with suspicion, and the coloured skin is so clear, so
immediate, and so ineradicable a mark of foreignness that
it seems inevitable it should provide one of the most adhesive
surfaces for prejudice to cling to.

In recent times, it is among 'white' people that this prejudice
has been most blatantly manifested and in them that it has been
most vehemently denounced; but it is not peculiar to them. Islam
very explicitly preaches the equality of all races, and its marriage
laws do not encourage racial purity; indeed the Arabs have on the
whole an honourable record of toleration. Yet it would be idle to
pretend that they have all and at all times lived up to their highest
principles. When in the tenth century their most celebrated poet
satirised the black eunuch who had become regent of Egypt, his
personal spite was all the more bitter because the eunuch had
previously paid court to *him*, but he clearly had a fund of racial
pride to draw on in himself and in his public—his best known
broadside ends with the mock excuse: 'White sires fall short of
worthy action; how then should it be with the castrated black?'[7]
In modern times too, when the French occupied Syria, some
Arabs felt that the crowning indignity was that African troops
were sent into Damascus; one of their poets said:[8]

> How I grieve for a homeland through which go prying
> Black gangs assembled from alien horizons.
> Do Senegalese barbarians despoil my nation,
> My fatherland, and do rocks not split asunder?
> The worst of calamities—and many are these—
> Is that slaves make free with freemen's bastions.

It is the sin of Adam rather than the sin of Albion that made
Britons interpret temporary power supremacy as the fruit and
measure of innate superiority. The myth is not distinctive, but it
can have distinctive twists. Of the nations which in our time have
held sway over others, the French expect to be admired, the
Britons to be respected, and the Americans want to be liked.

T. E. Lawrence[9] said of the English in the Middle East that they:

'assumed the Englishman a chosen being, inimitable, and the copying him blasphemous or impertinent. In this conceit they urged on people the next best thing. God had not given it them to be English; a duty remained to be good of their type.

The French, though they started with a similar doctrine of the Frenchman as the perfection of mankind (dogma amongst them, not secret instinct), went on, contrarily, to encourage their subjects to imitate them; since, even if they could never attain the true level, yet their virtue would be greater as they approached it. We looked upon imitation as a parody; they as a compliment.'

With Britons as with others, the assumption of superiority has taken its most arrogant forms amongst the Empire builders who were fawned on, among the inadequate who need to bolster their personality with a prestigious group label, and among the insecure who feel their interests may be threatened by the outsider. The immigrant intellectual may expect to move in circles where the cruder forms of prejudice will be held in check. He will not find all the barriers down before him, but he is likely to have a wide range of opportunity—wider, presumably, than in his native land or he would not be here. As elsewhere, he had better not be stridently self-assertive; but it will not be necessary for him to conform closely to local patterns. Indeed unless he can become entirely indistinguishable from his neighbours, he had better not try: he will attract less contempt if he is quietly true to himself.

All this may leave him comfortably within, rather than of, the society around him. To the gregarious, this may be profoundly frustrating. But is not their urge to belong akin to the group's tendency to exclude? Nothing in my experience has recommended to me the desire to wear a label shaped by the accident of birth. I am one 'who never to himself has said This is my own, my native land'. This was not of my own choice; but I have not found that it deadened my soul.

NOTES

1. *The Leisure of an Egyptian Official*, Hodder & Stoughton, London, 1948—first printed 1921.

2. Major C. S. Jarvis, C.M.G., O.B.E., pseudonym Rameses, *Oriental Spotlight*, *The Back Garden of Allah* (see footnote 4 below).

3. *Oriental Encounters*, W. Collins, London, 2nd impression, 1919.

4. *The Back Garden of Allah*, London, John Murray, 1943 (1st ed., 1939), p. 27.

5. Muḥammad Mandūr, 'Rusul ath-thaqāfah al-gharbiyyah', *al-Ahrām*, May 10, 1949.

6. A new Chair to be filled soon is likely to prove the exception, but this is because of special conditions attached to the financing of the post.

7. The poet was al-Mutanabbī, the regent of Egypt Kāfūr. The line quoted is in *Mutanabbii Carmina*, Fr. Dieterici (Ed.), Berlin, 1861, p. 695.

8. Khayr ad-Dīn az-Zarkalī quoted by Sāmī al-Kayyālī in *Al-Adab al-ᶜArabī al-Muᶜāsir fī Sūriyyah*, Cairo, 1959, p. 24.

9. *The Seven Pillars of Wisdom*, London, World Books, 1939, p. 355.

8 The Metaphysics of Anglicism

ARUN SAHAY

About five years ago I wrote a letter to *The Times* about George Orwell and suggested that he would not have developed a sense of anxiety at being an outsider at Eton if his family *had* belonged to the Indian Civil Service, the ruling caste of India, even if he was less well-off than other Etonians. But people refused to believe that anyone but the ruling elites of the British Empire ever entered Eton. It is such charming fictions that make up the English self-image: an image which they share with a lot of foreigners, who may or may not have lived in England. It does take a long time to know the English; although one of the first things that does filter through is that an extreme adaptability of action goes with an unchanging faith in the self image. I refer to the English, not the 'British', for I know only the English. Many of the English I have met seem to have a trace of Irish in their ancestry or are anglicised Scots. It has been difficult to determine if there is an Englishman who is, logically, English: perhaps a Welshman. Yet, such is the strength of Anglicism in a general cultural sense that it seems to take over other kinds of consciousness—not identity—in subtle and persisting ways. One loses one's passionate sense of success or failure, to become stoical in a quiet sort of way. The English word for this is, of course, 'civilised'. When one is talking about the English one is really talking about their elite: the masses of England are many different peoples, from the romantic, piratical Cornishmen to the coal-dusted heirs of the ancient Kingdom of Northumbria, absorbed into a peculiar mixture of political and emotional unity.

It is, of course, much easier to sum up the elite, especially if one is inclined to the same virtues. They believe very deeply that they are the best of the world. They are stoical and have a suppressed regard for excellence with a complete disregard of the passions of ordinary mortals. They even believe that education can cure all. Above all, they believe that the happiness of the human world is a function of the stability of money. I feel sympathetic towards these virtues in many ways. There is little need to assert oneself in this milieu, if one has the requisite qualities; money, talent and then charm. The foolish believe that the ultimate recognition that the English elite accord to a person is to invite him to a *tête-à-tête* with Joan Bakewell on *Late Night Line Up*, or to the front row of David Frost's crowded shows. The foolish also believe that the things discussed in public are significant and will influence their lives, and that the men who are 'popularised' by the press or the television are important. The discreet nature of the English social order is rarely noticed by the anxious foreigner and equally rarely challenged by the native. The discreetness is an expression of the innermost feelings of a political nationalism which is uniquely English. The English always talk around these feelings, and it astonishes them that they reflect a peculiar development of their character, emotions and experience. They do not understand that these feelings cannot be inculcated by others except as a defence against them, because the feelings are alien to other peoples' character, emotion and experience. Their various nationalisms are alien to the English, which they invariably interpret as a proof of the imperfect state of these nationalisms. Paradoxically, the English are much more curious about the rest of the world than any other people. It is thus not surprising, given the imperfections of the rest of the world, that they invented the idea of Evolution, which is a very tactful way of asserting their superiority. One can also see, incidentally, why the idea is so attractive to American intellectuals.

But, unlike America, life in England is not a colourful exciting experience. There is a quiet expectedness in politics, in everyday life and in the self-centredness of London, and above all, in the absolute importance of financial self-reliance which ensures the dullness and the quiet flow of life. If one is well settled the expectedness is reassuring; and the English are well-settled with their secure world-wide investments and the cleverness of their diplomats. The individual in England is not worried about the state of his environment, for he does not have to fight for his existential identity. He may from time to time wonder if something vaguely threatens it, but he soon forgets and resumes the cultivation of his many gardens and the use of his Do-It-Yourself kits.

The expected order of things, the cultivation of various interests, preoccupations and metaphysics have protected much of the genuine freedom that there is in England, but the price of freedom is a lessening enjoyment of natural inclinations and increasing involvement in the trivialities of everyday politics. Natural inclinations are always fickle, obsessive and disastrous in the end and the trivialities of politics build up into a tyranny, and if one is prudent, one would avoid natural inclinations and pursue the politicians' decisions *ad nauseam*. It is not that the English are particularly puritanical or interested in politics, they are simply prudent. Or, perhaps, they have educated themselves over the centuries to trust prudence more than their sensuality or religiosity.

All this characterisation is only an obvious introduction to a more acute analysis of the nature of Englishness and England and the anglicisation of the world. It may well go beyond the experiences of an individual's life, for the experiences of an individual are banal and unless they can be transmuted into art or knowledge they are without much interest. Thus, to be an intellectual and an ordinary individual is to live a contradiction, so subjectively one rationalises and reconciles and most of all justifies. It is not ordinarily possible to be an intellectual, for it is to be an exile from one's self, to search outwards and beyond. Even when intellect is introspective it simply turns out the seams of existence. The environment or the circumstance is incidental to the development of intellectuality. The identity of an intellectual, thus, if it is intellect-bound, is the individual's own: it just seeks an environment where its demands are responded to. It may or may not grow in that environment because a human being is not wholly intellect-bound. Intellect, moreover, is intrinsically destructive of the socially created loyalties and sentiments and assumptions: it creates its own. This may read as a mystical description of the 'free-floating intelligentsia', but the self-images of intellectuals have as little to do with intellect as the self-images of others have to do with the harsh realities of their existence. Again, it may seem that I believe in the goodness of reality, but, then, reality is what one continues to believe, in spite of what it may mean to others and what others may believe.

The paradoxes of belief and reality form, for me, the most interesting and mystifying aspect of life: not the obvious incidents of living somewhere, anywhere, but the superstitions of the rational as well as the irrational man, the civilised and the primitive, the white, the black, the yellow and the brown races of the world; the individuals, groups, nations. They are all paradoxical, contradictory, self-important, amusing and exasperating. Some day I might observe, record, read and understand all about them, but for the moment the paradox is the understanding of the English not as themselves but in contact with me.

To some extent, I have created the paradox by being in contact with them, their self-images, and the concept which has emerged from these phenomena. I and my contact with England is born of a very long liaison with the concept. The concept is a precise, slow development of a definition of my peculiar intellectual demands: for a sufficiently ambiguous language to express the paradoxes of my nature, the identification of certain character- istics independent of the natural human condition: poverty, wealth, inferiority and superiority of one human being against another. The concept that has emerged is that of Englishness, idolised in the notions of honour, decency and civilised behaviour. The concept is not an attribute of individuals, or of the nation from which it derives: it is an attitude of life cultivated by them, developed in an impossible world and, then, reified and believed in as a real characteristic of their being and organic life—and thus, weakening the power of the idea. But that is the fate of all realisa- tions of ideas: the paradox of existence and understanding.

This metaphysics can be illustrated both by parable and actual circumstance. It is difficult to invent a parable, so I shall restrict myself to an actual circumstance or two. The concept underlies the whole basis of English elitism. It is not an elitism of human beings but of a world view: the organisation of life, individual, and social, of governing, of nationhood. Those who defend it as their genetic right and those who wish to renounce this genetic right are both destroyers of this elitism. The world view which created the British empire, and sustained it for a while, died when the logical consequences were not understood. The empire was based on a distinction between the rule and the human beings who either ruled or were ruled. The rule itself was an idea which brought together diverse peoples and individuals in a formal relationship, which by its very abstractness, did not touch their ordinary human lives. Those few who either exercised power or lived in its shadow were, of course, touched by an inevitable madness inherent in the unreality of the circumstance: for, a human mind, it would seem, cannot live under an abstract shadow, it prefers to rule or be ruled, love or be loved, hate or be hated and use and be used by other human minds and bodies. This is another example of the paradox that ideas are corrupted by feelings. The empire should have led to a commonwealth: even when the commonwealth failed, the union of Europe should have developed. But the empha- sis is on the common market, mutual wheeling and dealing, and a consortium to fight the monopolies of power with a sneaking hope that some day the consortium will become a monopoly for the fittest. This is the reification of the concept which was inevitably growing when the idea itself occurred. The eighteenth century English politicians who studied and applied to their politics a modified Machiavellism did not perhaps realise the positive power of what they had interested themselves in—or perhaps they did. The appalling effects at home and abroad of their intellectual interests in the idea of government is what killed the idea: but it is providential that human beings do not get hold of permanently successful ideas. *Let them be permanently bewildered in their fate!*

However, the ultimate human condition is not my concern here. What I have wished to suggest in my metaphysical sketch is that the idea of civilised life that the English have developed is a valuable one. By eliminating the passions of ordinary mortals from consideration, it creates an atmosphere of genuine progress—even moral progress, if one does not insist that morality is a divine gift, nor, that human beings are or should be touched by divine qualities. Divinity, in contemporary English religiosity, is a peculiarly weak light, muddled with the control of 'permissiveness' and emancipation of the unfortunate. It is too much a demonstration and not a contemplation.

I find all piety tedious, and spiritual strength unrealisable. So the human resources which I can recognise and value are mundane: easily the most superior is the resource of intellect. This term is another of the ambiguities which the English use with such skill. I do not attribute it to effete dons, trendy journalists, difficult politicians or central European emigres. I find it applicable to all skilful men and women. Intellect does not make one a consistent rational being, it only allows one to sense things more intensively than those without it.

The English are intellectual in this sense in more ways than is realised by their allies or enemies. First of all, they have by tradition cultivated an instinct for storing things and ideas: skills can be stored and restored if they are valued. This trait, if missing from a tradition, can lead to self-impoverishment. However much one may learn things quickly, if one does not value learning and skill for their own sake, or if one only values them for the advantage they might bring, there will eventually be no enrichment, only bewilderment. There are many examples which clearly show the distinction and its contrasting effects. I shall not make a survey of the world in this paper, but the investigation leads to most intriguing conclusions; not one of them unjustified, if I may say so.

This particular notion of intellectuality which I favour is not, of course, an exclusive characteristic—no characteristic ever is. It has moreover its negative aspects. The skill that the English

have is spent mostly in politics, not in the formal activities of
Members of Parliament or local councillors and trade unionists,
but in the rituals of behaviour, avoidance of embarrassment and
emotional ties and in the pursuit of morality of various kinds. In a
word, ritualism; for morality—or its obverse, immorality—is only
possible in a ritualistic sense. If Malcolm Muggeridge, for example,
had understood Indian life, after reflecting on his exiled youth
and friendship with Nehru, he would have realised and preached
the inevitable logicality of Hindu ritualistic morality for social
cohesion, and not substituted a ritualised Christianity for it,
because the message of Christianity can only be read fully as an
intellectual isolationism of the individual—in either the sanctuary
of monasticism or the deep loneliness of Calvinism. But being
English, Mr Muggeridge has persuaded himself to believe and
preach the ritualistic message of social love. Social love has been
and is a peculiarly English religious impulse; it permeates the
whole life of the nation. If Ireland does not seem to subscribe to
it, it is because of the failure of Anglicisation to penetrate the
truly intense sadness of the Irish heart. Ritualism of the English—
social love of the good people, democracy of the politician, revolution of the student, righteousness of the taxpayer, avant-gardism
of the television theatre, inanity of the social worker, sex and
marriage of the sociologist, 'Schh . . you know who' of the adver-
tising, the solemnity of the stockbroker, integration of the race
relationist, investments of the trade unionists, the swinging votes
of the psephological doctor of philosophy, the protectionism of
the car worker, the decline of the shipbuilder, the recovery of
Rolls Royce, cries for Biafra and Bangladesh of the committed,
the Monday Club, the Young Liberals, Jeremy Thorpe (the
upper-class Liberal) Edward Heath (the middle-class Conservative)
Harold Wilson (the 'floating' intellectual Labour leader)—is
extremely methodical, cold and comforting. There will always be
an England if the power of ritualism remains. But will it remain?
There are people who believe that the ritual is real. It speaks to
them. It is an expression of their greatness: for example, the doctor,
the insurance broker, the building society manager, the heirs of
the empire builders. The doctor believes that he has the power of
life and death over one and he acts with a feeling of certainty in
his magical powers. He is innocent of his dependence on the belief
of the people that healing is a vocation. The vocation becomes a
privilege taken in the name of science from the individual's fear of
disease and death. Science, the vocation of knowledge and healing,
is used to exclude the rest of humanity by the narrow bigotry of

esotericism. A nation which values knowledge is in the danger of being strangled by a handful of self-deceiving ideals. Idealists without an understanding of social reality are self-opinionated fools and those who feel they must respect their sincerity, however misguided, have the death-wish in their souls. The probity of the world of insurance and the building society is the probity of the nation; but probity is also a love of money. Money as a commodity, without the benefit of human labour, is purely self-conceiving, an illusion which becomes real; it is an unstable substance—and contradicts the elitists' metaphysical doctrine of human happiness as a function of the stability of money. It is a contradiction which is good for the elite up to a point; but which can only be resolved by the producers of wealth and consumers of money. The ordinary English people do as much as they can to limit the illusory powers of money: by over-saving, making it cheap and too readily available to bear much interest. The probity is restored, the greed starved; but economists and their political patrons fail to understand why their theories do not make sense. Economists have failed altogether because their basic philosophy is based not on the greed of the investor, but on a transference of the greed to the producer of wealth—which they charmingly describe as the wage spiral. However, the restoration of stability to money by the ordinary people is their self-sacrifice in preservation of their freedom from the tyranny of greed; for which the elite used, not so long ago, to give thanks to God, by believing with the touching inversion of true believers that God was an Englishman.

However, if the English derive their metaphysics from their history, there is no shame in that. History has always been the matrix of metaphysics. Their real history is the history of the modern world. It is the understanding of this history that will make them reflect on their future, fight their ennui and nostalgia for an empire which was never theirs. The people who have risen to be the new middle classes are hardly the inheritors of the empire they wish to be; they are the children of Butler's Education Act, brought up to believe in the importance of the social structure, class, salary, tax relief and car-ownership. There can be no elitism in this plebeian paradise, obviously; there will only be a vague feeling that the middle classes are the trustees of civilised life. Middle classism is the end of creativity, risk and anguish, and the beginning of self-deception, false loyalties, crises of identity and lack of understanding. Human beings become items of love or prejudice, classified in ledgers of meaningless symbolism. There

THE METAPHYSICS OF ANGLICISM 149

is neither like or dislike of individual people, only social classification.

Education, it is said these days, is a middle-class thing, with more verbalism and more confidence, more ambition and more success. The aristocracy has been abolished in favour of traders, hairdressers, media-men and self-made rich young men. Even monarchy is a profession and supposed to earn a salary. It is, of course, true that there is more money and more education about. Education has more money spent on it, with more research, more books, and the apotheosis of 'professionalism'. There is less literacy, less thought and little skill, more geniuses, more invention of 'new' theories, doctrines and principles, of linguistic games, words without meaning, thought without sense; best selling lists without books worth reading. . . . It is like a world inhabited by liberated eunuchs: self-made and without dignity.

The strength of the English has, so far, been their peculiar combination of feudalism as the ideal and democracy as the realisation. Without their feudalism, the English would become impotent, and their democracy an oligarchy of self-made men, because feudalism is much nearer the human heart, and all forms of human society return to a natural feudalism. Thus, it would seem that those who think that to serve is to rule corrupt both the ideal of service and the idea of rule. To be ruled seems to be the natural demand of the most of the human race; and the English believe that the greatest sin that any part of humanity can commit is to be without leadership. The notion of leadership is one of the axioms of English metaphysics: it is inconceivable that people can co-operate without being directed. It is as a solution to the human problems created by this axiom that the abstraction, Anglicisation, was made. Human problems are problems of contradiction, and who, and what, can resolve a contradiction so fundamental as the individuality of being and the conformity of existence? Feudalism is the only possible way, it seems, to live with the condition of individual being and social existence.

The other forms that have been derived from this realised state of feudalism have led to disaster, and Anglicisation itself is nearly dead. The 'Little Englander' is unable to cope, for one of the conditions of the feudal emotion is to prove continually that the leader is capable of leadership.

One of the things that is really different in the world of today from yesterday's is the growing awareness of the ruled. The ruled may be more aware, but they are no more powerful against the necessity of being ruled. Who will, in fact, rule them? Obviously, themselves. The leaders of a group of people are not others, but themselves. Thus, one of the final paradoxes that one has to live with is the paradox of the leader being one of the led. It is towards this paradox that I have been working. That is, if the Anglicisation of the world has nothing to do with the English, it is their own characteristics that have been abstracted by themselves and the world.

The world and the English have had this paradoxical *affaire* without acrimony, in spite of their mutual episodes of violence, hatred and bitterness. To forget and perhaps to forgive is one of the most mystifying facets of human existence, which is not understood by those who are never mystified by life; and there are many in this world.

In fact, the metaphysics of the world can be reduced sharply to three basic elements: eternal individuality, the realisation of relationships and the aesthetic harmony between eternity and change; with three corresponding archetypal peoples: Indian, English and Chinese. They are archetypes because they are all completely self-contemplating and firmly rooted in their pre-conceptions of the world. There is a sense of mystery in their self-contemplation, no anxiety. It is this lack of anxiety in their souls that has left them untouched by their changing circumstances and by the cruelties of the human condition. While the Indian self-conception is an absolute eternal individuality, the English soul discovers itself only in relationships, rituals and connections of ideas, acts and things. There is no conflict, because to the English, eternal individuality is a perfect idea, which can only be realised in relationships, rituals and various ideas of organisation. The Chinese have always striven to harmonise this world into an aethetic form; but the rest of the world has been lost in combining and permuting these three central traits.

If I have reduced the metaphysics of the whole world to three basic elements, it is because one gains neither knowledge nor faith by wallowing in the minutiae of recurring life or by pro-pounding cliches. The 'macro' theorist and the 'micro' empiricist, the scientific philosopher and the practical politician, are only gadflies on the cosmos which they do not understand. This cosmos is the unity of the three elements, individuality, relationship and harmony of eternity and change. It is a unity which is created by the ordinary human being himself and not by his circumstances, nor his mentors, nor his rulers. It is his experiences, the experiences he creates out of his own contradictory nature, that are real to him. When his mentors and rulers divide the contradiction to get rid of it, they develop the aberration of belief inherent in the doctrine that science is knowledge. There is no knowledge, only belief, for human beings.

One of the traits that the English have which makes them perhaps the best people in the world to live with is: not claiming knowledge where belief will do. Many people think it is traditionalism. It is much more than that, it is to recognise that some things have no causes that human beings can understand. Certitude is an evil born of an inadequate nature. We can see much certitude in this age: in the feeling that going to the moon will mean much for the human race; in the idea that enlightenment and liberation are matters of legislative phraseology; in the notion that a sense of superiority is a social fact, not just an unrealised subjective feeling of individuals and nations. One can see why politics is the dominant problem of this age. Politics is the expression of an inadequate nature: it deals in certitudes and plays on the inadequacies of human beings. The English, unlike other nations, lack the cruelty of certitude which destroys the nature it feeds on. English politics is a necessary evil, a solution to destroy some of the inadequacies of human beings. It is a dangerous solution, but all life is dangerous. It is the understanding of danger and its control which is important. The ritualism, the seeking of relationships, is an unconscious attempt to control the danger, which inevitably arises out of the chaos of contradictory social relationships that human beings create.

English society, with its definition of order as a compromise with an impossible world, creates a climate of possibilities—for paradoxical gentlemen like me to speculate, study and confirm, or to reject within oneself what one does not care for. It is, perhaps, necessary for it also to create possibilities for the rest of the world to develop beyond the certitudes, to doubt and to be modest. It is not an unreasonable expectation which needs to be denied, nor a sentimental hope that the world will be a nicer place if it were civilised. It is a practical suggestion based on a fact which many people only sense, but hardly ever realise the significance of. The fact is that there is an intimate relationship between English philosophical thought and the social evolution of the people. The relationship between philosophy and life is so intimate that it makes the English either secretive or unaware of it in their own lives. However, they invariably attribute the connection to others, particularly to the Germans; whose outstanding philosophical thought has, in fact, developed in almost complete isolation from the sentiments of the people. German political and social history owes nothing to Germany's philosophers and social theorists. The history has developed from the German people's own impulses, without any appreciation of their intellectuals' gifts to them—in complete contrast to the English.

The 'undiscovered' history of England is the gradual unfolding of a philosophical view, in which ideas have dominated life throughout changing events. Past philosophers had immersed themselves in solving the practicalities of political and social change; and the greatest need in England today is for political and social philosophers, since in a misguided moment in this century it was thought that philosophy had died and should be buried in universities in dismembered parts. The earlier philosophers did not turn away, from lack of appreciation, to develop their intellectual emotions in the isolation of their thoughts; neither did they have to seek the begrudging recognition of an unintelligent political class as German philosophers had to.

Where else should one expect Milton to be needed but in England? Or the Reverend Thomas Malthus, or Bertrand Russell? Where else could George Bernard Shaw have become an institution, and made philosophical tracts into dramatic art? Shakespeare himself, GBS's alter ego, if he had not been masquerading as a poet and dramatist for so long, should be described as the greatest English political and social philosopher, whose views on Roman politics, Moorish love, England and St George have shaped the English vision of life in a way that Goethe never did for the Germans. Who has appreciated Dr Marx's philosophy except the English? His philosophical parable is only an analysis of modern English history, and has nothing to do with world revolution. And Engels, who saved him from a frustrating and miserable exile, was a Mancunian and not a Teutonic knight. Such a long and serious secretive love affair that the English have had with intellectuality cannot be hidden for ever. It is this love for ideas and their relationship to life that makes the English accept all those who come to England with ideas—in spite of what politicians say about their less gifted kinsmen.

This love is really a feeling of self-discovery, a faith in the enigmatic progress of humanity. Victorian England was an episode of intense love, for the English, in which they discovered themselves and their feelings for humanity in a way uniquely their own. It was a transformation characterised by the intellectuality of practical affairs and by the union of science and reality in a perfect moment of ideal relationship. It is to the Victorians that the English have to return to recover their own identity: not to the hypocritical, arrogant inanity of the caricature Victorian, but to the eccentric, curious men of ideas who helped to create for the world the possibilities which our technocratic rulers have debased into an incredibly grey and joyless power politics.

The rationalism of the Victorians was not the mindless order of a programmed computer, but the wonder, curiosity and humility of a searching mind. It does surprise me that the rationalism the Victorians created should not be recognised by the English as their protection against the cretinous foreign doctrines which seem to be making the world schizophrenically logical, without any sense of reality. The relationship of thought and action that is neither pernicious self-esteem nor ceaseless virtue of mechanical activism is an accidental offspring of a marriage between history and metaphysics. The English should bless this union.

9 Black Intellectuals in Britain

C. L. R. JAMES

The very title to which one has to write turns out to be prob-
lematical, as everything concerned with race. Is Vidia Naipaul a
black intellectual? Twenty years ago the answer to that would
have been simple. Not so today. There is a systematic persistent
tendency to call all members of the 'Third World' black. To
continue with another aspect of the problem: I doubt if there are
many black men who have made the impact on England that
Paul Robeson has made. He lived in England for many years
and was one of the best-known and best-loved black men who ever
was looked upon by British people as one of the blacks who had
made it. Yet Paul went back home to the United States and in
the last years of his life could not have been thought of as anything
else but an American citizen.

Once the complexity of definition has been established we can
go ahead cheerfully, knowing that many who are in ought to be
out and quite a few who are out ought to be in.

I shall begin at what can be called 'Modern Britain'. The period
of radical activity of the old type in Britain ended with the 'Cato
Street Conspiracy' in 1819. The Cato Street conspirators, from
one account, plotted in a garret the assassination of a cabinet,
the beheading of Castlereagh, and the burning of the Tower of
London. They were discovered, tried, convicted and hanged.
One of them was a Jamaican, Davidson by name. At their trial
they were defiant and created a sensation which, it seemed, helped
the government to win a general election. All of them were Deists
but Davidson the Jamaican, it seemed, had Methodist associations.
The 'Cato Street Conspiracy' and the part that Davidson played
are an inviting subject of study for those who are interested in
black intellectuals in Britain.

Another remarkable black intellectual who made a tremendous
impact on Britain was Frederic Douglass. At the height of his
reputation in the United States as a propagandist against slavery
Douglass paid a visit to England. He did an immense amount of

work in Ireland and England and in Scotland. He met most of the distinguished politicians and propagandists of the day and such was the effect that Douglass made that efforts were made for him to continue to live in England. Douglass felt that his place was at home where the struggle against slavery needed all the forces available. His English friends accepted this. But Douglass was still an escaped slave who could be re-captured by his master and once more be placed in bondage. English people subscribed the money for Douglass to be bought from his old master, and also helped him with funds to start a newspaper of his own. Few black intellectuals have the record Frederick Douglass made in England.

Douglass is an example of what it appears was taking place in England immediately after the days of emancipation. It is most notable in the works of William Makepeace Thackeray. In Thackeray's writings there are two notable episodes. In *Vanity Fair* a young woman of coloured blood, who was associated with the aristocracy and had enormous wealth, is sought by many lovers, who are not in the least disturbed at her colour but are more concerned with her wealth and aristocratic associations. Thackeray carries this attitude to blacks to an extreme in his novel *The Virginian*, a novel which deals with British settlers in America. The novel is dedicated to Sir Henry Davison, Chief Justice of Madras, India, and the inscription is dated September 7 1859. The characters in the book move continuously from the United States to Britain and back.

A notable character is a black called Gumbo. Gumbo is not what you would call an intellectual. He is an attendant on his English master. He is a great favourite with the domestic servants of the household, and Thackeray goes to great lengths to show the attitude of white young women to Mr Gumbo. I believe that the following passage should be more widely known.

'I believe Europe has never been so squeamish as regard to Africa, as a certain other respected Quarter. Nay, some Africans—witness the Chevalier de St Georges, for instance—have been notorious favourites with the fair sex.

So, in his humbler walk, was Mr Gumbo. The Lambert servants wept freely in his company: the maids kindly considered him not only as Mr Harry's man, but their brother. Hetty could not help laughing when she found Gumbo roaring because his master had gone a volunteer, as he called it, and had not taken him. He was ready to save Master Harry's life any day, and would have done it, and had himself cut in twenty thousand hundred pieces for Master Harry, that he would! Meanwhile, Nature must be supported, and he condescended to fortify her by large supplies of beer and cold meat in the kitchen. That he was greedy, idle and told lies, is certain; but yet Hetty gave him half-a-crown, and was especially kind to him. Her tongue, that was wont to wag so pertly, was so gentle now, that you might fancy it had never made a joke. She moved about the house mum and meek. She was humble to mamma; thankful to John and Betty when they waited at dinner; patient to Polly when the latter pulled her hair in combing it; long-suffering when Charley from school trod on her toes, or deranged her work-box; silent in papa's company—oh, such a transmogrified little Hetty! If papa had ordered her to roast the leg of mutton, or walk to church arm-in-arm with Gumbo, she would have made a curtsy, and said, 'Yes, if you please, dear papa!'

This is an extraordinary passage especially to us at the end of the twentieth century. There is a lot more to be said about *The Virginian*. Gumbo marries an English girl, takes her back to America. They have difficulties but she stands up militantly for her black husband. The family goes back to England. And the last page of the book tells us of a picture that has been drawn of Sir George Warrington, his wife and Gumbo following. And written under the piece is 'Sir George, My Lady and their Master'. So that although he continues to be a servant in England, everybody realises that Gumbo is the real master of the household.

It must be noted that during this period Thomas Carlyle, in particular, and James Anthony Froude in *The Bow of Ulysses*, were engaged in a most vicious attack upon the intelligence and character of black people, particularly in the Caribbean.

James Anthony Froude was a man of great reputation. And his book on West Indians aroused a great deal of wrath in the West Indies. A black schoolmaster named John Jacob Thomas decided to publish against Froude, and in 1889 he wrote a tremendous exposure of Froude, in a book aptly named *Froudacity*. Unfortunately, John Jacob Thomas, on a trip to England, fell ill and died soon after the book was published. The book had undoubtedly made a strong impression upon those for whom it had been intended. Recently it has been re-published by the New Beacon press, a book that is well worth reading eighty years after its original publication. Such a book can legitimately lay claim to distinction.

We move next to 1900, when Sylvester Williams, a Trinidadian and a lawyer, organised what can be called by some people the first Pan-African Congress. What is to be noted is that Sylvester Williams took such a step at that time is for us today quite a historical event. Two things are very notable for us about the Conference. It is a long time ago since 1900, but Dr Du Bois came from America to take part in the Conference. We note that apart from Sylvester Williams himself the most notable, in fact, the most famous of blacks in England, attended. He was S. Coleridge-Taylor, who was and still is recognised as one of the most notable composers in the Western style. His composition *The Songs of Hiawatha* is still an acknowledged masterpiece. What is to be noted about the Conference is the welcome it received from distinguished English people and its appeal to Queen Victoria who replied, 'Her Majesty's government will not overlook the interest and welfare of the native races'. Nevertheless, the most striking event of the Conference was the presence of W. E. B. Du Bois, as Chairman of the Committee on Address to the Nations of the World. Even in those days, Du Bois included in the address which he submitted the following:

'In any case the modern world must needs remember that in this age, when the ends of the world are being brought so near together, the millions of black men in Africa, America and the islands of the sea, not to speak of the myriads elsewhere, are bound to have great influence upon the world in the future, by reason of sheer numbers and physical contact.

Let the Nations of the World respect the integrity and independence of the free Negro states of Abyssinia (properly Ethiopia), Liberia, Haiti, etc., and let the inhabitants of these states, the independent tribes of Africa, the Negroes (people of African descent) of the West Indies and America, and the black subjects of all Nations take courage, strive ceaselessly and fight bravely, that they may prove to the world their incontestable right to be counted among the great brotherhood of mankind.'

The fact that Queen Victoria took official notice of the Conference constituted a recognition, but acquaintance today with the events and personalities startles us, not only by the fact that Dr Du Bois came from America to take part in the Conference, but behind the respectful tone of the whole event the document that he wrote indicates the power inherent in the drive for black emancipation. Between 1900 and 1914 there were various papers and periodicals published in England dealing chiefly with the political aspects of black emancipation.

It is not easy to make an adequate summary of this work which was done by men of African descent and East Indians. From personal memory I have one of them in mind, a Trinidadian who won an island scholarship, made something of a name for himself as a journalist in England and finally went to the United States. Despite all my inquiries I personally have been unable to find any trace of him. He was a natural born journalist, and people were saying that about him before he left Trinidad. He returned to Trinidad for a short visit in the early 'twenties, and I had the pleasure of meeting him. He was born too early. Had he lived in the present period—Lamming, Wilson Harris and Vidia Naipaul would have had a fourth name attached to these famous three. It is worth mentioning because I am quite sure that all who met him would have remembered this black intellectual and understood that, if not yet there, black intellectuals were on the way.

After the First World War, in fact during the 'thirties, black intellectuals began to make a serious impact upon British politics and the Labour movement. Beginning in 1932 I remember speaking incessantly on the case for West Indian self-government. My audience was not wide but it was interested in politics. Then Mussolini attacked Ethiopia. Jomo Kenyatta, Amy Garvey (the first wife of Marcus Garvey), Ras Makonnen, Wallace Johnson and some other Caribbean workers in Trinidad, formed the International African Friends of Ethiopia. English people were interested and we spoke in many places to somewhat small audiences. I got myself into a blunder. Being a Marxist I was naturally opposed to the League of Nations, but in the excitement of forming the organisation we passed a resolution demanding or supporting, I cannot remember which, those who were urging that the League of Nations take steps against the Italian Government.

There were certain political elements in Britain who were extremely glad that our organisation, which was pretty widely known among the limited circles who were interested in these matters, could be included among those who were urging the intervention of the League of Nations. But most of us who were in the organisation and who were supporting it, had a conception of politics very remote from debates and resolutions of the League. We wanted to form a military organisation which would go to fight with the Abyssinians against the Italians. I think I can say here with confidence that it would have been comparatively easy to organise a detachment of blacks in Britain to go to Ethiopia. Why it did not take place was because Dr Martin, the Ethiopian minister in London, with whom we had close and intimate relations, told us we would be better off doing propagandist work in Britain than in trying to form a military organisation to go to Ethiopia. We accepted his advice and about this time we made it quite clear that we were not looking to the League of Nations to give any assistance to Ethiopia. Our readiness to form a military detachment and our rejection of any appeal to the League of Nations created something of a political stir at the time.

I was moved to write the following letter which appeared in *The New Leader* of June 3, 1936. It gives a pretty clear view of what black intellectuals were doing at the time.

'Sir,

May I make my position in regard to fighting for Abyssinia clear?

Early last year I offered myself through the Abyssinian Embassy here to take service under the Emperor, military or otherwise.

My reasons for this were quite simple. International Socialists in Britain fight British Imperialism because obviously it is more convenient to do so than to fight, for instance, German Imperialism. But Italian Capitalism is the same enemy, only a little further removed.

My hope was to get into the army. It would have given me an opportunity to make contact not only with the masses of the Abyssinians and other Africans, but in the ranks with them I would have had the best possible opportunity of putting across the International Socialist case. I believed also that I could have been useful in helping to organise the anti-Fascist propaganda among the Italian troops.

And finally, I would have had an invaluable opportunity of gaining actual military experience on the African field where one of the most savage battles between Capitalism and its opponents is going to be fought before very many years. As long as the Emperor was fighting Imperialism I would have done the best I could. The moment, however, any arrangement had been come to which brought the country within the control of European Imperialism a new situation would have arisen, and I would have identified myself with those bands, hundreds of thousands of them, who are still fighting, and for years are going to carry on the fight against Imperialistic domination of any kind.

I did not intend to spend the rest of my life in Abyssinia, but, all things considered, I thought, and still think, that two or three years there, given the fact that I am a Negro and am especially interested in the African revolution, was well worth the attempt.

Unfortunately, Dr Martin, the Minister, told me that he thought my work with the International Friends of Ethiopia would better serve the struggle against Italy. When, however, that body decided to support League Sanctions and possibly lead British workers to what Marxists knew from the start would be an Imperialist war, I broke at once with the Society.

Faithfully yours,

London   C. L. R. James.'

This letter shows that we had gone a long way from Sylvester Williams' Pan-African movement of 1900. But it was a mere anticipation of the distance that black intellectuals would travel during the coming years. George Padmore arrived in Britain having broken his connections with the Communist International.

At the time I was reporting cricket for the *Manchester Guardian*. The next year I was to write *World Revolution, 1917–36: The Rise and Fall of the Communist International*. The writings on cricket and then the attack on Stalinism were to give the black intellectuals a certain status. The writings on cricket were much admired both by cricketers and the general public. The book on world revolution was a solid attack on the intellectuals in Britain, among whom as members or sympathisers of Communism were to be counted John Strachey, Stephen Spender, W. H. Auden, C. Day Lewis and others. We were a small group but we fought them on all fronts. Padmore was the chief. He had arrived at the end of the International African Friends of Ethiopia. With him was Ras Makonnen, Jomo Kenyatta, myself and maybe half-a-dozen others, chiefly West Indians. After my book *World Revolution* I published *Black Jacobins*, the history of the revolution in Santo Domingo, and then later a book which broke new grounds, *A History of Negro Revolt*, published in the series FACT under the editorship of Raymond Postgate. That series was sold monthly and this *History of Negro Revolt* could be seen on all bookshops and railway stalls the month that it was published. Padmore published *How Britain Rules Africa*, and I was astonished on reading the book a year or two ago to see that I had corrected the proofs. He wrote another book, *Africa and World Peace*, with an introduction by Sir Stafford Cripps. Padmore organised the journal *International African Opinion*, of which I was the editor until I left for the United States. We published various pamphlets, among which were *The Negro in the Caribbean*, written by Eric Williams and various others on Bechuanaland, on Kenya and on *The Native Problem in South Africa*. Jomo Kenyatta produced a study of the Kikuyu tribe under the title of *Facing Mount Kenya*.

Yet this imposing list of publications which brought the case for freedom for the colonised peoples was the less important part of our work. Padmore was tireless. He had had wide connections while he had been an official of the Comintern and it was curious that despite the vicious lying attacks that the Communists spread about him Padmore retained nearly all or practically all his connections. From Africa, the Caribbean and elsewhere they came to him and his organisation in a ceaseless stream. But what I think was even more important was that we allowed no opportunity of putting our case to pass us by. We had a lot of assistance from the Independent Labour Party, but wherever there was a meeting held by the Labour Party or a conference organised by the Communist Party or some trade union group, or a meeting of Liberals who were interested in the 'Colonial Question' we were always there. To present a resolution, to make a statement and to oppose our enemies. There were very few black people in Britain at the time. We held meetings at which a few dozen people turned up, often more whites than blacks. The fact that we had published books gave us some sort of status. At all these meetings we were there putting forward our line and opposing all who were not completely in favour of colonial emancipation in general and African emancipation in particular. There was no question about it. As far as political organisations in England were concerned the black intellectuals had not only arrived but were significant arrivals.

The black intellectuals as a distinctive body came to an end at the end of the Second World War. First of all there began with Nkrumah a series of independent African states which numbered, in ten years, fifty. This meant dozens upon dozens of black intellectuals representing their governments officially and unofficially in Britain. During the same period about a million and a half West Indians and Africans came to Britain to take part in British industry. It is impossible to select or mention special members. At the same time there began the emergence of black writers.

African writers like Ekwensi, Achebe, and that remarkable writer, Wole Soyinka, remained for the most part in Africa, their homeland. The West Indian writers, on the other hand, lived for the most part in England, and I personally doubt if in any English-speaking country there are three writers who can be said to exceed George Lamming, Vidia Naipaul and Wilson Harris. There are, of course, many other black intellectuals, notable young writers from South Africa. It would be a task, that I state is frankly beyond

F

me, to make any lists or distinctions which would not offend me, the self-appointed judge.

There are two other black intellectuals whom I feel I cannot omit. One is Dr David Pitt, who is a member of the London County Council. The other is Garfield Sobers, who has two claims to inclusion. He is universally accepted as the captain of any cricket team which represents or claims to represent cricketers from all parts of the cricket-playing world. I happen to believe that he is the most widely known black notability in the United Kingdom. Not to be able to link these two distinctions under the heading of black intellectuals in Britain would be, I think, an unforgivable mistake.

There is one figure which justifies the inclusion of Garfield Sobers in this list. Learie Constantine went to Nelson in 1929 and lifted League Cricket in the North of England to a status which astonished both spectators and critics. At the same time this astonishing man wrote books on the race question which made their way, not so much on their own merit but on his reputation as a cricketer. Constantine went on to become a barrister, earned distinguished positions at the Inns of Court and at the BBC, and in the end was made a member of the House of Lords. I knew Constantine very well for over fifty years, and it was his genius as a player which enabled him to use an acute intelligence and firm character to attain the distinctions which he did before he died. There is little doubt that but for his untimely death Sir Frank Worrell was clearly on the way to political distinction among the intellectuals of the day. The future lies before Garfield Sobers.

No list of black intellectuals in Britain can omit Andrew Salkey. Not only as a writer but as the black man in England who is the centre of all organisation, activity and public recognition of black writers in Great Britain. Close behind him is John La Rose, who has undertaken the enormous task of publishing books which revive and maintain interest in historical and contemporary writings. His firm, the recently begun New Beacon Books, is slowly but steadily making its way.

A few words about similar activities in France. One of the most famous names in French history is Alexandre Dumas, and this generation of British and West Indian people do not appreciate Dumas as previous generations did. Dumas was not merely a writer of romantic novels. He came from a most distinguished black ancestry. His father, a mulatto from French San Domingo, was a general of great distinction in the French revolutionary army. He died early and Alexandre entered the field of literature.

It is a common literary opinion that Victor Hugo was the first to win distinction with the new romantic plays that followed the French Revolution and the end of Napoleon, but as the Encyclopaedia Britannica says, *Henri II et son Cour* (Henry II and his Court) 'was the first great triumph of the romantic drama'. Later Alexandre won world-wide fame as a romantic novelist but he continued to be successful with drama. Critics of an earlier generation, like Andrew Lang and George Saintsbury, wrote about him automatically and frequently as one of the finest of the modern French novelists, and today, although his critical reputation may have declined, he is one of the most widely known of black men who have contributed to the civilisation of Western Europe.

Another notable writer is Rene Maran who won the Prix Goncourt in 1921 with his novel *Batouala*. He is not widely known today except among a special circle, but he is noteworthy for this reason. French intellectuals have always played an important part in revolutionary politics in France and Andre Gide in 1926 wrote a book famous for its exposure of French imperialism in Africa, *Voyage au Congo*. Rene Maran preceded him and when one reads both books today there is no doubt that Rene Maran more clearly understood and probably had a greater impact among French intellectuals as to what Africans needed from French civilisation.

There are two other French black men whose names are widely known even in British circles. One whose reputation has taken some years to be accepted in Britain, that is Aime Césaire, the author of the concept of Negritude in his famous poem, now translated in the Penguin edition, *Cahier d'un Retour au pays Natal*. Even more widely known in British circles than Cesaire and in fact a man accepted as one of the spokesmen for black people in Western civilisation is Frantz Fanon, whose book *The Wretched of the Earth* is now a bible among people in England as it is in France and elsewhere.

Response

PART TWO

Response

10 Stranger Upon Earth

PHILIP MASON

No one with any degree of sensitivity could venture on the task now before me without diffidence and indeed trepidation. I am asked to comment on a collection of essays in which 'non-white Intellectuals' discuss their experiences in England. And I am myself entirely English; my four grandparents and their sixteen grandparents were English. I am open at once to the challenge: 'Show your wounds!' and it is a challenge of which in part, though not wholly, I accept the validity. But it ought to be done and it is, I think, my *dharma* to face it.

Let me first state the background to my comments—my personal view. Man has spread more widely over the world than any other mammal and has reacted to a great variety of environments. The Eskimo has evolved physically into a type very different from the Nilotic. What is more, systems of law and custom, sets of values and morality have also evolved on different lines. Each people has thought its own system of evolved morality 'natural', while innovations and the systems of foreigners are 'unnatural'. So long as the physical obstacles to communication persisted, each could continue in this belief. If any Gulliver reached their shores, he must assimilate or perish, but as communications improved, peoples were brought in contact who had previously no knowledge of each other and were often horrified at what they found. The extreme example is the meeting of Cortes and his Spaniards with the Aztecs. The Aztecs thought it a meritorious act to tear out the hearts of large numbers of human beings to propitiate the forces of nature; the Spaniards thought this wicked and unnatural.

My personal view, about which I cannot be dogmatic, is that the human heart—or, if you prefer it, the psychological make-up of man in general—is very much the same wherever man is found. Love, hate, jealousy, the archetypal forms of self-assertion and desire, the need for comfort and companionship, are the ingredients present everywhere; the mixture is different in every individual but there is more difference between individuals in one group than between the 'averages' of groups. In fact, I do not think it is really sensible to try to compare 'groups' in this respect; a psychological average is a nearly meaningless concept. But *values* and ideas of proper conduct vary enormously; they can also change quickly, i.e. in a generation or two. The physical response to evolution is much slower but on the other hand in modern conditions physical differences are less and less relevant to survival. Unfortunately, most people have not had occasion to think deeply about this subject or to meet others from populations which look different physically. They therefore link physical differences with the other kind—differences of values and custom and in fact go further and expect people who look different to differ in intelligence and in psychology.

This is widespread if not universal; hardly any society accepts strangers unreservedly. In England the tendency is aggravated by deep-rooted symbolic associations of blackness with evil (which are common to Sanskrit, Arabic and Persian as well as European languages) and by memories of empire and the idea that blackness goes with primitive savagery. Hence arises the dilemma with which these essays are concerned. The inveterate custom of man is to label anyone he does not know and stick on a price-tag. This is not the behaviour of truly civilised man; it displays the mentality of the wolf pack, while the beginning of wisdom and the mark of civilisation is to treat each person as unique.

Thus I am wholly in sympathy with Bhikhu Parekh's warning about the dangers of generalising about Englishmen and Indians as though all members of each category were alike. However, I do think we can generalise about the kind of behaviour which is admired in one culture and not in another and I accept the truth of Parekh's subtle and perceptive analysis of much English behaviour. We do value control of the emotions in public; nor do I think this is something that developed only in the last century with the public schools and the empire—as has sometimes been argued. 'Show me that man that is not passion's slave' was first said on the stage nearly four centuries ago. We do also passionately value our privacy. I might add—and Krishan Kumar comes near this—that it is not merely negative; we find a comforting, indeed, an affectionate warmth, in a relationship which we know will not become too demanding. When I lean on a gate and talk about the weather and the crops to a neighbour, I know that in a year or so I shall know what he does about that back that sometimes bothers him and in another year about that nephew of his wife's who has never been quite right; we give each other plants and may lend each other tools or even do a little shopping for each other but we shall never ask each other to a meal. On the other hand, a stranger—

preferably from another continent—who writes to ask a question I at once ask to lunch. He will go away and never come again, so it is safe. It is a much more superficial relationship.

Although it may be specially English to want to defend privacy, surely we are not at all unusual in reacting to anything felt as a threat? A Sikh girl told me that the Sikh women in Southall who had been there longest said that when they first came people were kind and helped them in the shops. Later, when there were more Sikhs and they were more confident and several came into the shop together, noisily talking Punjabi, they met black looks. 'It would be just the same if strangers invaded our village in the Punjab,' one of them added, sketching the outline of a 'cyclical' theory of race relations which originated in California. Most contributors underline the point; it was quite different in the early fifties, before numbers made the indigenous feel threatened. This was instinctively understood, a dozen years ago, by Asian immigrants in West Yorkshire, whose leaders even then expressed the view that the indigenous would continue to tolerate them so long as there was no dramatic increase in the numbers of immigrants.

Four of the essayists in this collection—Dilip Hiro, Cachia, Parekh and Krishan Kumar—seem to recognise it as one of the facts of life, if far from a pleasant one for them personally, that there is inevitably difficulty about moving from one culture or set of values to another. Krishan Kumar, for example, recognises the complexity of the situation which faces him and perceives the analogies—none of them of course exact or complete parallels—between colour as an occasion for exclusion and class, language, culture and sex. Most pertinently, he refers to Disraeli, who, I have long believed, cultivated a mask of cynical brilliance to hide a profound loneliness arising from his 'otherness' among the English aristocrats who made him Prime Minister. Kumar has hit on a close analogy to one part of the dilemma of the 'non-white intellectual' (I dislike both words! They are both tags which label categories which have no boundaries), this is with the writer who has come through the indigenous British culture from a working-class background, who feels a stranger and a child when he goes back. This surely is a close parallel to the feeling that many Indians and Africans have when they try to go back to their own culture. It is deep in the roots of their being but they are out of it and cannot get back into it. In his case the crueller prong of the dilemma is that he feels that he belongs mentally in the English world but cannot wholly be accepted. It is being an outsider among people who *ought* to accept you that hurts. No one minds being left outside by people who obviously *are* different. I never felt lonely in camp among Indian villagers; I did sometimes feel very lonely in the white 'station' and the club. This I think plays a big part in the 'Lawrence of Arabia' syndrome which has been the special form taken by the 'Prospero complex' in so many British lives.

In a discussion of this kind, the great danger is to take as absolute terms which are really relative. To speak of being 'accepted', as I have just done, sounds as though it was a process which either happened or did not—as though there could be an answer: 'Yes, accepted' or 'No, rejected'. However, surely total acceptance is very rare in human relationships? Even sexually I think it is rare and the crooning love songs suggest a yearning for a total self-immolation on either side which only occurs between very mature and very unusual people. But this is near the heart of what I am trying to say and I shall come back to it and to these four essays which I find most sympathetic after some discussion of the one with which I find myself most in disagreement.

This is Sivanandan's, in which he expounds with even more than his usual brilliance, fire and skill, the sustained cry of anguish of Fanon, Eldridge Cleaver and Césaire. I have said elsewhere that I owe a debt to Sivanandan for helping me to some understanding of this agonised creed, and that debt I again acknowledge; some study of it is essential to anyone who tries to discuss race relations and this collection would be incomplete without it. But the longer I think of it the more convinced I become that its application is nothing like so wide as Sivanandan would like to think and that its conclusions, if they can be called conclusions, are not only negative and harmful to race relations, but harmful in a wider sense to a world in which there is little enough of goodwill, tolerance and understanding. First, as to application, the creed has its origins among West Indians and American blacks and for them the claim that they have been robbed of language, culture, roots and self-respect is true. For them the only ambition they were taught to cherish was to become more like the Man who despised them. This is not true to anything like the same extent of Africans; they have their tigritude, as Langley has pointed out. Who knows what dazzling developments may occur in Africa? To attempt to include in this family of metaphysical blackness Indians and Chinese is surely to abandon the use of reason altogether. Both India and China have ancient cultures of their own which have profoundly influenced the sense of values and the behaviour of Indians and Chinese today; I recall how astonished I was in Nigeria by aspects of Nigerian politics which made nonsense of my Indian experience. Family structure too is very different in different parts of Africa, let alone any comparison with India or China, or with the West Indies. Perhaps the greatest wrong done to the West Indians was the destruction of the African family. They have had to develop something new and different. To lump such widely different peoples together under the one label of blackness (which in the language of Fanon and Sivanandan means the quality of having been oppressed) is to put oneself on the level of Hitler as a labeller of people with misleading tags—and below the level of Powell, who is usually careful not to label so explicitly.

We are also reminded of Chisiza's remarks about the African personality. 'We cultivate the habit of loving lavishly, of exuding human warmth, of compassion. . . . Once so conditioned one behaves in this way not only to one's family but also to the clan, the tribe, the nation, and to humanity as a whole. . . .' Now I am sure that as he wrote those words Chisiza believed them; that was how he wanted it to be. No one with the least knowledge of African history could possibly endorse them as having affected the behaviour of African peoples to humanity as a whole. Tshaka was as ruthless of human life as Napoleon; indeed, the whole basis of tribal economy even for so advanced a people as the Barotse was the annual raid on weaker neighbours for plunder, slaughter and slaves. They behaved like the Vikings, who I suppose contributed to my genetic heritage. This was just as true of the Bemba, the Yao, all the Nguni peoples—and not very different on the West coast either. Nor does Indian history seem to me to show any marked moral superiority over Western; tyranny has alternated with anarchy and the Pindari raids were as ghastly as the Thirty Years' War.

We are all as bad as each other and no one has any monopoly of intolerance, or of fear or of hatred. Does Ceylon behave better to its minorities than Britain? Who is white (which in this language means oppressive and tyrannical) in Uganda? And who in Bangladesh? Who was white when the Ibos were massacred in Northern Nigeria? Heaven knows we all have enough to be ashamed of. The news from Ulster makes one sick, but it is not because they are white that Catholics and Protestants murder each other. One of the indelible impressions of my life is the memory of standing among the ashes of what had once been the Muslim quarter of a Hindu village and listening to the words of the two bandaged survivors—women who had seen their children killed and had been themselves left for dead. That had happened because there were stories of Muslims killing Hindus in East Bengal, 800 miles away. It confirms my starchy English belief that there are occasions when there is a good deal to be said for restraining the emotions.

I have a good deal of sympathy with Sivanandan's attack on modern art, but I think the label should be modern not Western. He contrasts it with African and Indian art which are 'anonymous', but so was European art in the Middle Ages, and it seems to me that when European art emerged from the Middle Ages the flowering of individual art, from Michelangelo to Rodin, from Chaucer to Hopkins, from Bach to Beethoven, was one of the greatest expressions of the human spirit. To throw it aside because Carlyle was so nasty about Quashee—and nasty is the only word that fits him on this subject—strikes me as rather like knocking down your brother's castle on the sands because someone has been disparaging about yours. It is no use consciously trying to go back to folk art; the self-conscious attempt stands false and immodest beside the genuine thing. What is distressing about the whole creed of Fanon and Sivanandan is that while in Algeria it could and did lead to an outcome, it cannot possibly do anything of the kind in Britain. It can only make things worse. It contemplates revolution, which must mean bloodshed and misery, with no indication of what will replace the existing order. But the apocalypse is post-poned until the white (which here means Anglo-Saxon) masses realise that they are really black (which here means oppressed and therefore good). This will not be soon; Sivanandan recognises that 'white radicals' are far from being his allies. Meanwhile, this kind of doctrine drops to the moral level of white prejudice, answering one set of stereotyped generalisations with another. Black is not always beautiful; it may sometimes be beautiful but then so may white; white is not always ugly; it may be very ugly indeed but so may black. As the operator twists the knife in his own wound, the cry of pain becomes a cry of hatred which feeds an answering hatred.

I return to the essays with which I feel more sympathy. First, while most of what Bhikhu Parekh says of Indian values and behaviour agrees with my experience, I cannot help wondering whether he does not idealise one aspect of the Indian family, not its importance for most Indians, which I am sure is overriding, but the absence of tension within it. As I read his essay, I was in the midst of Mulk Raj Anand's *Seven Summers*, one of those bio-graphical novels recalling the writer's childhood. His mother is of course a central figure, vivid and vigorous, a centre of love to the boy. But she hates her daughter-in-law and hated her mother-in-law, and, when she takes the narrator back to her native village—

which from her stories he had pictured as idyllic, a fairyland—she is verbally attacked by a jealous sister and retaliates vigorously. Her mother takes the sister's part and says: 'You were spoilt by your father and you still think you are his wife and not I . . .'—a thought which might well have occurred to a character in Ivy Compton Burnett but would have been indicated by the most tight-lipped of hints. After three quarrels, in which all the women shriek and weep, the mother takes her son home before the wedding she came to attend. One novel does not make a national culture but surely the tension between daughter-in-law and mother-in-law is something every observer of the Indian family has noticed. Those quarrels! There is a scene which I have never attended but which has been described to me so often that I feel as though I had been there. A letter has come, perhaps, asking when the young wife is coming to her father's house for what is significantly called 'leave' (*chhutti*), and in the argument that follows, voices rise higher and higher and abuse is hurled until suddenly she springs to her feet, bursts away from them and jumps into the well. It is an ineffective way of committing suicide—never successful so far as I remember—but an excellent cure for hysteria; by the time she has been pulled out the tension has dropped. I cannot suppose that one in twenty of such cases would reach my ears and quite a number did.[1] I also recall fathers whose sons ran away from home, brothers who were bitter enemies—but why go on? The point I am trying to make is that from outside the family it is the signs of tension that are observed and remembered, while from inside and in reminiscence it is the warm strength of what holds it together that is the reality. This does not affect Parekh's argument but it does mine. All families have tensions; all families have quarrels.

Here perhaps is the place to picture very briefly the kind of society I think we should be aiming at in England. It would be a kind of cultural federalism. The old homogeneous nation state, its political boundaries coinciding with its cultural, is on the way out; we are moving towards larger combinations of states and politically Britain will one day be part of a European federation. This will hardly diminish the demand for a greater degree of regional self-government but it will also mean an increasing variety of ethnic groups. It seems to me that far from trying to assimilate such groups they should be encouraged to cultivate their own identity and respect each other's; the ideal is the concept of the part-time Indian (in U.S. terms) who leaves his Indian identity behind in the reservation and comes into a wider world to earn money. This is much the kind of situation envisaged by Roy

Jenkins when Home Secretary; he defined it as: 'equal opportunity accompanied by cultural diversity in an atmosphere of mutual tolerance.' It is also similar to the pluralism envisaged by Michael Banton and quoted in one of these essays. Where I am sadly unhelpful is that I cannot honestly see any easy way of arriving at such a society. No slogan will work the trick. Communism has not made Russia more tolerant to the Jews or to national movements among the Czechs or Hungarians. I can only see the long uphill task of pegging away, by persuasion, advice and education, hoping to achieve wider toleration and understanding. It would be a great step forward if every Town Hall and Civic Centre in the country would abandon the ideal of assimilation, but it cannot be done overnight; this is still a country in which changes of opinion have to come about the hard way, by persuasion.

However, I do very tentatively wonder whether in the contemporary scene there are not two contradictory processes at work. We hear of polarisation, that is, of explicit attitudes becoming more extreme at either end of a spectrum and I do not question that this is happening. But is there not also going on in the middle-ground a process of getting used to each other and taking each other for granted, in buses and railway-stations and on building-sites, something altogether undramatic and never likely to get in the news? It is an almost unconscious process and it is liable to be upset by dramatic events, fiery speeches, and intolerant militancy; it can hardly be measured or recorded but the streets of London to me constantly provide indications of an almost imperceptible tidal movement at this level.

This is not much help to the intellectual, and I feel that each case probably needs a personal solution. Few will be able to equal the ironic withdrawal of Naipaul, but Dilip Hiro seems to aim at something not dissimilar, and Krishan Kumar to contemplate unwillingly something of the kind. It is so much easier to give advice than to take it—and I have no wounds in this war—that it seems an impertinence to wonder whether either should go so far. It is part of their situation to experience in a magnified form difficulties which are part of the condition of being human. Parekh writes of the difficulties he experiences in giving his son advice about how to behave at school, and of course these are accentuated by the otherness of being Indian. But I know hardly a middle-class parent who has not some similar story. My contemporaries are grandparents and most of us feel that our children are no better than we were at bringing up a family—if as good. Our role has been reversed in the course of a generation; traditionally children would try to escape from the strictness of parents to the indulgence of grandparents, who, thought the parents, spoiled them because they were not responsible. Now it is the grandparents who groan at the permissiveness of the parents. Freud said, however you bring up children it will be wrong, and the more sensitive you are, and the more prolonged your own formal education has been, the more you will agonise over your children's.

However, there is a much deeper level at which I wonder how far the sense of rejection and loneliness is not an inescapable part of humanity. In perhaps the most optimistic passage in any of these essays, Parekh speaks of the challenge of living in two cultures and trying to make the best of both. It involves, he says, continual self-recreation, and he recognises that some Englishmen as well as some Indians have this aim. Is it not universal? We conceal it as best we can, from each other and ourselves, but who is there who is not dissatisfied either with himself or with the way others regard him. So-and-so, we think, is a happy member of the gang—but is he really? As I read these papers, I kept recalling the beginning of Alice's dream in Wonderland. She is in a hall from which she is unable to escape; she finds a tiny door and she can unlock and open it; by lying on the floor she can peep through and see the cool lawns and fountains and flowers of a beautiful garden. But she is too large to go through the door so she locks it and wanders disconsolately away with the key in her hand. Soon she finds a magical way of reducing her size and hurries joyfully back to the little door—only to find that now she has left the key on a table where it is beyond her reach. This is surely a dream from the collective unconscious of mankind; I may be shut out of the beautiful garden by an angel with a flaming sword or by a little key that is always in the wrong place when I am the right size—but I must search till I find the way in. We feel we are strangers and children, as Krishan Kumar says; I am a stranger upon earth, said the Jewish psalmist nearly 3,000 years ago. Let me ram home the point not by sayings from my tradition but from India's. From Kabir, for instance:

> In thy home is the Truth. Go where thou wilt, to Benares
> or to Mathura:
> If thy soul is a stranger to thee, the whole world is
> unhomely.

And in the Bhagavad Gita:

> To him who has conquered his lower nature by its help,
> the Self is a friend
> but to him who has not done so it is an enemy.

Or to put it in its simplest and most mundane terms, it rests with the self to make the best of the situation or to turn the knife in the wound.

I do not underestimate the courage that the writers of these essays need, but for the Indian in Britain, given courage, there is a personal answer to be found. For the Indian in Britain there is the possibility of much that is rewarding within a purely Indian setting. I was recently at a party in Britain where the food and music and four-fifths of the company were Indian; it seemed to me that most of the people there would be called intellectuals, and that they were on the whole making a very good attempt at cultural federalism. There is available a base in Indian culture from which sorties can be made and personal contacts made. This is not much help to Krishan Kumar, who feels quite alien from that culture. His course can only be Disraeli's; knowing himself to be thought different because of an accident that does not make him feel different, he has to find his own special mask and role in the main society. The generalised scruples he mentions ought not to make him shrink from finding his Mary Ann. It is for the West Indian that the dilemma posed in these essays is most acute; what links him to the working-class Caribbean is little more than a shared history and a mood. But even for him, there is a personal choice to be made and he can add barbed wire and spikes to his estrangement or make it a gate on which he can lean to talk. Such talks may sometimes lead to friendship.

NOTES

1. Attempted suicide was an offence under Sn. 309 of the Indian Penal Code, in law punishable by a year's imprisonment. It would only be reported to the police if tension between factions in the village demanded such a move and the police would be unlikely to prosecute unless their conditions for keeping it quiet were refused. If they did prosecute, the proceedings were farcical; conviction was inevitable but the sentence would be 'confinement till the rising of the court', which meant sitting on the floor in the corner for an hour or two.

11 Black Intellectuals, Black Bourgeoisie and Black Workers

JOHN REX

On the face of it I do not possess good credentials for discussing the papers in this volume, for I am an English-descended South African of poor white origin, who has gained sufficient acceptance in Britain to be appointed as a Professor in a provincial University. Yet, paradoxically, these *are* my credentials, for my whole life has been shaped by that dialectic between the principles of class and race which my black co-authors are discussing. I know the exclusiveness and contempt which the wealthy and well-connected British show towards their fellow-countrymen who are in lowly employment abroad, yet find myself accepted in most circles in Britain as a clean-limbed and classless colonial lad. On the other hand, I have always lived with the fact of ultra-exploitable black labour, and know how easily British capitalists rationalise its use, while blaming the system of exploitation on their white employees. These are insights which neither bourgeois or academic black men nor black colonial workers, brainwashed into believing in British justice, actually possess. What I detect here, therefore, is a pained and growing awareness of how British culture and the British economy classifies black men, and what I want to do, after analysing the partiality of these insights, is to disillusion some of the contributors and seek to persuade them to accept the fact of British racialism in all its fullness.

The first thing to do, I think, is to object to the notion that there is a certain group of black men in Britain who are not like the others and in some way deserve different treatment from the others, because they are what are called 'intellectuals'. The claim is most commonly made by men who make their living by writing books, or by others who simply have high incomes, and, hence, have access to superior life-chances and an allegedly more cultured style of life to their fellows. When it is so made, those who make it seem to me to be beneath contempt. So far as I am concerned there is one and one only sense in which the term 'intellectual' might be used to describe a category of people whose experience is of any moral significance for the black community. This is when it is used to describe the situation of those black men who seek, through their involvement in the daily sufferings of their fellow men, to articulate the meaning of that suffering and to help them towards liberation. In this case, however, the so-called intellectual is not simply bringing his own pain and suffering to our attention. He speaks of his fellow men and for them. Thus the problem of the black intellectual becomes the problem of racialism as such.

Let us look, then, first at the upper-class and bourgeois black. He has, of course, no claim to special consideration beyond any other man, whether black or white. His real problem is that he has been encouraged to think that he has. He is a victim of the mythology of empire which could not and did not outlast the hey-day of empire itself. So long as the claim was made that the empire was not based upon racialism and capitalist exploitation, but on some kind of historic and civilising mission, there had to be a class of successor black men who would maintain all that was best in the British tradition after the last Governor had packed his bags and left. Moreover such men could come and stay in the best hotels or have their children educated at public schools and Oxford or Cambridge without difficulty. They could even go into Notting Hill without being harassed by the police. Theirs was a comfortable and secure life and usually they overconformed to English standards, gaining little knowledge of white working-class life, despising that which they knew. If it did occur that their rights were threatened by discrimination, if, for instance, one of their number was refused a hotel room, there was an outcry and the matter was rectified. A mistake had been made, a *class* mistake of not distinguishing these men from the ordinary dirty blacks whom you would not let into hotels anyway.

The upper-class Indian has seen this world disappear since the collapse of empire and the great West Indian, Pakistani and Indian migrations. No successor class is now recognised and *all* must face the possibility of rebuff in their search for high-class food and lodgings. Moreover, there is no class badge which enables a policeman or a landlord to distinguish the well-placed from the ordinary worker. Very shortly *all* black men will be liable to be stopped in the street to prove that they are not illegal immigrants and no hearty upper-class manner will cut any ice in the police station. Sadly, the privileged upper-class black has to learn what it is to be an 'uppety nigger'.

One of the most poignant experiences of this class, of course, is the sense of a changed atmosphere in Oxford and Cambridge. I once remember Dr Busia, before he became Prime Minister of Ghana, saying that the happiest days of his life had been spent in an Oxford Senior Common Room. I also remember a Creole Anglican Canon Professor in Freetown, who could not tell me the names of the rivers around Freetown, but who looked forward to his sabbaticals on the banks of the Wear near Durham Castle. The education which such men shared was the education of the British ruling class, for British rulers was what they were being educated to be. But what point can there be in the college offering, or the rich black student accepting, such education when there is no longer any old-fashioned British-style ruling to be done abroad. As a marginal man he must now be sidetracked into one of the more sly and cynical subjects like sociology. He may have some shadowy hope of being educated for a position of privilege, but what his lecturers are busy doing is telling him about the iniquity of privilege in Britain itself.

The smoothest educational production line in the old days, of course, was for the Indian ruling-class-to-be; and it was smooth because there were proud traditions in the Indian Civil Service and a more deeply ingrained illusion of the historic mission. Below the Indian Civil Service there was the Sudan Political Service, and, below that again, the hard-core Colonial Service in which racism was more open and explicit, and which selected only a small group of confused and ambiguous black men for the metropolitan experience. They were deeply puzzled by it all, and in any case many of them had to face, not the clearly elitist atmosphere of Oxbridge, but the utterly confusing class experience of Leeds, Hull or Manchester. They tried their best to puzzle it all out from the clues which were on offer, but in the end neither social practice nor cultural meanings seemed at all coherent.

Of course, it is by no means the case that all Indians came into the ruling-class category and all other colonials into that more confused group we have just mentioned. Of particular importance were that very large category of Indians, who were on the margins of the ruling class, wanting desperately to get in, but not knowing what was required of them. They could not, of course, recognise that what made most of their masters tick was racialism, and without this master-clue they put together sets of hypotheses which drew heavily upon the Englishman's own proud description of himself. He was reserved, but essentially firm and kind. Yet ultimately he was, like Calvin's God, inscrutable. One reaction to this situation was to become a culture expert, to make a profession of scrutinising the inscrutable. Another was to ease the tension by making a joke about it. Both reactions are to be found amongst non-upper-class black academics and both are represented in this volume.

One distinction which should be made amongst non-Indian colonials is between West Indians of African origin and the rest. For the descendant of the plantation-slave ultimately has problems like no other. What his ancestors suffered, over and above the world-historic fact of political enslavement for purposes of economic exploitation, was cultural castration. To the attempted remedies for this we shall have to return. But a cultural eunuch could do nothing of his own and for himself. He had to do his master's bidding and to seek a sphere of achievement within his master's culture.

While I was in Barbados I read in the local newspaper, the *Advocate-News*, a reader's letter whose implications for Barbados were really world-shattering. The reader asked whether it was not time that the West Indian, instead of playing the white man's game of cricket, found a game of his own. The striking contrast between the assumptions of that question and the paper contributed here by a West Indian Marxist intellectual and cricket writer merits some reflection. What I would suggest is that the ennoblement of Lord Constantine, in which C. L. R. James takes such pride, showed the colonial black man's dilemma and his ultimate humiliation in a double sense. On the one hand, his achievement was an achievement in the colonialist's terms, but on the other, it did not represent achievement in an area which mattered. It was a play activity only.

Phillip Mayer, in his important study of Xhosa immigrants to the South African town of East London, has indicated that there are two possible reactions to white conquest. One is that of what he calls the 'school' people who have assimilated the values of the mission schools and try, albeit in a stereotyped way, to attain white standards. Along with this goes a continuing fight against 'discrimination' which makes such attainment impossible. The other, however, is to adopt European ways and European clothes only for work and for the circumstance of economic enslavement, but to revert in the freedom of leisure-time to traditional African ways and to traditional African dress.

The reaction of the traditionalists of Mayer's study to the school-people is to claim that they have sold the pass to the White Man, and that it is essential to keep at least the forms of traditional culture alive in an alien world. At the present time this set of beliefs has been strengthened and has grown into a Black Consciousness Movement, which in turn has developed roots in political and trade union activity. Thus, the trade union and political struggle is to be fought, but the very terms of the struggle are defined in the black man's own terms. Such a development is at the opposite pole to the career of a black West Indian who is *symbolically* rewarded for his achievement in a *game*, which is *not his game, but that of his masters*. 'The future', C. L. R. James tells us, 'lies before Garfield Sobers.' Indeed it does, and it is quite compatible with continued exploitation of, and discrimination against, West Indian workers.

C. L. R. James, however, established an important connection in his piece, without recognising its significance. He tells us that we should be able to link the distinction of Garfield Sobers in cricket and that of Dr David Pitt in being elected to the LCC 'under the heading of black intellectuals in Britain'. Indeed, he tells us that not to do so would be 'an unforgivable mistake'. However, since Dr Pitt's career led him from the LCC to the Community Relations Commission, the question is sharply posed as to what the attitude of black men should be to the work of that body. No one would wish to deny that Dr Pitt is a man of the highest personal achievement or that he has worked hard for his West Indian people in Britain. What is at issue, however, is the institutional context in which he operates.

There have, in fact, been two important studies recently of the work of the Community Relations Commission and its local Councils. One by Hill and Issacharoff[1] sees the Commission as engaged in the worst form of tokenism in dealing with race relations problems (so much, indeed, that one of the authors actually left the project as a waste of time before the end of the research!). The other, by the American political scientist, Ira Katznelson[2], compares the sorts of political linkages established between black migrants and the so-called host community in Nottingham with those in the Northern American cities during the urban migrations from the Deep South in the thirties. The conclusion here is that, in Nottingham in the fifties and sixties, a process was going on through which the black community was deprived of leadership and a unidirectional control of the life of black men by white established. In fact, the view can be argued that the Community Relations Commission functions in a manner roughly equivalent to the South African Ministry of Bantu Affairs, although in a much more half-hearted and amateurish way.

The appalling thing about the papers in this volume is that the problem set for black men by the establishment of the Community Relations Commission is nowhere posed. In fact, 'intellectuals' in the black community might hardly have noticed its existence. One did not need a Community Relations Council to deal with the problems of Black Hampstead intellectuals, and the establishment of such Councils as well as their staffing by presumably 'non-intellectual' black men has passed without comment. In order to raise the issue sharply, however, we must now look briefly at what has been happening to the million or so working-class black people living in Britain, at what official Government agencies have done about it, and what black political intellectuals (in the sense in which we have used the term 'intellectual' to refer to those who articulate the grievances of the people) might do about it.

The actual situation with regard to discrimination against black men has been rendered less rather than more clear by academic research into the subject in recent years. Thus the proven fact of discrimination in the allocating of housing,[3] not merely by private enterprise but by Labour Councils, has been obscured by research projects into the importance of choice in re-housing, which emphasise the self-segregating tendencies of some Indian and Pakistani communities. The existence of a colour-bar and inten-sified exploitation of black workers in Loughborough is ignored in statistical studies of random samples of immigrant workers which miraculously fail to catch Loughborough in their samples. In addition, research in education both investigates the question of whether black children's presence in large numbers lowers white performance, and explains the high proportion of West Indians in ESN schools and low streams as due to the fact that West Indians are mistakenly thought to talk English, when, in fact, their language is utterly defective. What is needed now, perhaps, is some research into the research process as an instrument of racism.

There are, however, facts which are very well known to Britain's black working-class community despite such research. It should be the part of black intellectuals to bring them more widely to notice. The fact is that discrimination in the allocating of Council Housing still operates virtually unabated. West Indian families or just black families who apply for Council Houses must surmount all sorts of concealed hurdles to qualify and, if they do qualify, may still be offered slums awaiting demolition or whatever is the worst part of the housing stock at the disposal of the Council. In employment, black men can get jobs wherever the work is too tedious, dirty, or inconvenient to attract white recruits, but, when men who want to live permanently in England seek more skilled or responsible work, as at Loughborough, they face white strikers determined to keep them out. Indian and Pakistani children at school find out, instead of their language problems being tackled as a technical matter, as they would be, for example, for Greek-speaking Cypriots or Italian-speaking children, people talk of spreading *them* out more thinly; and West Indian children find that, even though they speak English, they do not speak it correctly or are classified as just too stupid to get on in school.

Add to this the fact that since the operation of the 1971 Immigration Act any black man may be stopped in the street and asked to show that he is not an illegal immigrant, and that, even the so-called liberal press, in campaigning against Powell, accepts the basic Powellite assumption that the mere existence of black men in their present numbers threatens the integrity of British society, and one has a reasonably clear picture of the position of the black worker in British society. It is surely one task for the intellectual in the black community to speak for these people who must live in overcrowded and insanitary rooms, literally fight to get decent jobs, have their children retarded in the schools and yet blamed as the source of most educational problems, and find themselves continuously harassed by the police. Dilip Hiro, one of my co-authors, is one of the very few black 'intellectuals' who has tried to do this in his excellent book, *Black British, White British*.[4] It is a pity that more educated black men and writers do not devote themselves to this task, rather than confining themselves to purely cultural matters.

Not merely writing is necessary here, but action. The fact is that a whole series of institutions have been created which succeed in co-opting potential black leaders and confining the area of their activity, if not actually employing them to work for discrimination. Notably, the Community Relations Commission faced with the demand of the United Nations that Britain should observe the year 1971 as a year to combat all forms of racial discrimination, redefined the year as one for racial harmony, so that local councils like that in my area could celebrate the event with exhibitions of West Indian Limbo dancing. The Race Relations Board moved from one derisory soft settlement to another, and, through its failures, probably made racial discrimination in the areas of housing and employment more secure after the Race Relations Act was extended to cover discrimination in those spheres.

Finally, there were a number of establishment agencies like the

Runnymede Trust which overtly challenged the growth of Powellism, yet at the same time covered up the facts about racial discrimination in places like Handsworth, Birmingham by arguing that the sufferings of the people there were only the sufferings of the poor in general.[5] Perhaps, however, the way ahead was indicated by another co-author, A. Sivanandan, whose incomparable work in the Institute of Race Relations and in support of *Race Today* helped to ensure that one 'intellectual' body should actually speak for black working-class people rather than spending its time ironing out the problems of the Institute's former capitalist sponsors.

I imagine that some of my co-authors may say that in raising these overtly political questions I have strayed from my brief. I do not think that I have. When I think about intellectuals and black people I am always reminded of some memorable words spoken on a memorable occasion by a distinguished friend of mine, the late Tennyson Hlabangana, during negotiations about the Bulawayo General Strike of 1948. The Minister of Justice, Mr Beadle, had come to Bulawayo to try to settle the strike. He heard Hlabangana and others speak and then said, 'Well, I'm quite prepared to talk to gentlemen like you, but not to that rabble outside'. To this Hlabangana, a Master of Arts, who apparently had a notable career lying before him, replied, 'I am one of that rabble, sir. They are my people'. I should like to name this the Hlabangana principle and commend it to some of my black intellectual friends in England.

Now there is, of course, another job to be done apart from the overtly political one. This is to undermine the racist elements in native British intellectual culture wherever they exist and to try to recover and build upon all that was important in the national cultures of the black countries before they were destroyed by colonialism. This is obviously the concern of Sivanandan and La Rose, but I would like to supplement what they say by drawing attention to more immediate dangerous tendencies of a cultural kind.

In 1967 I participated in Paris in a UNESCO experts meeting to draw up a statement on the nature of racism and race prejudice. We drew attention to the fact that the very success of UNESCO[6] in making biological theories of racial inferiority disreputable had created new dangers. For, although at that time highly systematised theories of racial inferiority seemed to have been repudiated, many new ways of rationalising racial discrimination had been found; and, even when there were no systematic theories, other justifications could be found in the new folk wisdom of working-class club humour.

Since 1967 the situation has deteriorated. It is no longer the case that academics do not argue for racial inferiority in psychological and biological terms and a new level of sophistication in the organisation of commonsense justifications has been achieved with the aceptance on national television networks of a programme in which black Englishmen make damaging jokes about black men in general.

Most immediately an intellectual challenge to academic liberals as well as to black men has been made by Jensen and Eysenck.[7] I have shown elsewhere[8] that, in setting up his defence of Jensen's position, Eysenck is guilty of the most extraordinary methodological crudities, and need hardly do so here. What is of interest, however, is what wide and favourable publicity Eysenck actually received. Nonetheless, when a later event occurred, namely the withdrawal by Leeds University of its offer of an Honorary degree to Professor Shockley, the *Guardian* referred to Eysenck as having been 'hounded' by academics. The *Guardian* offered no evidence of this hounding and apparently felt no need to do so. What this seemed to prove is that not merely can shoddy scientific arguments about the possible mental inferiority of black men get a hearing, but that they should get a privileged hearing in which any criticism is regarded as 'hounding'.

No one who has worked in British universities during the past twenty years and been concerned with questions of race could fail to notice the difference in the intellectual climate which now exists from that which existed in the early fifties. At that time the predispositions of academics were essentially anti-racist and any suggestion about the inferiority of black men was subject to a special scrutiny. So also were the early speeches of Powell. What I, at least, find now is that most academics are inclined to see Powell as a somewhat doctrinaire, but nonetheless an essentially consistent, man, and one whose views should be treated with respect, that criticism of work like that of Eysenck is immediately suspected of being prejudiced, and that there is a growing minority arguing that biological theories about men's social characteristics should be re-opened for investigation.

One of the responses of black intellectuals in universities to this situation has been, understandably, that they do not want to spend all their time talking about race, because part of their own claim against the racists is that black men can make an important contribution in other spheres of a politically neutral kind. I would be more impressed by this argument if I thought that the things which they were doing were in any sense more important, but, in any case, it looks to me increasingly that this *is* one of the central questions in all the social sciences and the humanities, and that anyone who tries to avoid it in his work, whether he be black or white, cannot really be a serious scholar.

If, however, I plead for overtly political activity by black intellectuals and for a very direct confrontation with scientific discussion of the question of race, I by no means want to detract from the importance of the very brilliant contribution to this volume by Sivanandan. Moreover, his political record is such that no one could possibly accuse him of taking an undue interest in exclusively cultural matters. What I think I should do in relation to his piece is simply to underline the centrality of what he has to say.

One of the problems about dealing with arguments like that of Eysenck is that what is at issue very often is not the question of whether or not he makes his case by this or that criterion of proof, but the whole question of where his language comes from, what criteria of proof and styles of argument he uses. Even more, when one turns to the way in which the question of race occurs in popular culture, it is clear that the very language which we use, which is the means whereby we create social reality, is shot through with value assumptions. My guess, to put it no higher, is that it is precisely in an individualistic or family-centred world where the individual is forced into a trap of always feeling that his prime duty is to his family or his mortgage company that racism flourishes. Moreover, just as petit bourgeois language and styles of thought have often been challenged in the past by the values and the thought styles of a working-class community, so the culture of the various black communities in Britain can and must be used to challenge the assumptions of the petit bourgeois and his masters, not merely at the point where racist thugs are on the street, but at the point where he makes out his banker's order to the building society. There is, therefore, a cultural task for the black intellectual and it seems to me to be very possible that within the context of vibrant political activity, the writing of a novel or a poem might, while not in a crude sense contributing to the political struggle, make effective political struggle possible.

On the other hand, it is important in thinking about the language and the cultural assumptions of clashing cultures not to assume that because everything which is to be set against the assumptions of Western European capitalism is necessarily to be commended. This is why I found the contribution of Dilip Hiro profoundly interesting. Clearly he found the cultural values which centre around arranged marriages and the seclusion of women in India stifling and frustrating, and the attractiveness of a society in which it was possible to get 'dates' with girls should not be underrated. I imagine that there are those who from some kind of puritanical, socialist or national convictions might argue that the titillating sexuality of Western society is wholly corrupt and that Dilip Hiro's naive confession of being titillated should be condemned. For my part, I do not think so. It should provide the basis for a more open discussion of sexual values than is part either of Hindu or Western capitalist society.

There is another reason, however, why Dilip Hiro's piece is not only engaging but important; he may not have realised it at the time, but the loss of his family's property in Sind was probably the best thing that ever happened to him. I feel that far too much intellectual discussion in Britain is conducted within the well-off upper classes and that, whatever importance one may attach to high culture and the perpetuation of tradition, living in unfashionable areas, being provincial, and having to make emotional and financial ends meet on one's own, is the beginning of wisdom in cultural matters. Like Dilip Hiro I have lived in Stockton-on-Tees, been to the Middlesbrough Labour Party and found comradeship in the Hull Tribune Group. They added a quality to my own life which, despite its studied self-importance, the life of my metropolitan friends seemed lacking in. It seems to me that the black intellectual who knows only Hampstead or Notting Hill would do well to follow Hiro's path. I am not saying that he would find British society less racialist, but he would learn something of the real values of working-class people which seem to me to be a closed book to a number of my co-authors.

I would wish to make a similar point about the failure of many contributors ever to engage with the actual life of the organisation of immigrant communities in Britain. This is as true of those with a Marxist orientation as it is of those with a more conservative outlook. In fact, however much we may wish it otherwise, the life of the immigrant community depends upon the activities of many individuals whom the more politically conscious and doctrinaire might regard as morally and politically dubious. However, we get nowhere by merely holding political seminars about these problems in universities. Let us be Marxist or Hindu or Africanist by all means, but let us make sure that our values connect with the real problems of the man in the lodging house. Otherwise they are likely to be so much hot air.

It seems to me in conclusion that a symposium like this one has great value in bringing different perspectives on race and class together. It also seems to me that whether they like it or not the contributors to this volume are going to see any privileges that they have whittled away in the years that lie immediately ahead, and that they will have to find their roots in the black working-class community. I cannot put this better than does Sivanandan:

'The coloured man . . . by virtue of his colour, has an instinct of oppression, unaffected by his class, though muted by it. So that the coloured intellectual, in resolving his contradiction as an intellectual, resolves also his contradiction. In coming to consciousness of the oppressed, he takes "conscience of himself", in taking conscience of himself he comes to consciousness of the oppressed.'

NOTES

1. Hill and Isacharoff, *Community Action and Race Relations*, Oxford University Press for Institute of Race Relations, London, 1972.

2. Ira Katznelson, *Black Men White Cities*, Oxford University Press for Institute of Race Relations, London, 1973.

3. Political and Economic Planning, *Racial Discrimination*, Harmondsworth, Penguin, 1968. *See also* John Rex and Robert Moore, *Race, Community and Conflict*, Oxford University Press for Institute of Race Relations, 1967.

4. Dilip Hiro, *Black British White British*, Eyre & Spottiswoode, London, 1971.

5. Augustine John, Race in the *Inner City: a report on Handsworth, Birmingham with comments from Robert Hollman, John Lambert and Dipak Nandy*, Runnymede Trust, 1970.

6. UNESCO, Four Statements on the Race Question, Paris, 1968.

7. A. R. Jensen, 'How Can We Boost IQ and Scholastic Achievement?', *Harvard Educational Review*, No. 39, pp. 1–24, 1969.

H. J. Eysenck, *Race, Intelligence and Education*, Temple Smith, London, 1971.

8. John Rex, *Race, Colonialism and The City*, Routledge & Kegan Paul, London, 1973, pp. 230–40.

12 Guests and Visitors

GEOFFREY GORER

Most of the dealings of any emotional intensity which non-white, or for that matter any foreign, intellectuals have with the English are with members of one of the English middle classes; and consequently it seems worth while exploring some of the values and strategies of the middle classes to see whether the unhappiness which some of the contributors to this volume have felt at the lack of intimacy which they have experienced is due to colour prejudice or is a repetition of the ways in which members of the middle classes treat people from outside their own group and is misinterpreted by foreigners who cannot understand the cues and implicit assumptions.

I have argued elsewhere[1] that the contemporary English man or woman's sense of identity depends above all on the certainty of his or her class position and the presence, real or fantasied, of members of other English social classes to confirm their own estimate. I have made or participated in a number of nationwide surveys in the last twenty-three years; and in none of them have more than 2% been unable or unwilling to place themselves within a seven-class structure. Among these refusals were a number of ideological statements of disapproval of the existing class hierarchy; but orphaned and unmarried women were often in genuine perplexity. As a generalisation one can say that English class position is determined by men but maintained by women. The father determines the class position of his sons and daughters at birth; at marriage the girls assume the class position of their husbands; so it is understandable that a woman without father or husband is genuinely perplexed. The role of women in maintaining the class position of their husbands and children, especially in the middle classes, should be constantly borne in mind. English men may easily strike up friendships with people outside their social class or of other nationalities at work or elsewhere outside their home; whether the husband's or son's friends will be welcomed into the home depends on the wife or mother.

In the last survey I made[2] respondents assigned themselves to social classes in the following percentages; and the differences over the last twenty years have been relatively very small:

Upper middle class (and the minute upper class)	2%
Middle class	25%
Lower middle class	8%
Upper and/or skilled working class	13%
Working class	50%
Lower working class	2%

In this essay I will not deal with the differentiations within the working class, significant though they are in the contemporary English political and social scene.[3] But I am assuming that the face-to-face contacts between overseas intellectuals and members of the working classes are slight and not emotionally important for any of the people involved; I shall concentrate on the middle classes, and particularly the two small groups who consider themselves upper or lower middle; a majority of English intellectuals seem to place themselves in one or other of these classes.

The English middle class, without a modifier, corresponds very closely to the classical and Marxist *bourgeoisie*; they are predominantly the traders and manufacturers and although, with the elaboration of technology, they may no longer own the means of production, they typically are property owners, living in houses they own (rather than rent) and, at least in theory, able to save enough to pay for their children's education, for medical attention, and to provide for their old age. As in nearly all other societies in a similar stage of technological development, the middle class generally live in fairly closely defined areas of the towns and, even more markedly, the suburbs. Middle-class life tends to be socially very self-contained and, except in the way of business, it is unlikely that foreigners, whether intellectual or not, will have any but the most superficial contact with members of this core class.

Those who consider themselves upper middle class or lower middle class are less numerous and in many ways much less confident about their social status. It seems useful to introduce here the Indian or Japanese concept of pollution. In both of these societies, at least in classical times, a person of high status or caste or sanctity risked having these qualities impugned or even destroyed by too close contact (even inadvertent) with a person or object ritually defined as unclean; and so they had to be continually alert to avoid such a polluting contact. The English upper and lower middle classes do not have the religious sanctions which shield brahmin or samurai, but they do tend to act as though prolonged contact with members of the social class immediately below them would undermine their status, certainly in the eyes of others and quite probably in their own. The feared polluters are other Englishmen in the first place; but these fears can be, and are, transferred to foreigners (no matter what the colour of their skin) who are permanently present in the country.

The position of the lower middle class is the more precarious as they tend not to have the property to back up their claims for deference; indeed today they are likely to receive less money for their services than do many members of the working classes from whom they wish to be so clearly distinguished. There is a large overlap between the English lower middle class and the American 'white collar workers'; both groups earn their salaries (the lower middle class tend to be paid monthly, the working classes weekly) by the use of their intellectual skills and never by physical effort which involves the larger muscles. As well as clerical workers, most of the auxiliaries to the learned professions and a large proportion of teachers are people claiming lower middle-class status.

In contrast to the working class, the lower middle class consider themselves genteel and refined (two attributes which tend to be mocked by members of the other English classes); they are far more religiously observant than the members of any other social class, with high membership of the various Nonconformist Christian sects; they tend to be vocally censorious and secretly envious and resentful of the members of the other more prosperous or more 'permissive' social classes.

Their resentment is in many ways understandable, for the rest of English society does tend to treat them with callousness and lack of generosity. Their training or apprenticeship is generally much longer and more arduous than that of a skilled worker and yet today they generally receive less money and no more deference; and the middle, and especially the upper middle classes react with great unkindness if members of the lower middle class presume to claim social equality. When the occasion arises for them to employ this middle-class model of the way to deal with strangers claiming social equality they have a tendency to be even more crudely callous than their models. Since they have relatively little money they tend to entertain in their homes only their kin or fellow-sectarians.

For the upper middle class, on the other hand, entertainment is the major informal technique for validating their status; and as hosts they (and as far as my knowledge goes, they alone) make the distinction between visitors and guests among the people to whom they accord hospitality. The distinction is between reciprocal and non-reciprocal relationships. As an aspect of their claim to be representative and important people, many members of the upper middle class feel called upon to offer semi-official hospitality to "all and sundry"; but they will not, as a generalisation, in their turn accept hospitality from these 'visitors'.[4] Hospitality will only be accepted from people with whom one can feel 'at home' and 'at ease'; when such people are in one's own home they are one's 'guests'. The distinction between perceiving oneself as a 'visitor' or as a 'guest' is a subtle one for English people of other social classes to make accurately and almost impossible for the non-English who have no analogues in their natal culture. I think much of the unhappiness recorded by some of the contributors to this volume is due to the fact that they considered themselves 'guests' while their hosts saw them as 'visitors'. They hoped they were embarking on a relationship of increasing intimacy, which their hosts had not even envisaged; the hosts felt that they had discharged all their obligations as ladies and gentlemen to the visitors they were entertaining by the hospitality they gave.

The differences between the upper middle class and the minute upper class in England depend almost entirely on pedigree. Owing to the system of primogeniture traditional in the English aristocracy, only the eldest son inherits the title and the lands. In the higher nobility (dukes, marquises and earls whose numbers barely reach three figures) the brothers and sisters of the heirs are accorded a 'courtesy title'; but this is not hereditable and the next generation will be plain 'Mister' or 'Miss' and are indistinguishable from other members of the upper middle class without research, unless they brag of their ancestry. The biggest divide within the English social system is that between the upper middle class and the middle class without a modifier.[5] Since the true upper class in England is so minute, I shall not refer to it further; what I still wish to say about the upper middle class should be understood to comprise the upper class also.

The upper middle class arrogate to themselves alone (and in general, until very recently were conceded) the right to the ascription of ladies and gentlemen. This ascription was not merely a claim for deference, though it was also that; the relatively inarticulate definition of these terms include an impressive concept of duties as well as an arrogant claim to rights.

Traditionally, the English gentleman could have nothing to do with trade, with buying or selling things (with the occasional

GUESTS AND VISITORS 193

exception of farm produce); to trade would be to lose status, to
derogate to the middle class. Throughout most of the nineteenth
century and up to the end of the Second World War most
gentlemen acted as though they were sincerely disinterested in
money; and this disinterestedness gave Britain and the Empire
one of the least corrupt administrations the modern world has seen.

The only occupations traditionally open to gentlemen were
those which involved dealing with people: the professions of the
Church, medicine and some branches of the law, the armed
services and administration. The educational system to which the
sons of gentlemen were subjected was held to confer on those who
survived it all the requisite qualities of 'leadership'.

The first duty of a young lady was to get married to a gentleman
(if she failed in this there were few possibilities for her except in her
different roles as kinswoman) and then to do all in her power to
forward her husband's career and to maintain his social status.
She typically regulated her husband's non-professional social life
and by her issuance and acceptance or refusal of invitations to
hospitality imposed the distinction between visitors and guests;
she would determine which, if any, among her husband's colleagues
or clients should be admitted to the intimacy of guest-hood, with
whom she would feel 'at ease'. This lady-like preoccupation with
excluding all the people with whom one did not feel 'at ease'
probably reached its apogee in the social clubs in the tropical
empire up to 1939. These unique institutions (as far as I know)
probably caused more unhappiness than any others in the colonial
world; but it should be stressed that it was not merely 'the natives'
who were excluded but also English men and women of lower
social class or occupation; and they were probably even more
resentful of the unkindness with which they were treated.

It has seemed useful to write at some length on the characteristics of the English upper middle class since they imposed their
patterns and values on nearly the whole of the tropical Commonwealth and Empire. The upper reaches of the Colonial and Indian
Civil services were very nearly upper middle-class preserves[6] and
their influence was paramount in the patterns they established in
administration, the armed services and—most important of all—
the education of the élite to be taken over by their successors
when the countries they administered were granted or achieved
independence.

It seems to me highly likely that most non-white English-
speaking intellectuals (except perhaps the very youngest) absorbed
during their earlier years of education an upper middle-class view

G

of English society—somewhat dated of course and sentimen-
talised—and that, when they came to England, they expected to
find themselves in the world of John Galsworthy. The *Forsyte
Saga* was an ingenious piece of flattery, portraying the English
upper middle class as they would like to have seen themselves; but
I have been surprised to discover in how many countries outside
England (even in the People's Republic of China) these books are
treated as great literature and as accurate portrayals of contemporary English life; I do not consider either claim justified.
However, if one expects to be warmly welcomed as a guest in a
Forsyte-like family and then finds oneself coldly and correctly
treated as a visitor by families of analogous status, the disappointment can well be poignant.

NOTES

1. *The Vicissitudes of English Identity over Time and Empire* in *Ethnic
Identity, Cultural Continuity and Change*, Wenner-Gren Foundation (in press).
2. *Sex and Marriage in England Today*, Nelson, 1971.
3. The relatively small group of talented young people who choose to
describe themselves as 'upper working class', rather than attempting to 'pass'
as upper middle class as their equivalents did a generation ago, tend to be easy
and free of anxiety in their contacts with people of other classes or other
societies. Few of them, however, would describe themselves or be described
as intellectuals.
4. It is perhaps necessary to stress that this is a generalisation. Individuals
in the upper middle class who are less anxious about their status or who feel
genuine liking for people outside their class may well accept hospitality from
people whom most of their peers would firmly treat as 'visitors'.
5. Nuances of vocabulary would seem to be the chief public markers of
membership of the upper middle or middle classes. This was explored in detail
nearly twenty years ago by Nancy Mitford and Professor Ross; but I consider
that they were inaccurate in supposing that the distinctions they had noted
separated the upper from the middle class, rather than the upper middle from
the middle.
6. The practical, in contrast to the administrative, branches found recruits
in most of the British social classes but they were not the trend-setters. The
upper middle classes played a very small role indeed in the settlement of African
colonies with temperate climates; most of the settlers were probably lower
middle class when they left England.

13 On Preserving the British Way of Life

JOHN PLAMENATZ

Nobody contests the legal right of a 'sovereign' state to decide whether or not immigrants are to be allowed to settle in it, or even its right to discriminate between settlers. Nevertheless, those who favour a policy of exclusion or partial exclusion feel the need to find arguments in support of it. They hardly ever say: 'It is enough that the people of the country should want to exclude the would-be immigrants, and there is no need to give reasons in justification.' As a matter of fact, the people never do want to exclude all would-be immigrants; they want to exclude only some, and they often differ considerably as to those they want to exclude. Besides, there have always been large movements of population in the world, and some of the richest countries have been quite recently settled or have taken in immigrants in large numbers to do work that the natives were unwilling to do. In parts of the world where democratic and liberal ideas are widely accepted, where it is taken for granted that there should be greater equality of opportunity among individuals inside the community, it is not easy to deny that there should also be greater equality among diverse peoples. Why should not people from poor countries be free to move into rich ones where there is a demand for their labour when people from the poorer classes in a country are free to move into the richer ones where there is a demand for their talents? Have not the rich and powerful countries, by their industry and trade, by their science and their social and political ideas, changed the conditions of life for all peoples all over the world? Have they not in the recent past created great empires, coming in uninvited among weaker peoples to rule them as conquerors and showing little respect for their ways of life? Such considerations as these have no doubt made it difficult for politicians and other leaders in democratic and liberal countries simply to assert, without more ado, a right to exclude would-be immigrants. They have felt the need to back up their assertion by putting forward reasons which they have believed to be compatible with their democratic and liberal principles.

In this country three such reasons have been put forward: the need to ensure that mass immigration does not aggravate social ills which are already acute (as for example the shortage of decent housing); the need to ensure that it does not exacerbate resentments which, even though they are often unreasonable, could in time prove fatal to our liberties; and the need to preserve the British way of life. It is the last of these reasons that I want to discuss.

Let me begin by admitting the obvious, lest some of my arguments should expose me to the suspicion of wishing to deny it. There can, of course, be good reasons for restricting immigration. It does sometimes aggravate ills which are already acute, even though the extent to which it does so is often exaggerated; it does exacerbate resentments dangerous to liberty, even though such resentments can often be diminished without restricting immigration; and it does change manners and attitudes in ways that the natives dislike, even though it also leads to changes they do like. I would not deny that the first duty of a government is to the people who already live in the country it governs, who have a right to expect it to put their welfare above that of would-be immigrants. If immigrants are allowed in as settlers, if 'outsiders' are allowed to become 'insiders', then they must not be discriminated against, but they can justifiably be kept out on the ground that letting them in would do more harm than good to the 'host' country. Even this principle would need to be qualified to be entirely acceptable, but I shall accept it for the purposes of this discussion. Most politicians and other 'opinion-leaders' in this country accept it, though not all their arguments are consistent with it.

The third of the reasons I mentioned for restricting immigration into this country, the need to preserve the British way of life, is at once the most persuasive and the vaguest. It is the most persuasive, not in the sense of being logically the soundest or the best supported by the facts, but in the sense that it is the most widely accepted. After all, there is plenty of evidence that immigrants, especially when they are coloured and come from poor countries, take jobs that the natives do not like to take because, necessary though they are, the jobs are badly paid or otherwise unattractive, and there is evidence too that these immigrants are not effective competitors with the natives for such scarce resources as adequate housing. The social ills that mass immigration is supposed to have aggravated have been carefully studied, and it would seem that, on the whole, immigration has not made conditions worse for the natives, though it has had bad effects from which the immigrants have suffered most. As for the argument that immigration exacerbates resentments dangerous to liberty, its persuasive power is diminished by its not being exactly flattering to the people to whom it is addressed. Do the British really care so little for their liberties and for the institutions which maintain them, that the resentments aroused by the presence of coloured immigrants among them are enough to move them to forms of behaviour dangerous to liberty? The British who in the recent past have aspired to teach the world, and especially the coloured peoples in their empire, what liberty is and how it is to be established and preserved! The most persuasive—or perhaps I should say, the safest—reason to give for restricting immigration especially when the immigrants are conspicuously different from us racially or culturally (or both together), is that immigration threatens our way of life. Just because this conception of a British way of life is vague—vaguer, for example, than the idea of an adequate supply of good houses or the idea of political and judicial processes that preserve the essential liberties—there is no hard evidence that coloured immigration is not a threat to it (which it conceivably could be); and the suggestion that it is, does not have implications unflattering to the British. Or if it does, this is not obvious. What, after all, should be more precious to a people than their 'way of life'? Is it not what distinguishes them from other peoples, what makes them one people? Is not a threat to it a threat to their identity?

There is, of course, a great deal in Britain worth preserving, as there is in France or Italy or India or China, or in any country with a rich cultural inheritance. There are human artefacts, buildings, pictures, objects of art, books and documents, and there is the countryside which owes so much of its beauty and its charm to what human beings have made of it in this long-inhabited island. There are also the customs, manners and institutions of the people, and ways of thinking and feeding that are characteristic of them and to which they are attached; and it is these that we have in mind when we speak of the British way of life. But these things are not the same over the whole country, and they are continually changing, and they are not valued equally by everyone. Scarcely anybody wants them to be everywhere the same or to be unchanging. What then in this great variety subject to continual change constitutes the British way of life? Britain is changing now in many different ways. Which of these changes are in keeping with its way of life, and which are not? Which among the many things now going on in Britain are authentically British? Who is to decide which they are? Are the learned men who have made a study of things British to decide? They may not agree with one another, and even if they do, their decisions may not be to the taste of the unlearned majority. Why should their preferences be imposed on the majority? Are the majority then to decide? But they too may disagree, and what they are agreed about may cover only a small part of what Britons cherish and wish to preserve in their own country. Or, to put it differently, every Briton may care deeply about many things British to which most Britons are indifferent. Everyone, native-born or naturalised, who cares deeply for Britain has his own image of the country. No doubt, his image has much in common with those of many of his compatriots, but how much of it is common to all their images, or even to most of them?

Britain has had a long history and has been subject in the past, as she is today, to many foreign influences. These influences have helped to make her what she is: but for them, her language and literature, her arts and sciences, her institutions and manners, would all be different. If being authentically British means being the product of native influences alone, then nothing British is authentically British, just as nothing French is authentically French. Things Chinese may, until a hundred years ago, have come closer to being authentically Chinese than anything British or French has come to being authentically British or French, but this is a privilege that the Chinese no longer have and apparently no longer value.

Even if we concede, as clearly we must, that things British can be authentically so though foreign influences have helped to make them what they are, we may still want to preserve them and may have reason to believe that they are threatened by foreign influences. The influences that threaten them will presumably be different from the influences that contributed to their making, but they may nevertheless be foreign. But, if they are foreign, why should we assume that they are brought in among us by immigrants? Even if there were no immigration, there would still be many foreign influences in Britain. There would be tourists and other temporary visitors, there would be Britons going abroad and coming back again with foreign tastes and ideas, there would be books, works of art and inventions. We should, no doubt, approve of many of these influences and disapprove of others, and those of us with a taste for that way of speaking might want to distinguish between the foreign influences that enrich or help to maintain the 'British way of life' and those that impoverish or subvert it.

Why, if the British way of life is to be preserved from hurtful foreign influences, should there not be censorship and also restrictions on the number of tourists, whether foreigners coming to Britain or Britons going abroad? What reason is there to believe that, in general, foreign influences are a greater threat to our way of life when they come in with immigrants rather than in other ways? One answer to this question might be, no reason; but that, whereas to impose a censorship or to put restrictions on Britons wanting to go abroad would be to curtail 'essential' freedoms long recognised in this country, to restrict the entry of foreign settlers would not be. Why should we forgo a remedy which our liberal and democratic principles allow us because we cannot use others which they forbid? Another answer might be that foreign influences to which we are necessarily exposed through ordinary and scarcely avoidable forms of intercourse with other peoples are one thing, while foreign settlers who come in in such large numbers that they are difficult to assimilate is quite another; for these settlers, while they remain unassimilated, form alien communities in our midst. We cannot discriminate, and we ought not to attempt to do so, between foreign influences that subvert our way of life and those that do not; we must leave it to people to absorb these influences or to reject them, as they think fit. But, in the interest of keeping Britain British, we can restrict the immigration of foreigners into this country when it reaches such proportions that it threatens to create unassimilable alien communities among us; we can do it and we ought to do it.

This argument, so it seems to me, is not a good one, if only because it is so difficult to decide what is meant by the word *unassimilable*. The native-born British differ greatly from one another in their styles of life and their ideas and feelings; they do so from region to region and especially class to class. They, presumably, are all 'assimilated'. But to what? Or, rather, what is it that is common to them all and distinguishes them from foreigners? Is it their speaking English as their mother tongue? Not all of them do that, for there are Welshmen whose mother tongue is Welsh, and there are, outside Britain, some five persons whose first language is English for every such person in Britain. Is it then the principles, attitudes and institutions which make it possible for them to live freely and peaceably together in spite of the many differences between them? There are other peoples who share these things with them, the peoples whose ideas of democracy and freedom are akin to theirs. To be sure, the British have contributed more than any other people to forming these ideas, but the ideas are no more exclusively theirs than is the English language or the magnificent literature produced in that language. If the immigrants, though they learn that language, subscribe to those principles, acquire those attitudes, take part in those institutions, still remain in important respects different from the rest of the British, why should we say that they are 'unassimilable' or 'unassimilated'? What should we point to in the ways they differ from the rest of the British to justify our denying that they are British, even though the undeniably British also differ from one another? How shall we discriminate between differences among people living in the same country, speaking the same language, having the same legal rights and obligations, and say that *these* differences distinguish outsiders from insiders and *those* do not? Since it is cultural assimilation which is in question, physical differences are presumably not relevant, unless they are indicators of cultural differences. Why should they be such indicators, unless persons who are physically different are so treated as to prevent their being assimilated; or, in other words, are so treated as to produce in them attitudes which are taken to be marks of non-assimilation?

I assume that people who want to preserve the British way of life are not keen to preserve everything that is characteristically British, for they will dislike at least some of these things. By the British way of life they mean, presumably, what seems to them valuable in what is characteristically British. Some things British they will value only, or very largely, because they are British, while others thay will value because they are admirable, or because they believe them to be so. But what is characteristically British and also admirable may be as much threatened by the native-born as by immigrants. If there had been no immigration into Britain in recent years, there would still have been considerable changes in the country, some of them for the worse. Much that is admirable and British would have disappeared in any case. Old things decay and new things appear in all countries at all times, and never more so than in advanced industrial societies in which the rate of social and cultural change is high; and there is good and bad both in what decays and in what appears. There are always irrecoverable losses as well as welcome gains. There are also, of course, changing standards, so that older people tend to think the losses greater than the gains. But, even if it were possible to decide by reference to unchanging standards whether or not the losses had outweighed the gains, it would still be open to question whether they were the more likely to do so the more foreigners were allowed to settle in the country.

To this it might be objected that the point is not whether change is desirable by reference to supposedly unchanging standards but whether it is welcome to the people whom it affects. If the natives do not like the effects in their country of the coming in of masses of immigrants, conspicuously different from themselves physically and culturally, why should they not restrict the flow of immigrants or even put a stop to it altogether? It may be that when they speak of 'preserving their way of life' they really have in mind no more than preventing changes they dislike. But if they want to prevent them, why should they not do so?

What then is the change they dislike? To what extent does it consist in *effects of immigration*, in unwelcome changes in the conditions of life that result from it or are honestly believed to do so, and to what extent does it consist in the mere presence in the country of people conspicuously different from the natives? No doubt, to some extent it consists in both the one and the other; but there is reason to believe that often it consists much more in the second than in the first, that what people really dislike is seeing the unfamiliar in familiar places. This, I suppose, can hardly be called a primitive reaction, since it is as strong among peoples who pride themselves on being civilised and sophisticated as among others; but it is unreasonable and unjust. It is particularly unreasonable when the immigrants come into the country to do indispensable work which the natives do not like doing; and it is particularly unjust when the natives have themselves been the greatest intruders upon others in the history of the world, when they have recently lost the largest of all empires.

The coming of aliens in large numbers, and even in small ones, can be deeply and painfully disturbing to natives, can subvert their institutions, unsettle their beliefs, and weaken their self-confidence. This, however, is much more likely to happen when the aliens are strong or rich than when they are weak or poor, when they come as conquerors than when they come to take the worst paid jobs and live in the least comfortable and most ruinous houses. There are more Indians and Pakistanis in Britain today than there ever were Britons in the Indian sub-continent, but who can doubt that the British did far more to subvert native ways of life over there than the Indians and Pakistanis have done, or are likely to do, over here? It is their interest to fit into our ways, or to adapt their ways to ours, so as to disturb us as little as possible. They cannot afford to behave among us as we used to do among them.

My last sentences are not an attack on imperialism, which has much to be said in its favour as well as against it; they are merely a reminder of a simple truth.

14 The Immigrant Intellectual

EDWARD SHILS

The life of a man in society is hard. It is hard in the society into which he has been born and in which he has lived all his life. The life of a person who leaves his society often seems to him in some respects even harder. The life in his new society is usually hard but it is usually in a very significant respect better than what it was or appeared to him to be in his native society. The quest of an improved standard of living or the desire to escape from restrictions and damages inflicted because of religious beliefs or ethnic qualities is usually attained in the society to which the immigrant comes. But with those improvements, which are often obscured by complaints, there are also deprivations. Although his income in the host society is almost invariably better than what was earned in his society of origin—except for exiles who are expelled physically or who fled for their lives—satisfaction over the attainment of a higher standard of living does not inevitably come. The employment which he finds is very likely to be in an occupation which is not well regarded by the host society. This is only one of a large number of stresses to which a newcomer to a society is subjected.

I

The newcomer is usually ignorant of the language spoken in the host society and even if his language of origin is of the same linguistic family, the dialect which he speaks obstructs his intelligibility and marks him off from those who are native to the host country. His perceptible distinctiveness in complexion, dress and demeanour renders him easy to identify as a foreigner and accordingly to exclude from convivial association and friendship. As a result, his contacts with members of the host society are restricted and he is confined to the company of his former fellow-countrymen who share his handicaps. Although this protects him it also exacerbates his sense of being alien to his surroundings. The communal life which he can lead is deformed; the sex and age ratios of the immigrant community are often deformed by the selectiveness of emigration; climatic conditions and the arrangements of buildings affect the pattern of his pleasures. The pleasures themselves are often looked at askance by the members of the host society who come into contact with them. They are thought to be outlandish and quaint at best, repulsive or immoral at worst. Religious institutions must be reconstructed; sometimes they cannot be reconstructed because they depend on traditions, skills, persons and social arrangements which cannot be transferred.

Then there is a sense of loss, a sense of being cut off from primordial things, from the familiar landscape, from the ground on which one was born and where one's ancestors lived and died. There is pain and yearning about this as long as it can be remembered and even after it becomes vague in memory. There is a sense of being an alien in the new society. Slights, derogations, difficulties in understanding what is said and sought by the members of the host society contribute to this, but they only accentuate it, they do not create it.

In addition to all this, there is the obvious and enigmatic fact of ethnic difference. Even in societies which were at one time ethnically heterogeneous in the assembly of their population, the passage of time, the sharing of a continuous and bounded territory under a common authority and the bearing of a common name, precipitates a tendency towards the formation of an imagery of a common ethnicity. Immigrants have to live in a country for quite a long time to share this supposedly common ethnicity. Differences in language, dress, bearing and conduct render the difference obvious to both host and immigrant. The immigrant is aware of his appearance and it adds to his sense of alienness. Skin colour, hair and facial features where these are obviously different, confirm it.

To the extent that the immigrants keep to themselves, they feel their ethnic alienness, but they cannot really keep entirely to themselves. They have come to work in the host society and this forces them into association with established members of that society. The low status of their employment is brought home to them by the omission of acts of deference and indeed by many acts and words of disparagement by members of the host society under and with whom they must work. Outside of work, they cannot wholly withdraw from contact with the host society. They must make purchases, apply for social services, send their children to schools, seek the aid of or attempt to evade the ministrations of the police; they must walk in the streets and use the vehicles of public transport; they attend cinemas which are not always owned, operated or attended only by members of their own ethnic group. They must in short do many things which bring them into contact with natives and which provide the occasion for being treated derogatorily. They learn and they develop a culture to keep injury at a minimum by reducing their exposure to unpleasant situations and diverting, where they can, their resources and affections to more tolerable situations. The burdens of daily life, a limited range of aspiration and attention and a modest conception of what they are entitled to in the host country help to render bearable the stresses which are the price paid for economic improvement or freedom from persecution and improvement.

This is the way it is for the uneducated immigrants who perform menial services, who supply relatively unskilled manual labour and who in most immigrant communities form the majority. If the immigrants are educated persons and are qualified or seek to be qualified for occupations which require intellectual attainments, the situation is somewhat different. It is usually more complicated; it is in any case likely to be more painful.

II

Immigrant intellectuals are of diverse types. There are established mature intellectuals who already have acknowledged accomplishments to their credit and who immigrate because they find their own countries disagreeable or the host country more attractive— for any number of reasons. Henry James and Alfred North Whitehead, who crossed the Atlantic in opposite directions between the United States and Great Britain and Ivan Turgenev who settled in France are three notable instances of this type. Akin to these are the intellectuals who settled in the host country voluntarily but before they had become established as productive intellectuals. James Joyce, T. S. Eliot, George Bernard Shaw, Ezra Pound, Joseph Conrad are in this class. W. H. Auden and Christopher Isherwood are marginal members of this class since they had already published a certain amount before emigrating from England. The American 'expatriates' in Paris during the twenties and thirties fall into the latter classes: Ernest Hemingway and Henry Miller were the two who subsequently became most famous.

Then there are the intellectuals who have to leave their native countries because they have been exiled by the government and would be imprisoned if they remained, e.g. Alexander Herzen,

Peter Kropotkin, Karl Marx. Many immigrant intellectuals became immigrants by fleeing from a foreign conqueror or from a tyrannical regime which deprived them of the opportunity to do intellectual work and which might have imprisoned or executed them had they remained in their native country. In the twentieth century the refugee intellectuals who fled from Italian Fascism and later from National Socialism were very numerous. Some of the most distinguished figures of modern scientific scholarship and literature are to be found among them.[1]

Not falling into any of these classes are the intellectuals who are not themselves immigrants but who come of immigrant parents. Many of the intellectuals of Jewish origin in Great Britain and the United States are offspring of immigrants who came from Eastern Europe; these intellectuals were either born in the host country or came there in childhood. The generation of the Israeli intellectual class above the age of thirty comes largely from this latter group or from the refugee group.

African, Asian and Caribbean intellectuals in Western countries are seldom the offspring of immigrant parents.[2] They have usually become immigrants early in their careers as intellectuals. Many came to the host country for university studies and remained. Some have come because they wish to practise their intellectual activities in the host country. Some are refugees from political persecution or from political regimes with which they are unsympathetic, but by and large, these are relatively uncommon.

The immigrant intellectual who has come to the host country on his own initiative either as a student or after the completion of his studies—and also the exiled immigrant intellectual—differs from the uneducated immigrant in the very important respect that much of his culture is already the culture of the host country. Whereas the uneducated immigrant came to the host country primarily to find more remunerative employment and to join his kinsmen and fellow-villagers who preceded him, the immigrant intellectual is usually drawn by the desire to acquire or to be in the presence of some elements of the culture of the host society. The immigrant intellectual begins with some anticipation of being 'at home' in the host country. He comes with a 'place' in an institution which is in some respects very much like the higher educational institutions of his own country or even if he is not a student, he already possesses a certain amount of some particular part of the intellectual culture of the host country in which he hopes to participate.

It is in the nature of intellectual culture, especially in modern times, that it is shared beyond national boundaries. It is capable of movement across national boundaries and it is capable of being shared by individuals of diverse nationalities or ethnic provenience. This does not mean that all of the intellectual culture of any particular society is also equally possessed in any other society. Much of intellectual culture of any given society is local or parochial in its reference and idiom and only the intellectuals of other societies who specialise in its study or cultivation know about it. This is true of national history and a great deal of the corpus of novels and poems. Major literary and philosophical works are shared by a public which extends across national boundaries into many societies. Mathematics and the natural sciences are similarly shared. There is, of course, much asymmetry in the sharing of intellectual works. However, it is important to note that the societies which are the seats of production of the most known intellectual works are also the societies to which intellectual immigrants tend to come when they can come voluntarily and are not constrained by the threat of violence or by legal barriers to settlement.

This community of intellectual culture, partial and limited though it is, is one important condition of the immigration of intellectuals. The sustaining and derivative intellectual institutions of the host society, i.e. its universities and research institutions, its journals and its publishing enterprises, its intellectual, especially its literary, circles and the style of life associated with them are part of the image of the host society which draws the intellectual from abroad. It is not just the charisma attributed to a society in which great intellectual works have originated which draws intellectuals from other countries; it is also the prospect of a superior intellectual conviviality which might be enjoyed directly. The practical advantages of proximity to those institutions also exercises great attractive power. At the centre there are connections to be made with literary agents, editors and publishers; it is easier to arrange for the publication of one's works there. It is easier to find opportunities for gaining supplementary income through marginal or quasi-intellectual activities such as broadcasting, writing for popular magazines, book reviewing, etc. A student of an academic subject might be able to find employment as a tutor or as an assistant or even a permanent academic appointment.

The ordinary uneducated immigrant departs from his home society because he thinks he can find employment both regular and more remunerative in the host society or else he foresees safety from persecution. He foresees little else there: he expects no welcome; he has no sense of affinity with the host society—only with the fellow-countrymen and especially with his fellow-villagers and kinsmen who are already there. He might also in addition to the more practical anticipated advantages, be attracted by the vague prospect of a more lively, more excitingly enjoyable society. Occasionally, a political idealist driven into exile or a persecuted religious believer has ideas about the political freedom and the religious tolerance prevalent in the society in which he takes refuge but most ordinary uneducated immigrants know little of the society to which they go. They are voyaging into the unknown.

The intellectual immigrant is not voyaging into the unknown, at least he does not think that he is doing so. He is going to a society, the intellectual culture of which, at least some parts of it, have a place in his mind. He might know of certain famous works and authors of publishing houses and journals and of their more eminent editors, he might know of professors in his subject and of their universities. A good part of his education and his intellectual life in his own country was focussed on these through the school and college syllabuses and through the conversation of his like-minded contemporaries. This was true of Americans going to France in the period between the First and Second World Wars, or an American going to England at any time since the eighteenth century. It would have been true of a Russian going to Germany or France in the middle decades of the nineteenth century. It is still true.

There is a community of modern culture transcending national boundaries and having nothing to do with conquest or colonisation. The diffusion of modern mathematics or biology as subjects of school education and academic study has nothing to do with conquest or colonisation. The appreciation of Graham Greene or Jean-Paul Sartre or Saul Bellow in Poland and Yugoslavia is not a result of British, French or American colonial expansion in Eastern Europe or the Balkans, any more than was the popularity of James Dean in Tunisia or Turkey at the end of the 1950s. Intellectual culture spreads both through propagation and through being sought by those who want to receive it. It is not an imposition; it would fall flat and lifeless if it were nothing more than a set of books which had to be read in order to pass an examination for admission to the Civil Service. The immigrant intellectual was not an inert object before immigration; they were not simply shipped overseas by their elders.

The immigrant intellectual who is not transplanted by his parents while he is a child or who is not fleeing from persecution to any place which will take him in is attracted by the imagined prospect of a congenial, stimulating intellectual environment such as he believes to be lacking in his home society. He believes, rightly or wrongly, that the type of intellectual work and life to which he aspires is disregarded or even despised in his own country. In the envisaged host country, he imagines it, rightly or wrongly, to be highly and widely esteemed. In his imagination he sees himself fitting into that intellectual society without any trouble. He sometimes anticipates a freer, less familially bound personal life; he might think that he can enter more freely into sexual relationships.

The reality usually turns out to be rather different. Unless the intellectual immigrant is already eminent in his achievements he always has to endure prolonged obscurity. Like most aspirants to intellectual careers, he encounters the obstacles of indifference from the outside and the limits of his talents from the inside. He does not gain access to the circles in which, at home, he had hoped to have ready acceptance. Like other literary intellectuals at the beginning of their careers, he has difficulties in gaining a livelihood. Like the less educated immigrant he finds himself thrust back into the company of his fellow-countrymen because he already knows them or makes contact with them easily and because the native intellectuals show little interest in him. Within the bohemia of aspirant writers or in the circles of postgraduate students, he seeks out or gravitates towards those who have come from his own country, who share his sense of alienness, who have similar grievances and sometimes similar homesickness.

In some respects, the immigrant intellectual is like some of those intellectuals who have come from the lower classes within a society. There are of course major differences; the native intellectual of lower class origin has nonetheless some problems which resemble those of the immigrant intellectual. Both are in partially alien cultures, both admire certain parts of the host culture in which they seek acceptance and acknowledgement, both are apprehensive of showing 'the cloven hoof' of their origins which would reveal their unfitness for acceptance. Both occasionally yearn for what they recall as the intimacy, protectiveness and genuineness of the societies in which they had their origin which they contrast with the coldness and artificiality of the host culture. Both also are resentful about their exclusion; they are critical of the intellectual culture and its institutions which place them at a disadvantage. Both sometimes come to the point at which they reject *in toto*, or at least so they think, the intellectual culture which had previously prevailed.

The society to which the immigrant intellectual—the immigrant across class or national boundaries—emerges is something rather different from what he first thought it was. The particular features of the intellectual life which he imagined to be all-pervasively characteristic of the host society turn out to be very exceptional. The god has feet of clay; most of the host society is philistine, ugly, unintellectual, and that is a disappointment acutely felt. The intellectual institutions lose some of their imposingness as their limitations are perceived. Some immigrant intellectuals become more royalist than the king and they see nothing more perfect than the intellectual culture of the host country; others come to hate the intellectual culture and institutions to which they aspired. The hatred is not always found among the failures just as the affirmation is not always associated with success: but affirmation of the host culture among those who have sought to be in its presence has become less common now than it was sixty years ago. As long as British intellectual culture admitted very few persons from beyond the traditional middle-class limits and as long as its bearers regarded their intellectual culture and its institutions as self-evidently superior, it maintained its ascendancy. When both of these conditions changed, hostility became more acrid. British and French intellectuals now commonly derogate their own society and much of its established intellectual culture. In the United States, a similar phenomenon has been endemic for many years. The centre has been eroded by the realisation of widespread aspirations to gain admission to it. This is an encouragement to the immigrant intellectual to express his discomfiture by joining in the chorus of derogation.

The derogation of the intellectual centre is a poor remedy for the griefs of the immigrant intellectual. It is like scratching a wound; it brings momentary relief while aggravating the condition it would relieve.

In an intellectual culture which has a clear ascendancy, an immigrant intellectual who, like Henry James, was distinguished before his arrival, or who like T. S. Eliot and Joseph Conrad were able to establish themselves, confronted a fairly well-delineated standard to which he felt under obligation to conform. It was this which attracted them in the first place and although conformity was strenuous, it had its rewards.

The situation of the present-day immigrant intellectual coming from 'white-skinned' former colonies such as Australia, and North

America or from the 'coloured' former colonial territories in
Africa, Asia or the Caribbean, seems both easier and harder at the
same time. On the one hand, the attenuation of the once exigent
standard of the upper and upper middle-class intellectual culture
which prevailed from the latter part of the Victorian period to the
Second World War reduces the oppressiveness to which newcomers were subjected. Newcomers now have more freedom and
they also have available to them the pleasure of expressing their
revulsion against the host culture and society—but this gain is
also accompanied by a loss. Those who come to the centre out of
fascination by its power suffer disillusionment. They are in varying
ways and degrees left at loose ends.

Another reason for the hard lot of the immigrant intellectual is
that, more than ordinary uneducated persons and despite what is
sometimes said about them by their detractors, intellectuals are
idealistic and attached to their nationality of origin as well. To a
greater extent than uneducated persons who are more parochial
than national, intellectuals value their national society, however
much they derogate it and denounce it. Immigrant intellectuals,
except for those from the United States, do not like to say that
they immigrated because they did not wish to stay in their native
countries. (The American immigrant intellectuals are often
'second-time' immigrants; many come from immigrant families
and their attachment to American society, which had no compell-
ingly ascendant intellectual culture, was rather labile.) If they are
literary intellectuals or humanistic academic scholars, their subject
matter is very often some aspect of their native society and culture.
Novelists find it very difficult to write about the host society; it is
more feasible for them to write about their native society or about
some marginal zone where the native and the host societies overlap
with each other. It is a little easier for social scientists to lighten
their preoccupation with their native societies, especially if their
branch of social science is relatively formalised. If they are
scientists and their subject matter has no clearly visible connection
with their own society, still they acquire enough of the general
intellectual culture of their own society through their education
and their family life to be sensible to it. They are rendered more
aware of their native society by their sojourn in their host society.
Their identification with it is broadened and more sharply de-
lineated when they live in the contrasting host society.

They cannot shed their attachment to their original society.
They are made more aware of their primordial bond by what they
see as their exclusion from the intimate intellectual circles of the

THE IMMIGRANT INTELLECTUAL 211

host society and from their alienness in the larger society. They settle for the company of their own intellectual fellow countrymen or of other intellectual immigrants who have suffered similar exclusions and similar hardships in making their way as intellectuals. This is especially true of freelance or independent intellectuals since intellectuals who work in scientific or academic institutions are thrust into a framework of colleagueship or fellow-studentship with natives of the host country. Even then the immigrants tend to form their own convivial circles into which they take a few natives with particular interests in the immigrant society and culture of origin. There happier thoughts of home mingle with rueful reflections on the state of affairs in the host society. Only those who are most recognised in the host society become socially assimilated; the more transnational their subject matter, the greater the likelihood of cultural assimilation.

III

Now all these observations apply to intellectual immigrants in general. They apply to intellectuals who come from states with a long history of sovereignty and from countries of the same linguistic family, of a more or less common religious, literary and philosophical history as the country to which they came. They apply to Americans in Paris in the twentieth century. They apply to Russians and Poles in Western Europe and America in the nineteenth and twentieth centuries, to Americans and Canadians and Australians in Great Britain in the nineteenth and twentieth centuries, to Argentinians in Spain and Brazilians in Portugal in the nineteenth century. They might apply to persons from Gaul and North Africa and the Iberian Peninsula in Athens and Rome in the last centuries of the Roman republic and the first of the empire. They might apply to Byzantine scholars in Italy in the sixteenth century and to continental immigrants in England in the sixteenth and seventeenth centuries. The history of the immigration of intellectuals and the families from which intellectuals have come is varied and it has taken many forms. In consequence of the expansion of Europe into Asia and Africa and in consequence of the trade in black slaves with the Americas, it has acquired another variant in the past two centuries.

Whereas the expansions of states in antiquity was usually confined to areas of the world, the populations of which had the same pigmentation as the populations of the expanding societies, this changed with great age of European exploration and colonial conquest and with the world-wide expansion of European trade. Certain elements of European intellectual culture were transported and to some extent took root in these areas. Whereas the immigration of intellectuals, other than missionaries, had been to countries belonging to the same religious tradition, the modern intellectual immigration between populations of different pigmentation was also a movement between societies of deeply divergent religious traditions. The religion of the European intellectual immigrants was widely received only in a few parts of Africa and it can be said that by and large the effort to proselyte Asia and Africa to Christianity was not successful. The intellectual culture brought by missionaries, teachers and administrators struck deeper roots. European languages were acquired by the small but significant sector of the population of each area of Asia and Africa where Europeans ruled. In the Caribbean the African languages were practically forgotten and were replaced by the European languages. With the languages came some knowledge of European literature, some knowledge of the history of Europe and of the European age of the colonised country, some mathematics and science of a European sort. The small numbers of natives who entered the learned professions had of course to master the European or metropolitan language and to master the substance of the particular profession as well, whether it was medicine or law or engineering.

Such education as was provided was not intended to generate a flow of productive or creative intellectuals. Training for occupations requiring some European culture—often fairly elmentary— and for the practical-intellectual professions was the objective. Nonetheless as in Europe and America, this practically intended training inevitably secreted, as a by-product, an aspiration towards productive intellectual activity in the European medium and in European genres and fields.

This implantation of European culture occurred at the same time as a growth of a new sentiment of 'national' identity with an ill-defined positive reference but with a clear negative identification. The territorial foci tended to be those of the colonial administration, which were usually without deep indigenous precedence. The criteria of self-identification became colour and residence within the territorial boundaries set by colonial rule. The primary line of distinction was not between adjacent territories but between the indigenous ruled and the alien ruler whose different pigmentation became a very significant criterion of identifying the self and distinguishing it from the other, the enemy.

The intellectual in the colonial countries acquired a culture which he accepted unquestioningly or which he admired, while at the same time he was identifying himself by criteria which emphasised his difference from the bearers of that culture. It was moreover a difference with overtones of antagonism and defensiveness. The traditional indigenous culture which had been neglected in this modern education was transfigured as part of a new identification of the self. There was a latent tension between these two cultures but it did not always become actual. Immigration helped it to become actual. It was not by chance that the ideas of Negritude and of the need to extirpate colonial culture by purgative violence evinced this tension in most acute form. The ideas of Negritude were developed by immigrant African intellectuals in the Paris area. The ideas of Frantz Fanon were similarly the product of his years as an immigrant intellectual.

The attractions of the intellectual culture of the metropolitan centre are reinforced by the prestige of economic, political and military power of that society. This attraction still exists although the power has diminished. The culture of the centre has its own charismatic quality but the decline of power diminishes the force of the culture. Power which is weak, power which has abdicated or been defeated loses its capacity to command deference. The suppressed resentment against successfully ascendant power comes into the open when that power ceases to be ascendant. Some of that resentment turns against the intellectual culture which has been historically associated with that now diminished power. Nonetheless, African and Asian intellectuals continue to be attracted by the possibility of study, residence and employment at the former centres of empire.

The intellectual culture remains very attractive, and those who are enmeshed in it, however they resent it on the grounds of its association with a hated and once humiliating power, find it difficult to resist its attractions. Once they have acquired it and become committed to it by submitting to its fascination, the only way in which they can effectively cultivate it is by being at the metropolitan centre. There they hope to find the market for their productions, the company of like-minded intellectuals and acceptance—social and intellectual—by those for whose approval they seem to care. Even if they do not intend to remain, and even if they have very specific and limited professional interests, they acknowledge the deference which will accrue to them for having been at the centre. Being a 'been-to' or 'Europe-returned or England-returned' still has its attractions.

Only a small proportion of those who come stay; even a smaller proportion intend to stay. Of those who stay only a small number obtain academic appointments or are successful in having their writings published. For those who are successful, the stresses of being out of or neglecting their own country, in living in a society to which they feel alien, even though they admire it, of conducting their intellectual life in an idiom which, rightly or wrongly, they sometimes believe is not quite appropriate to them, are painful but bearable. For the less successful, there is no comparable compensation.

Colour aggravates every one of these stresses. Indian intellectuals were always to some extent 'colour-conscious'; they have become more so in recent years. It used to be that Indian intellectuals were at pains to discriminate themselves from black Africans. Now more of them are more willing to accept classification as 'black' or as otherwise falling into the same category as Africans. This recent increase in the prominence accorded to pigmentation has moved hand in hand with the intensification of the demands of American Negroes, and the campaign against the remains of white dominion in black Africa.

It is very difficult to avoid the definition of the self in terms of colour, the envisioning society does nothing to discourage it but as an obsession, it adds to grief. There are probably few immigrant intellectuals from Asia, Africa and the Caribbean to whom colour and their own origin mean very little. Similarly there are not many who are successful intellectually, and this is not to any significant extent because of their colour. The combination of colour and failure intensifies unhappiness: but failure is as common in intellectual life as it used to be in small industrial and commercial enterprises.

Intellectual production is a wasteful process. It is like medieval agriculture in which many seeds have to be sown in order for far fewer plants to be reaped. Birds, winds, animals, huntsmen and soldiers, either scattered or ate the seeds or trampled on the plants which grew from them. A great number of intellectual exertions on the part of a great number of intellectuals is necessary for a few significant works to be produced. This is true regardless of whether the intellectuals are autochthonous or immigrant; it is true whether they are of one pigmentation or another or of many different pigmentations in the same society. There is bound to be failure and wastage and the grief and disappointment which attend failure in any sector of life and in any society. In intellectual matters and in an epoch in which individual achievement and creativity are so highly prized, failure is distressing. The company of failures is demoralising. It is difficult to persist under conditions of discouragement. Makeshift jobs, surrogates for intellectual accomplishment, do not assuage the spirit. This must be added to the other burdens of being an immigrant intellectual.

IV

There is really no satisfactory solution to the problem of the immigrant intellectual, the intellectual career being as hazardous as it is, the immigrant intellectual possessing his multiplicity of difficultly poised attachments and the metropolitan society being itself hard-faced or at best uneasy in the presence of a markedly different pigmentation.

If the intellectuals of the once colonial countries were to remain at home they would have the pleasures—and the burdens—of being there. They would have their kinsmen and the social and physical scenery to which they are accustomed. If they were civil servants, they would have stable and well-remunerated employment in which authority is exercised and they would have the esteem which follows after these much desired things. If they were to pursue the academic profession in their own country they would probably be employed and would be relatively well-remunerated compared with most of their fellow-countrymen. If they are literary men writing in their own vernacular language, they would be able to use an idiom for which they feel affection and they would be close to a subject matter with which they would be at ease. If they were to write in the metropolitan language, they would still have their subject matter around them. They would also have the sense of not having deserted their own 'people' in the desolation of their troubles. They would not feel 'unfaithful' to their impoverished 'people'.

However, if they were to stay at home they would not be satisfied by these gratifications; they might not even notice them. Their kinsmen would press in upon them and demand more from them than they would wish to give; if they were literary men who write in the metropolitan language, which is the language of their former colonial ruler and the language in which they received their modern literary culture and the genres in which they write, their audience at home would be small and the publishing firms and reviews which might publish and review their work so few and feeble that they could do little to bring them before the audience of the larger world.

If they were academic scholars or scientists, they would feel cut off from the main centres of work in their fields. The numbers of colleagues with whom they would share interests at home would be too few to continue to be stimulating, particularly if they were contrasted with the imagined stimulus of being at the metropolitan centre. Those who work on subjects which require field work in the locality would be well placed but they too have learned to count on foreign visitors or trips overseas to stimulate them. They would often think themselves disregarded at home, their intellectual gifts and accomplishment passed over, their talents wasted in obscurity and they would think of the metropolis as a place where intellectual achievements are highly respected and given an appropriate prominence in the public mind. Some observers say that the conditions and achievements of scholarly and scientific work in Asian and African countries are improving and that there is less justification for an intellectually ambitious young person to spend so much time overseas. It is also possible that the slowing down of the expansion of the universities in the rich countries will reduce the 'brain drain'. Nonetheless, the attractions of life in a metropolitan country remain great and the pressure for emigration continues. There are at least 1,000 Indian academics teaching and doing research abroad, mainly in the United States and Great Britain and Canada—apart from those doing postgraduate studies and a substantial proportion of the main Caribbean and West African literary men are living out of their own countries.

It is not easy to accept this resolution of the problem. Complete assimilation into the host society is probably not attainable even in as absorbent a country as France. In Great Britain and the United States, the complete social assimilation of Asians is not likely; for black African and Caribbean intellectuals it is even less likely in this time of stress. Professional assimilation is more of a possibility, especially in the academic world. Yet in Great Britain, even white intellectual immigrants are not so assimilable. At the same time sensitivity about barriers to assimilation has increased. The willingness of whites in the wider public and in intellectual circles to accept coloured persons has increased too, but it has not kept pace with the rising standards of what is acceptable in the circles of coloured immigrant intellectuals.

This discrepancy is somehow connected with the increased 'politicisation' of immigrant intellectuals. Whereas in the past, they tended to hold themselves aloof from the host society, expecting little or nothing from it, they have now begun to participate, at least in opinion, in the political life of the host society. They

THE IMMIGRANT INTELLECTUAL 217

had expected nothing from the host society except sympathy for the cause of 'colonial liberation'. Now, being somewhat more partisan, more enmeshed in what they think is a 'world-wide struggle of the third world' for its own emancipation, more courted by white radical groups and more infused with the traditional doctrines of white revolutionism and anti-imperialism, they are less inclined than ever to accept the ascendancy of the culture of the host society into which they have immigrated.

Many of the intellectuals of the formerly colonial countries are unhappy about the political and economic life of their own countries. Most of them are in one way or another progressivists and they think that their countrymen have not been enabled to make the desired degree of progress; for this they blame the political leaders of their countries. Sometimes, they fall out with their political leaders and think it safer to live abroad; the metropolitan centres offer them refuge. Discontent with the political leaders of their countries is often coupled with the belief that the misfortunes of their country are a result not only of the experience of having been colonised but also of a newer type of misfortune called 'neo-colonialism'. The metropolitan powers are held responsible for this, with the indigenous political elite being either dupes or collaborators with this 'neo-colonialist' policy. This view of the political universe is by no means entirely shared by all coloured immigrant intellectuals, but in a vague way it is seeping into the outlook of many who are generally rather sober and matter-of-fact. The ideas of 'neo-colonialism' which some immigrant intellectuals from Asian and African countries accept can only add to their distress. The patriotism of the immigrants was already affronted by the defection which is entailed in their more or less deliberate decision to settle in the metropolis. Their attachment to their native society is already in conflict with their desire to become established in the metropolitan society which goes on despite rebuffs, wounds and failures. The 'neo-colonialist' view of things appeals to them because it explains the difficulties of their countries; it censures the host society against which they have many reasons to be resentful and it provides an interpretation on a cosmic scale of their own misfortunes. But despite its attractiveness, it resolves no problems.

V

There might well be no definitive resolution of the problems faced by the coloured immigrant intellectual in predominantly white host societies. To pursue the path of intellectual achievement offers alleviation but no resolution as long as the members of the host society do not regard intellectual achievement as the sole criterion of assessment. It is this which produces the experience of unending alienness.

The intermittent meeting with disparagement called forth by no more than the perception of their colour seems to be an almost universal experience among the immigrant intellectuals who have settled in Great Britain. It is not absent in France. It is certainly not absent in the United States, although Africans and Asians seem to be treated more considerately in non-intellectual circles than American Negroes; in academic or intellectual circles there is sometimes 'reverse-discrimination' which can be almost equally objectionable.

The fact that so many immigrant intellectuals are in universities or otherwise engaged in intellectual occupations reduces somewhat the chances of affront but it does not eliminate them. Although academics and other intellectuals are probably less inclined toward aversion against their fellow human beings on grounds of colour, they too are not entirely free, and coloured immigrant intellectuals sometimes come up against this. Life moreover even for an un-married fellow of an Oxford college cannot be lived entirely without contact with the outer society; for those who live in large towns, who travel on public transport and who shop in ordinary retail shops, there are many occasions for affronts. Nor is it entirely a matter of affront. Marriage and the raising of children in the host society raise serious problems of the attenuation of one's ancestral culture and even of its loss—and this quite apart from the position of being a 'coloured' person in a 'white' society.

The entire experience is nerve racking for those who take such matters to heart or who allow themselves to be 'thin-skinned'. Human beings have not learned to live at ease with whatever is most central to their existence. Sexual and familial relations are recurrent sources of torment. Where religion is taken seriously that too disturbs the spirit, turns men against each other and them-selves. Nationality and ethnicity which seem to be more trivial and more peripheral to what is essential in human life show, by the tenacious and consuming passions to which they give rise, that they are not peripheral. Colour seems to be an especially trivial ground for action towards a fellow human being or oneself. Yet colour has been taken with the utmost seriousness. It is indeed serious, if it seems to be connected with some qualities of existence which human beings regard as belonging to the very centre of their existence on earth.

If ordinary men and women cannot overcome their tendency to attribute importance to it, it might seem excessive to urge intellectuals to do so. On the whole they have not been very good at transcending the passions of ordinary men and women. Yet their commitment is to the production and appreciation of the truths of science and scholarship, the beauties of language and the riches of imagination. In none of these does pigmentation have a moral standing. It behoves intellectuals—white, black, brown, yellow, grey, pink or of whatever the tint of human skin takes on—to disregard it and to adhere steadfastly to their calling. I know that this is calling on human beings to overcome a propensity which is deep in their minds, that it is urging the victims to be indifferent to injury and the others to renounce the pleasure of inflicting injury. It might be against the grain but it is not contrary to the striving for truth, and the creation of beautiful objects in word and form. That striving requires concentration and discipline of the mind. It requires entry into a community in which other considerations are secondary, so at least in a small part of life, the significance of colour as a criterion for the assessment of human beings might be annulled or set aside.

NOTES

1. The immigrant intellectuals who fled from National Socialism are well studied in Bailyn, Bernard and Fleming, Donald (Eds), *The Intellectual Migration—Europe and America, 1930–1960*, Harvard University Press, 1969. No comparable studies have been made on the Russian intellectual emigration which followed the Russian Revolution of 1917.

2. Mr Krishan Kumar is one of the few of this type up to the present. The number is bound to increase.

15 Postscript

BHIKHU PAREKH[1]

As the controversy concerning the number of immigrants to be allowed in Britain is coming to an end, the far more important question as to how she is to deal with those already settled here is at last beginning to receive serious attention. Since the debate has not yet developed a firm vocabulary and a settled body of assumptions, it would be fruitful to analyse, in the light of the foregoing chapters, the direction it is beginning to take and the dangers lying therein.

I

Let me begin by registering a protest against the language used to describe the immigrant community. It is amazing how often the term race is used to describe the situation in Britain. Britain is said to be a 'multi-racial society'; she enacted a 'race' relations act, setting up a 'race' relations board; and her social ideal is to achieve 'racial' harmony. Now there are several grounds on which the term race is objectionable. First, on any racial typology, Indians and Pakistanis belong to the *same* race of Caucasoids as do the British and therefore there is simply no question of race relations so far as they are concerned. As for West Indians there has been much 'racial' intermingling between them and the British. The free sexual relations of the British settlers in the West Indies with their black slave women have meant that nearly one-fifth of Jamaicans and Barbadians have some white blood in them.[2] The reverse process, although not always mentioned, has also occurred. Over ten thousand negro slaves in London, after their emancipation, intermarried with the white community and became biologically assimilated. One wonders how much negro blood courses in British veins.

Apart from its empirical inaccuracy in the British context, the term race is, as is generally recognised, highly misleading. It is basically a biological concept and probably has some taxonomic value for the biologist although, in view of so much racial intermixing over centuries, even this is doubtful. When used in politics the term is particularly obnoxious. To a layman ill-versed in scientific controversy, it suggests that each racial group is a distinct and unique biological unit, the patterns of behaviour and thought of whose members are determined by their genes. As acknowledged by most biologists, however, the fact is that the genes men share in common are overwhelmingly greater than those that make them physically distinct,[3] and that human behaviour is capable of considerable adaptation. The term race suggests further that racial mixing and mating are undesirable, and there is no evidence for this whatsoever. What is more, given the past history of European States, the term evokes powerful emotions and images and renders dispassionate discussion of relevant issues difficult.

Like the language of race, the language of colour too is inappropriate and misleading. The non-white population is universally referred to as 'coloured'. The basic objection to this term is that every man is coloured, white being a colour just as much as black or brown.[4] To confine the term coloured to non-whites is to suggest that white is in some sense so different a colour as not to be a colour at all. Why the whites are not called coloured is difficult to say. Perhaps an unconscious racism is at work here. To accept white as a colour is to acknowledge the white man's shared humanity and equality with men of other colours, and, since throughout their long encounter with non-whites the whites have treated them as animals or as children, they perhaps cannot bring themselves to accept that they belong to the same species as the 'coloured'. Whatever the explanation it is obvious that to call a man 'coloured' is to suggest that he is reducible to his colour, that his colour is the only significant thing about him, that colour, like leprosy, is a disease which the poor man suffers from and from which the white man is miraculously exempt.[5]

Sometimes the so-called coloured people are referred to as 'immigrants'. This term is less offensive than the other two, but it too is misleading. British history is a history of successive waves of immigrants. It is not therefore clear why only the members of the 'coloured' community should be called immigrants. It might be rejoined that they are so called because they are recent arrivals— but then so are many whites. In fact, since 1945, two out of three immigrants in Britain have been white, and yet, as is well known, in newspaper headlines and government records the reference to immigrants invariably means a reference to the 'coloured' immigrants. What is more it is not true that the 'coloured' people are recent arrivals. Although a very large number of 'coloured' people have arrived in Britain in recent years, a fairly large number have been resident here intermittently for over 400 years. The

H

Gentleman's Magazine in 1764 put their number at about 20,000 in London alone.[6] Since the population of London then was probably 650,000, the 'coloured' people amounted to nearly 3 % of the total population. Already in 1788, Philip Thicknesse, a former army officer in Jamaica, was saying that 'London abounds with an incredible number of these black men, who have clubs to support those who are out of place . . .' and who are to be seen 'in every country town, nay in almost every village'.[7] When many West Indians, initially brought to Britain as slaves or servants, were emancipated, they got absorbed into British society and have lived here ever since. Indians started coming to Britain at the turn of the century, and quite a few of them have been resident here since the First World War. It is also odd that the children of recent immigrants should be referred to by that strange and self-contradictory expression, 'second-generation *immigrants*'. Since they are born and raised in Britain, by no stretch of imagination can they be called immigrants.

Sometimes immigrants are referred to as 'guests' and the local community as their 'hosts'. Although those using these terms are well-meaning men, clearly they have not thought the matter out carefully. To call a man a guest is to suggest that he is temporary and will not only leave one day but can also be 'persuaded' to leave if he overstays his welcome. In other words, to refer to immigrants as guests is to place them under a moral obligation to leave and, by implication, to confer on their hosts a moral right to throw them out should they fail to do so in time. Men who have no intention of leaving the national 'household' and who wish to become members of the national 'family' can hardly be called guests. Further, the language of guest and host not only imposes obligations on each party that it does not wish to accept, but also forces them into an artificial relationship which is difficult to keep up for long and which prevents the emergence of a natural and healthy relationship. As long as immigrants regard themselves as guests, they continue to expect their hosts to take the initiative and do not explore the ways in which they can adjust to the wider society. Also, as long as the wider community looks upon, or is made to look upon, itself as a host, it is constrained, even blackmailed, to feel concerned about men who do not really mean anything to them. The language of 'guest' and 'host' is obnoxious for another reason as well. Immigrants were encouraged or allowed to come to Britain to do the menial and dirty jobs which the natives shunned. Most of them eke out their livelihood by working as sweepers, cleaners, cooks and factory workers, and live in pretty miserable conditions. To call those men guests who live by serving their masters, who cook for, serve and wash their masters' dishes, who live in what are sometimes no better than servants' quarters, and who are sometimes treated with undisguised contempt, is a perverse and inhuman joke.

The point of this terminological exercise was to show that the apparently innocent and even well-meaning terms contain an ideological bias and can appear highly offensive to those they are meant to describe. It might be of some interest that when their opinion was canvassed on the possible title of this volume, all the contributors consulted objected to the term coloured, a few were sympathetic to the term black, and a much larger number to the term immigrant, although they all felt that even this last was discriminatory and 'racialist'. In this chapter we shall use the term immigrant and reject the rest.

II

There are basically three views concerning how Britain should deal with the immigrants settled in her midst. Some argue that Britain cannot and should not accept them and urge their repatriation. Others consider this undesirable and would like to see them fully integrated into British society, but differ as to what integration precisely means and involves. Some think that it implies assimilation, understood in its strict sense of obliterating the cultural identity of the immigrant and requiring him to adopt British values and practices, while others take integration to involve the creation of a plural society in which the immigrant is free to retain his cultural individuality consistent with the general demands of law and order. Let us briefly examine the logic of the repatriationist, the assimilationist and the pluralist argument.

In June 1969 Enoch Powell described repatriation as a matter of 'extreme urgency and importance', and even proposed a separate ministry to deal with the 'problem'. He estimated that about 600,000 to 700,000 people would be involved, costing the country around £300 million, 'only the cost of eighteen months' aid to underdeveloped countries at the present rate'.[8] The idea of repatriation is clearly so bizarre that one might be inclined to dismiss it out of hand; but when one remembers that Britain has tried it in the past with success, one sees how essential it is to take it seriously and refute it in detail. The first proposal for repatriation was made as early as 11 August, 1596 when, according to the *Acts of the Privy Council*, 'Her Magestie understanding that there are of late divers blackmoores into this realme, of which kinde of people there are allready too manie, considering how God hath blessed this land with great increase of people of our owne nation . . . those kinde of people should be sent forth of the lande'. The Queen appointed Casper Van Zenden to transport them out of England. Again, when Lord Mansfield's famous judgement inspired a few liberal masters to free their slaves, many of the latter found it difficult to obtain work and lived a wretched life. Unwilling to do anything, the government repatriated around 500 of them to Sierra Leone in 1786, and many more to the West Indies. Again many Africans and Asiatics brought to Britain to assist the war effort in 1914 were sent back at the end of the war. Mr Powell is not a new phenomenon in British history.

It is difficult to see why repatriation is considered necessary. It is totally irrelevant whether people are compelled or merely encouraged to return, since the basic question is whether repatriation is an acceptable policy in principle.[9] Mr Powell and his followers are rather muddled and seem to want to repatriate the immigrant community on one of the four following dubious grounds.

First, they sometimes argue that immigrants are a burden on the country's resources and lower its standard of living. This argument has been knocked down so conclusively by so many so often that only an ignorant person would want to repeat it. All available statistics show that immigrants put in far more than they take from the nation's resources, that they generally take up only the jobs the whites are unwilling to take, and that but for them many vital areas of the nation's economic life would grind to a halt.[10]

Second, it is sometimes argued that immigrants are *incapable* of being integrated into British society and that their continued presence is a threat to her way of life.[11] This argument, again, is clearly false. A large number of Indians and West Indians have adopted and cherish British culture. Indeed the latter have no other culture but British. It is also difficult to see in what sense the coloured minority presents a threat to the British way of life. A way of life is a complex of, among other things, language, social traditions and conventions, and cultural artifacts. As John Plamenatz points out,[12] the immigrant is a threat to none of these. Indeed, the threat to the British way of life comes precisely from those who, in advocating repatriation and in assassinating a minority's character, flout the values of tolerance and mutual respect which are an integral part of it.

No doubt the presence of the immigrant does call for some degree of adjustment on the part of the wider community. The nation might have to exempt Sikhs from wearing helmets; political parties might have to issue their election literature in Urdu or Bengali or Gujarati; and the white community will have to get accustomed to seeing some women dressed differently and some sections of the community speaking different tongues and celebrating their distinctive religious festivals. In other words, the presence of the immigrant does require some degree of pluralisation of the British way of life.[13] It is difficult, however, to see why this should be considered a threat or should arouse any anxiety. Liberal society has always cherished diversity and welcomed every attempt to loosen its monolithic cultural unity. In any case British way of life is no longer as homogeneous as it used to be, and was never as homogeneous as its erstwhile champions would like us to believe.[14] As a matter of historical fact the so-called British way of life has always been a federation of three distinct ways of life—the Welsh, the English, and the Scottish—held together by an agreed body of political conventions. The English have, no doubt, generally enjoyed considerable cultural hegemony, but this has never prevented the Scots and the Welsh from cherishing their distinctive cultural heritages. In recent years, their cultural consciousness has become even more articulate and has generated demands for greater autonomy. Even in England there is an increasingly greater diversity of manners, dress, food and life styles than a few decades ago. People, mercifully, feel less nervous and self-conscious about their provincial origins, accents and manners. If one interpreted such pluralisation as a threat, the coloured minority is certainly a threat, but then so are the Welsh and the Scots, and to a lesser extent, the Jews, the Poles, and the Irish, who have all refused to surrender their identity. Indeed the 'threat' is likely to increase, now that Britain has cast her lot with Europe. Anyone determined to arrest the pluralisation of the British way of life will therefore have not only to oppose British entry into the Common Market but also to cleanse British culture of *all* alien elements. Those familiar with recent European history well know where this is likely to lead and how foredoomed and futile such an enterprise is.

The third ground on which repatriation is advocated is much less respectable and consists in saying no more than that the white majority finds immigrants 'strangers' and simply does not like their presence. If the argument were carried to its logical conclusion, we would be justified in asking the removal of everyone who appears a stranger. A number of Englishmen dislike Jews and find them strange, and so they will have to go. A number of them find the working class objectionable, and so they too will have to be removed to some remote island. Mr Powell talks of 'sharp differences, recognisable differences',[15] but does not condescend to clarify if he would extend the reference to 'recognisable' differences to the Jews as well and even perhaps to the Scots and the Continentals whose accents are unmistakable. It is also worth noting that the logic of the Powellite argument requires an international exchange of population, since there is no reason why Indians, Malays and Nigerians should not find the British in their midst recognisably different.

Finally, repatriation is sometimes advocated on the ground that the presence of the coloured minority constitutes a potentially explosive situation. This is a strange argument. Repatriating the immigrant is likely to create as explosive a situation as the one that is feared, and with far greater certainty. Therefore the advocates of repatriation are really asking us to prefer a greater and far more certain evil to a lesser one! Besides, it is not the simple presence of the black[16] minority but the white majority's attitude to it that is likely to drive the latter into desperate acts of violence. The answer to this problem is to create greater understanding between the two communities. Further, the talk of an explosive situation is likely to be self-fulfilling. As anyone with any knowledge of the mood of the immigrant community knows, Mr Powell has unwillingly expedited the emergence of a black power movement in the country and has even led some of them to ask seriously if they should not start arming themselves against potential trouble from their white neighbours. The warning against an explosive situation strikes an odd note, coming from the lips of those who are themselves effectively contributing to it.

The proposed policy of repatriation should not only be rejected because its advocates have failed to make out a case for it; it is objectionable on several other grounds as well. Repatriation means sending a man back to his own country and therefore cannot make any sense with respect to those so-called second generation immigrants for whom Britain is their fatherland. This also means that even after large-scale repatriation several thousand 'dark strangers' are bound to remain and therefore its basic objective of keeping Britain white is not going to be served. Repatriation, further, is bound seriously to harm Britain's national interest. The countries affected will want not only to expel Britons settled in their midst but also to nationalise British investment and divert their trade to other European countries, a situation a predominantly trading nation can hardly contemplate with equanimity.

Repatriation then is impracticable, morally unacceptable, and politically inexpedient. Since the immigrant is therefore here to stay until as far as one can foresee, the only proper way to treat him is to accept him as an equal, entitled to the same rights and opportunities as the native, and neither as a stranger against whom one can legitimately discriminate, nor as a guest to whom one accords the privileged treatment due from a host. Instead of regarding him as an outsider operating on the periphery of society, to be treated with condescension and patronising humanity at best and with muted contempt at worst, we should incorporate, integrate, him into the wider community and treat him on equal terms with the native in all areas of life, whether economic, social, political or cultural. Common sense, morality and national interest point to full equality and integration as the only sensible policy.

The question, however, is as to what precisely integration involves. As we remarked earlier integration is defined in academic and political debate in either assimilationist or pluralist terms. The assimilationist view which makes the integration of the immigrant contingent on his surrender of his cultural identity is objectionable on a number of grounds. Historically speaking it is not true that a minority has been integrated into British society only when it has surrendered its cultural identity. The Jews, for example, have been more or less fully integrated, and yet they have rightly resisted assimilation. As a survey showed not very long ago, over 70% of them strongly object to marriage outside the fold, nearly as large a percentage of them bring up their children on strict religious lines, and only 19% of them belong to non-Jewish organisations or clubs.[17] This is also true in varying degrees of other immigrant groups like the Irish and the Poles whose retention of their cultural identity has not prevented them from enjoying full membership of British society.

The assimilationist view must be rejected on other grounds as well. In denying the minority the right to its culture, it reduces it to the status of second-class citizens and this is unacceptable for obvious reasons. In the ultimate analysis the assimilationist argument rests on the same assumption as the segregationist: both alike are intolerant of differences and consequently assign the minority a subordinate position. Besides, if systematically carried out, the process of assimilation involves an unacceptable degree of interference with individual liberty. For example, it requires turning schools into centres of ideological indoctrination and producing ideologically pure textbooks; and this is not only undesirable in principle but, what is more to the point, it must surely be unacceptable to assimilationists themselves who, being generally conservatives, are chary of investing the government with more power than absolutely necessary. The most well-known and futile attempt to assimilate minorities was made by the Americans between 1910 and 1920. This '100% Americanisation of the immigrant' programme involved, among other things, lessons in civics and the American way of life, suppression of minority languages, elimination of minority language press, and aggressive hostility to minority cultural associations. Predictably it provoked such strong resentment that it had to be ended, leading subsequently to the flowering of immigrant culture.[18] Further, it is not clear into what the minority is to be assimilated. One can be assimilated only into what is capable of coherent and clear formulation. Unlike America, Britain does not have an overarching ideology of national culture. Her way of life essentially depends upon unspoken understanding and unarticulated habits of behaviour, and these are incapable of clear definition. In forcing the British into an unfamiliar, even 'alien', habit of self-conscious rationalism, the assimilationist exercise is likely to do far more harm to the British than to the minority. It is also worth remarking that no assimilationist has so far faced the full implications of his position. If the minority is to be fully assimilated, it should be encouraged to intermarry with the white majority. After all, culture is assimilated far more effectively in the family than in schools and places of work, and therefore a 'coloured' child is likely to be fully assimilated if either of his parents were white. But then the assimilationists, most of whom are little-Englanders and strong advocates of British racial purity, balk at such a thought, and cannot persuade themselves to accept the most effective means to their cherished goal!

In rejecting assimilation and emphasising the value of cultural diversity, we need to be careful not to swing to the opposite extreme of full-blooded pluralism which has found strong support both in immigrant circles and among some white liberals. It is contended that the immigrant community should be free to live as it pleases, and that the general community has no business sitting in judgement on its beliefs and practices, as long as these do not harm anyone. It is therefore argued that the general community should do no more than lay down a framework of law and order within which each ethnic minority is to remain fully autonomous. Full-blooded pluralism, although a commendable liberal doctrine, can easily have reactionary consequences, especially when it protects a minority from outside criticism and arrests its growth. This is what has happened, e.g. in India where successive governments, apprehensive of provoking Muslim opposition, have not dared to interfere with even those Muslim practices that are almost universally recognised to be evil. If this kind of pluralism was insisted upon in the British context, we would have to say that Muslims settled here should have a right to polygamy, to summary divorce, and to refuse to pay for their divorced wives' maintenance. We would also have to admit that orthodox Hindu and Muslim parents should be free not to send their girls to schools, or to stop sending them when they are in their teens, or to send them in veils, or not to let them take part in mixed or any kind of sports. To most of us, immigrants as well as natives, this should be unacceptable.

Now this, of course, raises an extremely difficult question as to the areas of life in which uniformity should be insisted upon, and those in which diversity should be tolerated and even encouraged. But unless the problem is faced we are in danger, as recent events have shown, either of enforcing uniformity where it is totally unnecessary (e.g. asking Sikh bus conductors or motor cyclists to discard their turbans) or of tolerating unacceptable diversity (e.g. tolerating the continued absence of Hindu girls from schools). It would not do merely to say that uniformity should be required only in those areas where individual actions are likely to harm others' interests, since interest is an extremely loose notion, and is likely to be defined differently by the various cultural communities involved. Whose interest, for example, is affected if a Hindu father refuses to send his daughter to a school? His refusal does not seem to hurt anyone in any obvious way; and at any rate *in his view*, his action is intended to protect his and his daughter's interests by, for example, preventing premarital emotional and sexual involvement.

As we cannot pursue this difficult question here at any length, a few general remarks should suffice. British society, like any other society, has a certain definite conception of the good life to which its members subscribe and which influences the way they live. Although its members hold and endeavour to live up to different personal ideals, there are certain basic values to which they all adhere, and which form the basis of their decisions concerning what personal ideals they can legitimately hold. If someone held that it was his ideal to have a harem, or to starve himself to death, or to sell himself as a slave, or to drug himself into a state of torpor, nearly all Britons would consider it a bad ideal, indeed, not an ideal at all; and this is so because they believe that there are certain basic values to which each of them should subscribe. His ideals may go beyond but cannot fall below them. In other words these values act as regulative principles of ideals, and define the limits of pluralism. British society is therefore entitled to insist that every one of its members, immigrant as well as native, must conform to what it regards as its basic, minimal, values. What these values are and how they can be elicited are difficult philosophical questions which we cannot pursue here, but we will all agree that monogamy, legal and moral equality of all men, equality of sexes, and basic civil liberties are some of them. It has taken Britain centuries of struggle to secure these values a firm institutional basis, and she is morally entitled to insist that nothing should be done to weaken her adherence to them. No immigrant practice in conflict with any of these values can therefore be tolerated; and conversely, any practice that does not so conflict should be left free. If immigrants, like the aborigines of Australia, had their own separate area to which they wished to remain confined, the argument will not have the same force. But they are, rightly, concerned to play their full part in British society, which therefore can legitimately ask that they should accept those values that it regards as constitutive of its conception of the good life, indeed, of its moral and political identity.

Modified pluralism, that is, pluralistic integration within the framework of a generally accepted conception of the good life, should be the ideal governing Britain's relations with her immigrant population. In the ultimate analysis pluralistic integration entails that the Briton's perception of his identity should be revised. If Britain is defined as a white society, and a Briton as a white man whose mother tongue is English and whose kith and kin are settled in Australia, New Zealand, Canada, South Africa and Rhodesia, the non-white minority, and for that matter even the Continentals, and Americans settled here, are bound to feel, and are bound to be regarded by the rest, ultimately, as outsiders, as at best only partial members of the national 'family'; clearly persons who do not speak the same tongue, nor share the same physical features, and do not have the same relatives cannot be said to belong to the same family. The national family therefore needs to be redefined to accord with social reality. Only when it is acknowledged as a matter of course that a Briton is not by definition white but could be black, brown or yellow, that he might speak Swahili, Mandarin or Hindustani as his first and English as his second language, and that his 'kith and kin' might be found in Bombay, Barbados and Ibadan as well as in Salisbury and Wellington, can the non-white minority feel as authentically British as the native, and can be so accepted by the latter. Naturally the radical revision of its self-image is painful to any community, especially to one so homogeneous and insular as England, but there is no alternative if the ideal of pluralistic integration is taken seriously.

III

Integration of a group of people is always a difficult process; pluralistic integration is even more difficult. Schematically speaking, pluralistic integration, by which I mean acceptance of the immigrant as a full member equally entitled to the liberties and privileges enjoyed by the rest of the community, requires three things. First, he should enjoy full equality in legal, social, economic and political matters—in what one might call the material side of life. Second, his distinctive cultural identity should be respected and provision should be made to meet its basic demands. Third, nothing should be done to denigrate his humanity or to undermine his self-respect or to make him feel that he is less than a full human being living on the community's sufferance. The process of integration can therefore run into difficulties at each of the three levels.

The PEP and other surveys have conclusively established that the immigrant is subjected to discrimination in several vital areas of social life. This must surely be a matter of concern to anyone who aims at his integration into the wider community. As long as a fully qualified immigrant is denied a job or promotion, as long as workers refuse to take orders from him, local councils refuse to allocate him houses or allocate only those due for demolition, as long as building societies refuse him mortgage or charge him an illegal fee, he can hardly be said to be integrated into the community. These and other areas of discrimination[19] have rightly aroused a good deal of concern. It is the more intricate and elusive obstacles to integration, especially those presented by a misplaced assimilationist zeal and ugly racism, that have gone relatively unnoticed and deserve to be stressed.

The immigrant's background, habits, aspirations, emotional constitution, and the structure of his family are different from those of a Briton, and these create problems[20] for the immigrant child that require sensitive and skilful handling. As several recent cases have shown, educational institutions can easily make the mistake of applying culturally biased intelligence, aptitude, general knowledge and other tests[21] to immigrant children and classify them as subnormal, or stream and grade them wrongly, or fail to identify their real needs and problems. It is alarming that while nearly 54% of the immigrant children in ordinary schools are West Indian, nearly 75% of the children in schools for Educationally Subnormal Children (ESN Schools) are West Indians. Children in ESN schools are supposed to have an IQ of between 50 and 80 and rarely learn anything more than discipline and the 'three Rs', deemed necessary to prepare them for repetitive and simple manual jobs. Since many of the children in these schools never return to the normal schools, these schools are in effect meant to educate docile, socially adapted and cheap, mainly black, future servants. Even in the ordinary schools, teachers sometimes show hostility to black children and discourage them from undertaking difficult mental work in the false, although sometimes sincerely held, belief that the 'poor chaps' will have a nervous breakdown if stretched.[22] The children either internalise the image and *become* retarded, or revolt and get slapped down.[23]

It is not generally recognised how much of what is taught appears biased and offensive to an immigrant child. Nursery rhymes and children's stories, Dr Dolittle stories, for example (in which Prince Bumpo cries over his blackness and promises to give Dr Dolittle half of his kingdom and 'anything besides you ask' if only he will turn him white)—which represent black colour and black man as evil and undesirable, and always give the black man a good and 'deserved' beating, could be profoundly upsetting to a young child.[24] History lessons and textbooks dealing with British colonial history often depict 'natives', interpret general British policy and specific events (like, e.g. the Boxer Rebellion or the Black Hole of Calcutta), and describe other societies before the arrival and after the departure of the British in a way that could hurt black children deeply. When a history master, who had explained the partition of India in terms of the inability of the Hindus and Muslims to get along with one another, was asked by a curious Indian boy if in his view the British had in any way exacerbated the situation, he got angry and asked the boy to keep his 'politics' out of history. A West Indian history teacher once remarked that his white pupils complained to the headmaster and threatened to boycott his classes for presenting the British treatment of slaves in a bad light.[25]

Beyond the material and cultural problems lie yet others which are much less tangible but often much more disturbing. The immigrant cannot ask to be loved, but he can justifiably demand that his dignity as a human being should be respected, and that no attempt should be made to bring him into contempt or to lower his self-esteem. And yet the climate of opinion around him conspires to do precisely the opposite. He is constantly hounded, denigrated, depicted as a villain responsible for the nation's malaise, and burdened with a sense of guilt for disasters with which he has nothing to do. He is told that he is an intruder in another man's house, that he is a thief stealing the nation's wealth and sometimes women, that he is a parasite upon the nation's social and welfare services, that he spreads disease and insanitation and poses a mortal threat to the nation's life and well-being. Indeed his breeding habits are made a subject of careful statistical analysis, and the 'smell' of his food and the way he sleeps and relaxes are considered subjects worthy of national attention. It is almost as if the nation refused to accept him as a full human being, entitled to respect and dignity and to the ordinary civilities of a cultured society.

In countless ways the immigrant is treated as subhuman and is made to feel unwanted. Not very long ago, the dockers protesting outside Parliament shouted, 'Blacks are monkeys to be trampled upon'.[26] The inhumanity shown to the British passport-holding Kenyan Asians, and the fact that they were shunted back and forth or detained for weeks as if they were chattels, without any effective public protest, is a further evidence of racism.[27] The relatively humane treatment accorded to Ugandan Asians only reinforces the point. These people who were legally entitled to enter Britain were not admitted in their own right; they had to be classified as 'refugees', and turned into objects of pity before the nation could be persuaded to exercise Christian 'charity' towards them. The airlift of Asian families was described as 'mercy flight', and Britain was presented as a neutral third party providing shelter to the brown victims of a Black Hitler, thus carrying the white man's burden all over again. It is remarkable how the example of Hitler's slaughter of Jews was constantly invoked to explain and interpret the condition of the Ugandan Asians. General Amin was depicted as a Hitler; his motive, like Hitler's, was said to be one of preserving African racial purity; and Asians were seen almost as brown Jews, innocent victims of mad black fury. It was almost as if the nation was living the Second World War all over again and atoning for its tragic dereliction over the plight of the Jews. The retrospective application of the Race Relations Act of 1971 and the recent government directive that immigrants could be asked to produce their passports to obtain national insurance cards, are further steps in the racist direction. Without such a card a man cannot work, and thus his passport has to be produced for obtaining a job. Some local authorities are requiring that immigrants should produce passports before their children are admitted to school.[28] There are also cases of immigrants being stopped in streets and asked to show their passport. This is almost to introduce the notorious pass laws.

Racism[29] is not confined to the public realm; it appears in countless small ways as well. A white couple with many children is said to have a large family, whereas a similarly situated black couple is said to breed like rabbits. White immigrants to Britain, who have always outnumbered black immigrants, are said to come in 'large number', while the blacks come in 'hordes' or 'waves'. Middle classes living together constitute a suburb, miners a community, and the immigrants a ghetto. Racism appears in the way the immigrant is cheated by, say, a shop assistant as if honesty in her view was not to be practised with respect to him; it appears in the way promises given to him are broken as if a promise given to a black man is not binding; it appears in the way he is gratuitously insulted as if his feelings deserved no consideration; it is expressed in his social ostracism, in the way his favours are taken for granted and those by the white man to him considered to require more than equal in return, in the way his social graces and intellectual skills are treated as unusual in 'someone like him', in the perverse glee taken in not being able to spell or pronounce an immigrant's name correctly, in petty abuses over the fence, in refusing to take him seriously on any question, in accusing him of having a chip on his shoulder when he refuses to be patronised, in expecting him always to be smiling and polite in apparent gratefulness for the privilege of being allowed to appear in the white man's presence, etc., etc. A West Indian sociologist listed over a hundred subtle and not so subtle ways in which he was 'put in his place' within the short span of a week. Not that he was prickly or oversensitive, or was looking for racism where it did not exist; he was simply recording its manifestations which, although subtle, were unmistakable to anyone endowed with a modicum of pride. Such instances are all individually trivial but can be cumulatively shattering and generally enough to make an immigrant's life unbearable. If he ignores them, he is in danger of losing his self-respect and dignity; if he reacts to them on each occasion, he is in danger of getting consumed by the fire of his rage.

IV

How the immigrant can be integrated into British society is an extremely difficult question. Earlier we listed three levels at which integration needs to be achieved. Each requires different strategy.

As for discrimination it is obvious that law alone is not enough, since it operates in terms of general categories to which there are bound to be exceptions. One can punish a hotel manager for refusing to take a coloured tenant, but it would be unfair to fine an old lady for refusing to rent him her only spare room. Similarly one may fine a factory manager for refusing to hire a fully qualified coloured worker, but it would be wrong to fine a housewife for not hiring a Nigerian or an Indian to help her with household work. That would be to remove one form of human suffering by creating another.

However, these limits to what the law can do can be easily exaggerated and used to deny its educative and moral role. If we as a nation abhorred a certain type of conduct it is our duty to say so and to do all within our power to stop it. Law is one way a nation affirms its collective commitment to an ideal. Law, further, plays an important creative role in forming a nation's character. National character is formed in more or less the same way that individual character is. Developing character is primarily a matter of developing habits and dispositions, and these are generally created not by individuals making conscious and deliberate Kantian-type choices but by an intelligent blend of persuasion, habit and discipline. A child acquires character, not by reflecting on the intrinsic rightness and wrongness or on the long-term consequences of his every action, but by being made to behave in a certain way by a combination of arguments and authority. In acting in this way over a period of time, he develops the habit of so acting. The habit gives his moral consciousness a firm direction so that certain types of conduct alone appear to him right and proper, and their opposites, which had once attracted him, now appear morally unacceptable and outrageous. With habit, in other words, comes the conviction that a certain type of conduct alone is right, and the conviction that an action is right generates the desire to do it because it is right. It is therefore wrong to argue that one must first cultivate a desire to act morally before one can act morally. Conduct often generates its own appropriate motives and desires; as Aristotle rightly observed, we become just by performing just acts and brave by performing brave acts. The liberal argument that one cannot make a man good by an act of

Parliament rests on a dubious analysis of the nature of human action and of character, and involves too neat a contrast between motive and conduct to be acceptable. What is true of the individual is also true of the community. By prohibiting and punishing certain types of action, the law creates a climate of opinion where some degree of moral opprobrium comes to be attached to them. It weakens the pressure of unenlightened public opinion, gives its subjects courage and incentive to resist it, and releases them from a self-perpetuating vicious circle that pushes reluctant individuals into meekly conforming to a dominant pattern of behaviour. In these and other ways, members of a community develop a habit of behaving in the desired way, and might even come to find it unthinkable that they should ever have behaved differently. The ending of, for example, slavery, suttee, thugee, and inhuman factory conditions testifies to the creative moral power of law.

The government can therefore legitimately be expected to play a much more positive role in ending discrimination and securing equality of opportunity than it has done so far. It can compel local authorities to be more fair in its housing allocation and require them to provide full information about their policies. It can insist on equal pay for immigrant and white workers, on the standardisation of working conditions, and on the immigrant workers having full access to skilled and well-paid jobs. It can use its contracts with the industry to pressure it into accepting a certain number of immigrants. It could also increase its meagre help to the deprived and immigrant-concentrated areas; this in no way gives them privileged treatment but only brings their standard of living up to the level enjoyed by other parts of the nation. It can also invest the Race Relations Board with greater power to investigate complaints and prosecute those responsible for discrimination, and investigate on its own initiative companies and factories that show no immigrants on their roll. It is intolerable that Community Relations Officers, operating with a ludicrously small sum of money and with a ridiculously small staff, should take months to investigate a small complaint and should allow themselves to be fobbed off with a feeble statement by the party proved guilty of discrimination that he loves his 'coloured' victims and will not harm them again. The Board is so hamstrung by the restraints imposed on it that out of over 800 complaints made to it in 1972, only five could eventually be brought to court.[30] The standards of proof demanded are so excessively high, and require so many unbiased witnesses, statements, recent evidence of con-

8

POSTSCRIPT 237

tinuing discrimination, etc., etc., that they can rarely be met. Often all this takes such a long time—over a year in several cases and sometimes even several years—that the Board or the complainant sees no point in pursuing the matter any further.[31] And even when the complainant is tenacious enough and his case can be proved, his net gain is often meagre. If the complaint concerns a house or a job, they are almost invariably gone by the time the case is decided, and the courts sometimes award such a derisory compensation that it is no solace for the hardship and distress suffered.[32]

When we turn to the immigrant's cultural and moral problems, the situation is more intricate. The government has a limited role here, and much depends on the goodwill of the parties involved. Teachers, headmasters and local authorities can be encouraged to show greater appreciation of the problems and needs of the immigrant children in their care. The government can give a lead here by appointing a commission to collect relevant data and recommend policies concerning the special problems of these children. Greater contact between immigrant parents and teachers, giving the former representation on the governing bodies of schools, greater exchange of information between teachers of immigrant children across the country, greater role by black teachers in articulating their problems, acquainting teachers with the background and problems of immigrant children; all these are ways in which psychic damage to immigrant children can be avoided. A critical examination of the bias revealed in textbooks is also necessary, not as a sop to immigrant feelings (that will be academically suicidal), but in order to present a truthful and more balanced picture of Britain's past history and to provide for all children a non-racist and non-parochial education. Children who grow up reading that Asiatic contribution to man's control over nature is 'negligible' and African contribution 'non-existent', or that these societies, before they were 'civilised' by the Europeans, spent their time killing one another, or that their moral and political achievements are inconsequential can hardly be expected to be other than prejudiced to the non-white community in their midst. By contrast, children who are taught to appreciate non-Christian religions, Asian and African music, art, literature and languages, and the great cultural and social achievements of non-European peoples are likely to grow into sensitive, curious and sympathetic adults capable not only of treating all their fellow men with kindness and understanding but also of living a rich and varied life. Both the best elements of the liberal tradition and the interests of the immigrants point towards making education non-parochial and universalist.

We referred earlier to the racist streak in British consciousness, and contended that, although some sections of society are free from it and that it is generally held in check by British sense of fair play, it does keep appearing, and increasingly so in recent years, in the Briton's relations with the immigrant. Racism, whether white, black, brown or yellow, is always repulsive, but it is especially so in Britain where against a fundamentally humane and liberal background, its ugliness stands out most markedly. Since racism must be a source of deep concern to everyone who cherishes liberal values and since it generates many of the problems discussed earlier, we shall discuss at some length its nature and the ways to combat it.

Most social psychologists interpret racism as a form of prejudice one 'race' entertains against another, and argue that, although it represents an extreme form of prejudice, it is essentially the same type of phenomenon as the prejudices encountered in other walks of life—the prejudices, e.g. which the middle class has against the working class, the Englishman against the Frenchman, or which some men have against long-haired or bearded or dark-haired men. The black man is, it is argued, an archetypal *stranger*, and that the white man's prejudice against him is no more than an extreme form of prejudice he entertains against strangers. This view seems to me to be totally mistaken.

Prejudice is a partial rejection of a man on the basis of his real or supposed specific or specifiable characteristic. A white man may be prejudiced against a black man because he thinks he is lazy, sexy, dirty, mean, unclean, unintelligent, etc., etc., even as a black man might be prejudiced against a white man because in his view he is selfish, inhuman, merciless, devious, emotionally undeveloped, etc., etc. Since prejudice is based on some assumed characteristic of the victim, it can be countered by showing that he does not in fact possess this characteristic, or that it is not really obnoxious, or that he can be helped to get rid of it. Racism belongs to a very different category. It involves a *total* refusal to accept the victim as a full human being entitled to the respect due to a fellow human being, and implies that his belonging to a particular race has so corrupted his humanity that he belongs to an entirely different species. A white Southerner in America is not merely *prejudiced* against the negro; he *rejects* the negro's humanity and refuses to acknowledge that they both belong to the same species. To say that Hitler was *prejudiced* against Jews or that his prejudice differed only in degree from my prejudice against, say, a bearded or a red-haired man is totally to misunderstand and misrepresent the basic issue involved. What Hitler did was to refuse to accept Jews as his fellow human beings and looked down upon them almost as worms that could with moral impunity be trampled upon. Colonial powers, similarly, did not just entertain prejudices against natives, but saw them as belonging to a different species, to an altogether different level in the scale of civilisation. The examples of the treatment meted out to the immigrant discussed above reflect a similar attitude. Racism, to put the point differently, is not the same as racial *prejudice*, and it degrades and dehumanises the victim in a way that ordinary forms of prejudice do not.

Combating racism, then, involves not simply ending discrimination or eradicating prejudice but something totally different; it involves securing from the white community a full recognition of the humanity of the black man who, although deficient in this or that respect as all human beings, white and black, are, is still a human being with dignity and pride and entitled to proper respect and regard. Racism therefore cannot be combated in ways that social psychologists have proposed for eradicating prejudices, since what is required here is not to establish the simple point that the black man possesses or lacks some specific characteristic on which the white man's prejudice is based, but to get him to appreciate their shared humanity. It is this failure to comprehend the distinctiveness of racism that is largely responsible for much of social psychology's inability to suggest effective ways to combat it. Indeed, as long as it remains *social* psychology, that is, as long as it remains rooted in the assumptions derived from the study of isolated individuals or of groups within the *same* cultural milieu, and remains innocent of the historical dialectic of the political relations between different communities, it is by its very nature incapable of understanding the phenomenon like racism which is, as we shall presently see, historical and political in its origin and nature. Fanon and Sartre are two of the very few writers to have understood the nature of the problem, but their analysis is vitiated by some highly dubious psychological and political assumptions.[33]

Racism was a result of the dramatic historical encounter between the white and the black man in a colonial context, and can only be understood in historical terms. The image of the black man as an inferior creature was a product of several factors of which two deserve mention. The first was economic and the second cultural. Colonialism was by its nature a master–servant relationship and was fundamentally exploitative in nature. Colonies were largely suppliers of raw material and consumers of imperial industrial products; and the native bourgeoisie, such as it was, played a subordinate role to imperial interests. Not only did colonies remain poor but also their economy remained tied to European economy and was seriously distorted. The simple fact that even after decades and, in some cases, centuries of colonial rule they are still very poor and undeveloped is a sufficient proof of this. The vast disparity between the level of existence of the native and his European master, and their relationship of command and obedience, made it impossible for the two to meet on equal terms. Each knew his place and kept to it.

The second, cultural, factor carried the process further and turned economic subservience into cultural and moral inferiority. Convinced that they represented the highest level of human civilisation, the British (and for that matter Europeans) defined the civilised man in familiar liberal terms, and predictably the non-European peoples turned out to be uncivilised. Since a civilised society was defined as one that had a strong and centralised state, a firm sense of national identity, a competitive capitalist economy and a high level of technology, and a civilised man as one who had drive and ambition, who was competitive, individualistic, calculative and ruthless in the pursuit of his interests, non-European societies and their members were by definition un-civilised. Non-European societies naturally found these ideological definitions impossible to resist. No doubt, there was some resistance and scepticism in the beginning, but it collapsed before systematic European indoctrination carefully carried out by educational, legal, political and economic means. To be fair the natives themselves were sometimes a willing party. They were impressed by European self-confidence, power and energy and were only too eager, as the biographies and autobiographies of their leaders show, to imbibe the ways of thought and life that had made these possible. So gradually the black man began to inter-nalise European values, and with these, the European image of him. The white man said that the black man's religion was super-stitious, that his morality was primitive, his social and legal insti-tutions backward and his traditions uncouth, and the black man agreed. The white man said that the native was uncivilised and barbaric, and the black man, again, agreed. The white man said that the native could become fully human only if he got Western-ised, and the native concurred. The bewitched native, judging himself on the basis of European values and ideals, felt that he could not respect himself if he failed to live up to them. Since these values were not an outgrowth from, and therefore unsuited to, his temperament and background, he naturally found it difficult fully to live up to them. However hard he tried he failed, thus reinforcing his own and his master's belief that he was naturally, inherently, an inferior creature. Bemused into believing that he was less gifted and therefore less of a man than the white man, he felt a profound sense of inferiority in his presence and could not feel or act like an equal in his relations with him; the white man, for his part, could not see how he could accept a man of proven inferiority as his equal. Once the black man's soul was conquered, the stage was set for the racist belief that he was lacking in those vital qualities that made a man fully human.

Since racism was a product of, among others, these two powerful and mutually complementary forces of economic and political power and cultural domination, the answer to it obviously does not lie in analysing the white and black man's personality structure and asking how they can be made less 'authoritarian' and 'deferential' respectively, nor in hoping to eradicate the white man's 'prejudices' by giving him more information on the black man's cultural and personal background, nor in exhorting both to treat each other as brothers, nor in trying to *prove* to the white man that the black man is, for example, clean, healthy, intelligent and 'civilised'. In trying to sell the latter as an acceptable human package this last approach not only perpetuates the repulsive initial inequality at another level but also degrades him even further. While all these and other methods may succeed in establishing better relations between isolated members of different races, the problem of racism is too profound to be tackled by such simple-minded ahistorical and apolitical approaches. If what we have said above is correct, the answer, if we may so call what is no more than a tentative suggestion, is to be found in radically altering the politico-economic and cultural relationship between the white and the black man which generated racism in the first instance.

As long as the black man remains wretched and powerless he is unlikely to command any respect. Unless therefore the immigrants settled in Britain can organise and become a powerful force in British economic and political life, they are unlikely to be taken seriously. Further, the destiny of the black man in England is integrally tied up with the Third World, in that the latter's success or failure inevitably affects the way the white community looks upon him. As the changing British images of the Chinese, the Japanese and the Jews during the past two decades show, the respect enjoyed by an individual follows the power and success of his nation. Unless therefore the countries of the Third World acquire economic and political power such that they cannot be taken for granted, that is, unless they undergo profound political and economic changes and succeed in totally redefining their parasitic relationship with the West, the black man's demand for equality and respect will be met with nothing more than patronising condescension at best and downright contempt at worst. People who lack the will to take charge of their destiny and to stand up for their rights may be flattered for their 'moderation' and 'civilised' behaviour by those whose interests they serve, but they never evoke respect.

At the cultural level the black man's demand for the full recognition of his humanity rests on his ability successfully to recreate his identity and to assert his individuality at the deepest existential level. Men who have no pride in their history and its heritage and are content to conform to others' image of them are culturally insubstantial and lack the necessary basis of self-respect. Recreation of identity is an extremely complicated and painful process, requiring a patient and intelligent recomposition of one's historical heritage by putting together the scattered fragments of the ruptured past. Fanon and Sartre have rightly emphasised the value and necessity of this, but they have gone wrong in their account of what it precisely involves. They argue that the black man's ontological self-recreation requires that he must reject European culture absolutely and uncompromisingly, and assert his own without discrimination. This is a mistaken and dangerous counsel.[34] Centuries of contact with Europe have left deep marks on the black man's consciousness, which he simply cannot blot out or wish out of existence. For better or for worse, he is deeply influenced by European culture, and can never revive his cultural virginity. Even assuming that he was able to do this, it will only impoverish him, since there is much in European culture that is noble and worthy of respect and from which he stands to benefit. Indeed as the black man begins to rediscover his past, he is bound to find that not everything there is valuable and worth preserving. Of some of his customs and institutions, he is bound to feel ashamed (e.g. treatment of women, or of the socially and econ-omically underprivileged); he is also bound to find some of the beliefs and attitudes of his society morally offensive (for example, its attitude to the poor, to the outcastes, to animals and to those in power). He is also bound to find that his pre-colonial past is not a golden age as he fondly believes; along with much that is great and worth cherishing, it was also disgraced by tyranny, oppression, violence and exploitation, comparable in their magnitude and inhumanity to those perpetrated by the imperial powers.[35] Indeed, the more he digs into his past, the less contemptuous he is likely to be of his colonial heritage, and the more he is likely to realise that some European influences have been for the good, that some European values are nobler and higher than his own and that he should therefore incorporate them into his heritage. The answer to European cultural hegemony, in short, is not to be found in the black man's aggressive and undiscriminating assertion of his native traditions and values but in going beyond and transcending European culture by recreating his identity on the basis of the best that *both* his own society and Europe have to offer.

So far as the white community is concerned, it is inconsistent of it to claim to abhor racism, and to do nothing to remove the very conditions which foster it. If it is *seriously* worried about its racism, it should therefore do all in its power to help the black man achieve economic and political power and cultural self-respect. It could stop treating meanly the representatives of the Third World settled in its midst as successive British governments have done, and show them respect and humanity. It could go further and end its exploitative relationship with the Third World, and help its members achieve decent human existence. It must stop thinking in terms of foreign 'aid' which, far from helping poorer nations, is really a process by which they help the rich nations sustain an ever-rising standard of living, and join them in a spirit of partnership in combating the terrifying economic legacy of colonial rule. At the cultural level, the white community can encourage the black man to develop his own distinctive identity by taking sympathetic interest in his culture, social institutions, beliefs and historical achievements. And this it can do only if it stops imposing culturally biased standards of evaluation on the Third World, reflecting the familiar divine pretension of the West to define and create the black man in its own image, and acknowledges that each community has its own distinctive mode of life which, subject to certain universally operative moral principles, is entitled to equal respect.

Lack of any real concern in Britain and elsewhere for the dire economic predicament of the Third World, and the cultural narcissism underlying academic, journalistic and other approaches to the Third World offer little ground for optimism. If lucky, we might succeed in creating better 'race relations' in Britain, but we are unlikely to end racism.

NOTES

1. I have benefited from the comments made by Dr Gordon Hutton, Dr Ivar Oxaal, Mr Colin Creighton and Mr Robert Copper. Some of the points made here were discussed with Professor John Plamenatz, to whom I am also grateful.

2. Dilip Hiro, *Black British, White British*, Eyre & Spottiswoode, 1971, p. 123.

3. Phillip V. Tobias, 'The Meaning of Race', in Paul Baxter & Basil Sansom (Eds), *Race and Social Difference*, Penguin, 1972, p. 40. See also the UNESCO declaration of 1964, *ibid.*, pp. 68ff.

4. It is worth observing that, scientifically speaking, black is not a colour at all.

5. If some people are to be called coloured, then fairness demands that those not called coloured should be called colourless!

6. *Gentleman's Magazine*, Vol. XXXIV, 1764, p. 492.

7. Quoted in Michael Banton, *White and Coloured*, Cape, London, 1959, p. 55. He was also complaining against white women's open and excessive fondness for their negro slaves and servants.

8. Paul Foot, *The Rise of Enoch Powell*, Penguin Special, 1969, p. 125.

9. The attempt to couple repatriation with an offer of financial help, far from making it more acceptable, makes it even more obnoxious, in that the offer is really an impertinent attempt to ask a man to name his price for getting out of the country.

10. See, e.g., Peter Evans, *The Times*, July 17, 1970, and various Runnymede Trust Publications.

11. Tom Stacey, *Immigration and Enoch Powell*, Tom Stacey Ltd, 1970, p. 133.

12. Chapter 13.

13. Editorial in *The Political Quarterly*, Vol. 39, 1968.

14. See Gorer, Chapter 12.

15. Tom Stacey, *op. cit.*

16. Here and elsewhere I use the term black to refer to anyone who is not white. Personally I find these terms most disagreeable, but there are no others.

17. Ernest Drausz, 'Jews in Britain: Integrated or Apart?' A paper presented to the Fourth Annual Conference of the Institute of Race Relations, September 19, 1969.

18. The story is well told by E. G. Hartmann, *The Movement to Americanise the Immigrant*, AMS Press, N.Y., 1967.

19. For a detailed account of these, see Hiro, *op. cit.*, pp. 251ff.

20. See Dr G. Stewart Prince, The Emotional Problems of West Indian Immigrant Children in England (ACE Forum, 6, *Education in Multi-racial Schools, 1970*), and A. C. R. Skynner, *Report on Preliminary Conference on Special Psychiatric Problems Presented by some West Indian Immigrant Families*, held at the John Scott Health Centre, London, January 31, 1968.

21. See for example, Bernard Coard, *How the West Indian Child is made educationally subnormal in the British School System*, New Beacon Books Ltd, 1971; R. T. Goldman and F. M. Taylor in *Educational Research*, Vol. 8, 1966; V. P. Houghton in *Race*, Vol. 8, No. 2, October, 1966; and F. P. Watson in *New Society*, January 22, 1970, and July 16, 1970.

22. Despite their initial disadvantages immigrant children in fact manage to do as well as and sometimes better than their white peers. See Sir Edward

Boyle, Race Relations: The Limits of Voluntary Action, in *Race*, January, 1968, p. 297.

23. Bernard Coard, *op. cit.*; Maureen Stone, *West Indian Children in an ESN school. Why are they there?* Mimeographed; and P. Williams in *Educational Research*, 1965.

24. See e.g. Ken Worpole's exposure of the limitations of the 'Ladybird' series in *New Society*, December 23, 1971.

25. See Stephen Hatch in *Race*, Vol. 4, 1962; Frank Glendenning in *Race Today*, February, 1971; *The Teacher*, November 19, 1971; *The Guardian*, October 26, 1971; *New Statesman*, October 29, 1971; and Felicity Bottom & Jennie Laishley, *Education for a Multiracial Society*, Fabian Research Series, No. 303, July 1972.

26. *The Observer*, April 28, 1968.

27. To avoid misunderstanding I do not use the term racist to refer to a man who holds that mankind is divisible into different races, each with its own distinctive genetic structure and culture, since one can hold such a 'scientific' theory without drawing any moral and political conclusion from it; nor do I use the term to refer to a man who holds that some races are intellectually or in some other specific respect inferior to others, since they well might be, and the person holding this view might go on to advocate policies designed to remove their inferiority. I use the term racist to refer to a man or a body of men who hold that some races, however identified, are inferior not in this or that respect but *qua men*, and that therefore their interests and feelings do not deserve to be regarded as *equally* important with those of the other so-called superior races. As I use the term, racism refers not merely to a body of beliefs but also and primarily to the type of conduct it generates. Thus a person who believes that the 'coloured' people are intellectually inferior, and then goes on to propose positive discrimination in their favour is not a racist, but he who, on the basis of this belief, argues that they should therefore be treated as less than fully human and may be exploited with a clear conscience, is.

28. *The Guardian*, Editorial, June 21, 1973.

29. I argued earlier that the term race is misleading, but since a large number of people do actually think in such terms, it becomes necessary to use it, and its derivatives, to describe their attitude.

30. *Report of the Race Relations Board for 1972*.

31. Chris Mullard, *Black Britain*, Allen & Unwin, 1973, pp. 82f.

32. In the Bradmore Working Men's Club case, a black telephonist who was refused admission to the Christmas party, although possessing a proper ticket, was awarded in way of compensation the money value of her ticket—25p!

33. For a detailed critique of Fanon, see my *Fanon's Theory of Violence*, in Bhikhu Parekh (ed.), *Dissent and Disorder*, World University Service of Canada, 1971.

34. For this paragraph, I have drawn on my *Fanon's Theory of Violence*, *op. cit.*

35. See Chapters 10 and 14.

Index

247